THE NAZI SPY RING IN AMERICA

Other Titles of Interest from Georgetown University Press

To Catch a Spy: The Art of Counterintelligence
by James M. Olson

*Spying in America: Espionage from the Revolutionary War to the
Dawn of the Cold War*
by Michael J. Sulick

*Spy Chiefs: Volume 1: Intelligence Leaders in the United States
and United Kingdom*
edited by Christopher Moran, Mark Stout, Ioanna Iordanou,
and Paul Maddrell

*Spy Chiefs: Volume 2: Intelligence Leaders in Europe, the
Middle East, and Asia*
edited by Paul Maddrell, Christopher Moran, Ioanna
Iordanou, and Mark Stout

Spy Sites of New York City: A Guide to the Region's Secret History
by H. Keith Melton and Robert Wallace, with
Henry R. Schlesinger

THE NAZI SPY RING IN AMERICA

Hitler's Agents, the FBI, and the Case That Stirred the Nation

RHODRI JEFFREYS-JONES

Georgetown University Press / Washington, DC

The publisher is not responsible for third-party websites or their content. URL links were active at time of publication.

Every effort has been made to trace the copyright holder for the unidentified press photograph of Kate Moog Busch and to obtain permission to reproduce it in this book. Please contact Georgetown University Press with any inquiries or information relating to this image or the rights holder.

Library of Congress Cataloging-in-Publication Data

Names: Jeffreys-Jones, Rhodri, author.
Title: The Nazi spy ring in America : Hitler's agents, the FBI, and the case that stirred the nation / Rhodri Jeffreys-Jones.
Description: Washington, DC : Georgetown University Press, 2021. | Includes bibliographical references and index.
Identifiers: LCCN 2020008216 | ISBN 9781647120047 (hardcover) | ISBN 9781647120054 (ebook)
Subjects: LCSH: Germany. Wehrmacht. Amt Ausland/Abwehr—History. | United States. Federal Bureau of Investigation—History. | Espionage, German—United States—History—20th century. | World War, 1939-1945—Secret service—Germany. | World War, 1939-1945—Secret service—United States.
Classification: LCC D810.S7 J395 2021 | DDC 940.54/87430973—dc23
LC record available at https://lccn.loc.gov/2020008216

♾ This book is printed on acid-free paper meeting the requirements of the American National Standard for Permanence in Paper for Printed Library Materials.

21 20   9 8 7 6 5 4 3 2 First printing

Printed in the United States of America.
Cover design by Faceout Studio, Tim Green.
Interior design by Blue Heron, Paul Hotvedt.

For Alex and Ava,
and in memory of Lily Pincus

CONTENTS

PREFACE

Reacting to the carnage of World War I and to the rise of Adolf Hitler, the US Congress passed Neutrality Acts in the years 1935–37. The nation vowed never again to take sides in a European war. Yet in the year immediately following the final and most draconian of those acts, opinion changed on the subject of neutrality. One reason for the transformation was the exposure in 1938 of a Nazi spy ring operating in the United States. Leon Turrou, a special agent with the Federal Bureau of Investigation (FBI), was instrumental in securing that exposure and launched a campaign to warn the American people about the Nazi menace.

The case resulted in increased powers and funds for the FBI. Yet the bureau's director, J. Edgar Hoover, turned against the ace detective who had once been his favorite. Hoover undertook a decades-long campaign to blacklist Turrou and to ensure that he would never become a household name. That is one reason why the story unraveled in this book is unfamiliar and has not been heeded by historians writing about US foreign relations.

The ensuing pages attempt to restore the balance and to tell the full story of German espionage directed against the United States. They identify the master spy with a dueling scar who directed operations against US targets. They unravel some of the case's mysteries: Who was behind the "Mata Hari" plot to seduce young army officers in Washington, DC? Was anybody innocent in the McAlpin Hotel murder plot? Why did our chief protagonist, Leon Turrou, deny he was Jewish?

The story tells of fast cars, louche liaisons, and a critical tip-off by the British Security Service (MI5). At the same time, it carries a serious message about spies from a totalitarian country who tried to subvert democracy in the United States and, in the end, inflamed public opinion to the detriment of the fascist cause.

In January 2013 under the terms of the Freedom of Information Act, I applied to access FBI documents relating to the Nazi espionage case. It was a big ask. The name of one spy whose story I shall tell, Jessie Jordan, appeared on no fewer than 14,500 pages. Jon Russo of the FBI Information Management Division labored over a two-year period to supply me, in a manageable format, with digital copies of the documents I needed. Richard Bareford generously helped me obtain and wade through the FBI's file on Leon Turrou. Still more archival help came from Rod Bailey and Andrew Jeffrey, who shared with me their expertise on MI5 files.

Individuals who encouraged, criticized, or otherwise helped me were Robert Anderson, Doug Charles, Jeremy Crang, Owen Dudley Edwards, John Fox, Fabian Hilfrich, Dolores Janiewski, Andrew Johnstone, Kenny Kevin, Knud Krakau, Marianne Mooijweer, Kathryn Olmsted, David Silkenat, Jill Stephenson, Pat Storey, and Bertrand Vilain.

My diligent research assistant Leonie Werle, a graduate student at the Free University of Berlin and a worker at the German Resistance Memorial Center in the same city, showed initiative. Andrew Lownie showed why he is a top boutique literary agent. At Georgetown University Press, Don Jacobs suggested improvements after reading the book and has been a good shepherd. My wife, Mary, keeps me on an even keel by never reading my books and is a source of joy and support beyond compare.

To all the foregoing, my deepest gratitude.

This book is for my latest grandchildren, toddlers Alex and Ava. May they never witness crimes like those of the 1930s. And it is in memory of my godmother, the late Lily Pincus, who escaped Berlin just in time and who was always a source of wisdom and strength.

1
LONKOWSKI'S LEGACY

The time was midevening, September 27, 1935; the place, Pier 86 on the Hudson River in New York City. The guard wearing US Customs Service badge number 572 was Morris Josephs. His gaze fell upon a familiar scene: passengers, relatives, and friends milled around in an excited throng, anticipating the departure of the North German Lloyd steamship *Europa*.

Just after 8:30 p.m., Josephs, a keen musician, spied a smooth-faced man in a dark hat carrying on board what appeared to be a violin case. Citizens of that mobster-ridden era knew how Thompson submachine guns fit snugly into such receptacles, and the customs guard stayed alert. After a short while, the smooth-faced man left the ship and walked back down the pier with the object still tucked under his arm. At 8:50 p.m. Josephs arrested him. Upon closer inspection, the parcel, which was not even a violin case, contained neither a gun nor a Stradivarius. It did, however, contain copies of military plans.[1]

The man in the dark hat was Wilhelm "Willy" Lonkowski, code name Sex. When the American press belatedly found out about him, one journalist declared that he was "the cream" among spies. Lonkowski certainly had one useful attribute, a talent for obscurity. After months of intensive if belated investigation, an FBI special agent finally lamented, "Little is known concerning the personal history of Lonkowski."[2]

No FBI agent ever knowingly encountered Agent Sex. Yet over the years a partial picture emerged of this most secretive of secret agents. Lonkowski was slender and tall, with brown hair and blue eyes. He had a long nose and floppy ears. He suffered from stomach ulcers, exacerbated by the anxieties of long years of espionage. His heavy drinking did not help his medical condition, though it was an operational advantage that he was a "cold soak"; that is, he could remain sober while plying the keepers of secrets with drinks that loosened their tongues.[3]

Like several spies in our story, Lonkowski came from contested territory. He was born in 1896 in Worliny (in German, Worleinen), a village Prussia claimed following the eighteenth-century partition of Poland that then passed to the unified state of Germany in 1871. In World War I, he served as an airman in the Imperial German Army and suffered grievous injuries when a French pilot shot him down. Just before the end of hostilities, the recovering aviator married Auguste "Gunny" Krüger, the daughter of a barber from Obernik, also in East Prussia.

After the war, Lonkowski tried to carve out a career as an aircraft designer. He never explained why he became a spy. The embittered patriotism of a wounded and defeated soldier no doubt played its part. Patriotism had a special twist for a man who came from the German-Polish borderland with its threatened identities. Adolf Hitler would promise a greater Germany under Teutonic control, an aspiration that appealed to ethnic partisans. Like other German spies, Lonkowski may have felt aggrieved with the United States for its role both in helping to defeat his country and in the subsequent peace settlement that punished Germany on the grounds of war guilt.

Lonkowski's agency, the Abwehr, inherited a tradition. Prussia had a history of espionage. Frederick the Great (1712–86) once dismissed a military foe with the words, "Marshal de Soubise is always followed by a hundred cooks, [whereas] I am always preceded by a hundred spies." The Versailles peace settlement threatened to end that tradition. According to its provisions, German military activity was supposed to be confined to specified units and excluded spying. But old ways returned. In 1921 Friedrich Gempp, who had been the deputy to the wartime intelligence chief Walter Nicolai, took charge of a group of ten officers and together with support personnel formed the Abwehr, which literally means "defense" but soon expanded its mission. By 1935 staff numbers had reached 150; three years later, 1,000.[4]

The Abwehr sought technical data to enable Germany to rebuild its military. In September 1926 Gempp singled out Lonkowski for a mission to the technologically advanced United States. While Germany was hitherto renowned for the quality of its technical education, such education was stagnating due to a lack of money and to resistance from the nation's traditional elite.[5] By comparison, the United States by the mid-1920s had demonstrated it had the prowess and the means to outstrip its European rivals.

On March 27, 1927, the secret agent had arrived at Hoboken, New Jersey, carrying a passport in the name of Wilhelm Schneider. This was one of a string of aliases that included William Sexton, the mundane origin, through abbreviation, of his later operational code name Sex. Lonkowski and his wife were gifted individuals. Gunny knew about hats, and once they had both settled in Long Island in 1929, she managed a millinery shop and then a dress emporium in Queens Village. Willy could repair and tune practically any musical instrument. He worked at this trade for the Temple of Music store in Hempstead, Long Island. More significantly for his mission as a spy, he worked between 1929 and 1931 as a mechanic for the Ireland Aircraft Corporation at nearby Roosevelt Field and then for Fairchild Aviation Corporation in Farmingdale, New York.[6]

According to Willy's cover story, the childless Lonkowskis accumulated enough capital working in the United States to enable Willy to return to Germany in February 1934, where he engaged in wire manufacturing. His cover story held that he then sold the business and returned to the States on January 18, 1935, with considerable funds. That would have been a remarkable feat, given the brevity of his stay in Germany. The truth is the money came from the German foreign intelligence service. The time had come to reinvigorate Abwehr spying operations in the United States.

Lonkowski built a formidable spy network. He was able to recruit German Americans working in the defense industry. Managers in that industry had been glad to hire well-trained workers and, perhaps reassured by the supposed demilitarization of Germany, did so with scant regard to security checks. While working at the Ireland Aircraft Corporation, Lonkowski also secured work there for the future secret agent Otto Hermann Voss. A native of Hamburg who had trained as a machinist and had served with the Imperial German Army's Company of Engineers in World War I, Voss was an airplane mechanic and keen yachtsman who worked for a succession of US defense industry businesses after his arrival in the country in October 1928. He and his wife, Anna, whom he married in 1934, socialized with their neighbors the Lonkowskis.[7]

On one such occasion, Willy introduced Voss to Karl Eitel, a German agent who worked as a steward on the steamship SS *Bremen*. Built for the North German Lloyd Line and launched in 1929, the *Bremen* achieved a cruising speed of twenty-seven knots and until 1932 held the Blue Riband, which was awarded for the fastest transatlantic crossing. It was the pride of a resurgent German maritime industry. However, the *Bremen* and its sibling ship the SS *Europa* served as vehicles for propaganda, censorship, and espionage. When the Nazis gained power, they installed storm troopers, or political bosses, to enforce totalitarian discipline on these and other German ships. They banned magazines such as *Harper's* that expressed free American opinions, and the atmosphere became so poisoned that passengers began to shun the shipping line.

In July 1935, just two months prior to Lonkowski's arrest, the *Bremen* took center stage in the international fight against fascism. Communist-led members of the International Seamen's Union in New York wanted to protest the imprisonment of Lawrence Simpson, an American sailor whom the German authorities had arrested for distributing anti-Nazi literature in Hamburg. The protestors looked for a target and found one close at hand. Activist Bill Bailey described the great German ship that dominated the waterfront: "Her bow jutted up, looming over the street. Large, powerful floodlights in various parts of the ship directed their beams at one spot: the jackstaff that held the Nazi swastika." Demonstrators boarded the ship, and Bailey was one of those who tore down the swastika and cast it into the cold, black water of the Hudson River.[8]

The New York seamen's protest sparked imitation anti-swastika demonstrations across the world. What had started as a communist-inspired movement soon won wider sympathy. When the case against the flag vandals went to court in September, Louis B. Brodsky, a Jewish New York magistrate, dismissed the charges and condemned the swastika as a piratical emblem. Hitler reacted. At the annual Nuremburg Nazi Party Rally that month, he declared that the swastika would replace the imperial tricolor as Germany's official national standard.[9]

Ships such as the *Bremen* supported not just the Nazi apparatus but also the Abwehr's operations. The commanding officers of German passenger ships knowingly facilitated the transport of spy couriers with their letters and bulky documents. The British Royal Navy had intercepted Berlin's messages and broken its codes in World War I, and transatlantic cables remained an unreliable means of sending secret data. Sea transport in Nazi Party–disciplined ocean liners was slower but more secure.

Karl Eitel agreed to serve as a courier for Lonkowski, for example, by delivering a letter asking Berlin for more money. By way of reverse traffic, Eitel relayed to Voss the German authorities' desire for specified US military technical secrets. In the course of six subsequent meetings, Voss supplied Eitel with design details and photographs of army training planes under construction at the Seversky Aircraft Company, covering the wings, fuselage, engines, and landing gear. Voss had himself reengineered the landing gear to make it stronger.[10]

Germany paid Lonkowski generously. He received $500 a month, with bonuses for particularly useful intelligence. With his expenses paid, Willy was able to reward his informants handsomely. He claimed to have dispensed to a single group of spies as much as $30,000 in one year. Perhaps he exaggerated, but the material benefits of the advanced technology that his agents purloined from military-associated industries were of great value to his employers. Neither the US government nor the nation's industries were prepared for such an espionage onslaught, and Lonkowski had a sharp eye for opportunities. From Johannes Karl Steuer, an inspector at the Sperry Gyroscope Company in Brooklyn, he solicited information on bombsights. Johannes Kögel, a foreman at the Kollmorgen Optical Corporation in Brooklyn, may well have supplied him with data on periscopes.[11]

Another of Lonkowski's recruits at the Ireland Aircraft Corporation was Werner Georg Gudenberg. A native of Hamburg and a trained coppersmith, Gudenberg first stepped ashore in the United States on October 22, 1928, having arrived in New York on the SS *Deutschland*. By the end of the year, he was foreman of the fuselage and fitting department at Ireland Aircraft. Under Lonkowski's tutelage, he would obtain secrets from a contact in the Boston Navy Yard and scheme to lure German-born technicians to return to the fatherland, where they would be induced to divulge the secrets of US military technology. In still another venture, Lonkowski set up an agent in Montreal, instructing him to forward rolls of film to Germany and later to spy on the Canadian aviation industry.[12]

Lonkowski was the Abwehr's main man in America, yet he was not in overall control of German espionage operations in the United States. The Abwehr abided by what was a valued principle of good security—compartmentalization. The left hand was not allowed to know about the right hand, lest the right hand had fallen under the control of a rival agency making it liable to betray the secrets of both hands. For such security reasons, Willy did not control Abwehr operations in California.[13]

For the same reason, he may not have known about the Abwehr's effort to get hold of a code-deciphering machine developed for the US Navy Department by the gifted American code breaker Agnes Driscoll (née Meyer). Together with Poland and Germany, the United States was in the early stages of developing computer-driven encryption and decryption. Agnes Driscoll—a later FBI report noted drily that she was "of German ancestry"—obtained a secret appropriation of $6,250 from the US government in recompense for her contribution. But that was less than she had claimed. Furthermore, she suffered an automobile accident at this time that temporarily incapacitated her, and she may have felt aggrieved when the Navy Department stopped her salary during the period of her recuperation. According to FBI sources, the woman who is today remembered as a pioneer of US cryptography sold the device for $7,000 to the Abwehr, prompting jubilation in Berlin.[14]

The Driscoll mission was never directly traced to the Lonkowski network. The same was only partially true of another high-technology venture. Wilhelm Canaris, head of the Abwehr between 1935 and 1944, commissioned this operation. He entrusted its execution to Nikolaus "Niki" Adolf Fritz Ritter.

A native of Rheydt in the Rhineland and the son of a university president, Ritter had been twice wounded while fighting as an infantry officer in World War I. In the course of that conflict, he spent some time in the United States on the staff of Franz von Papen, who, as a military attaché in Washington in 1914–16, ran sabotage operations against British and Canadian installations. Von Papen later became the chancellor of Germany and facilitated the rise of Hitler.[15]

In 1924 Ritter arrived in the United States on an immigration visa. Tall, blond, and blue-eyed, he stirred feelings in an Alabama girl named Mary Aurora "Lady May" Evans. Two years after his arrival, they married. They had a boy and a girl and seemed a happy family, but following the stock market crash and in the Great Depression era, Ritter's business ventures enjoyed indifferent success. An official at the German Embassy suggested that he resume his military duties. Ritter returned to Germany and, on September 1, 1936, became an agent of the Abwehr, attached to its Hamburg office. Under the tutelage of Hilmar Gustav Johannes Dierks, an experienced intelligence officer, he won the confidence of his superiors and would receive the Iron Cross for his intelligence work against the United Kingdom.[16]

If Ritter conformed to one facet of the typical Abwehr profile in having served in World War I, he subscribed to another by engaging in extramarital activities. Soon after he joined the Abwehr, the man described by an associate as "a very brutal, ambitious individual" developed an interest in his secretary. Aurora frowned on his secret service work, and his marital infidelity was the last straw. In 1938 she divorced Nikolaus, and the following year he remarried. Nikolaus had custody of the children each summer, and he banned his wife from returning to the United States. Aurora was bitter about her former husband's behavior. When she obtained a job at the US Consulate in Hamburg, it would be only a matter of time before she told American officials what she knew.[17]

In July 1937 Canaris had ordered Ritter to spy on Aurora's native land. According to Ritter's later account of the mission, he was not keen on the assignment. He claimed it was because he was fond of the United States, even if he had reservations about what he termed the Americans' tendency to treat women like royalty (evidently he had not treated Aurora that way). But an order was an order, and he obeyed it. At first, things did not go well. He was violently seasick on the Atlantic voyage, and when a German American journalist recognized him as he passed through immigration, it might have blown the whole operation. Perhaps he had not quite gotten over his queasiness as he reacted by changing his name to Mr. Landing.[18]

Initially Ritter's aim was to establish contact with Frederick "Fritz" Joubert Duquesne, someone Canaris identified as having been involved in secret service work in World War I. Duquesne had been the intelligence officer for the Order of '76, a whites-only, anti–New Deal, pro-Nazi organization founded in March 1934. Aurora recalled that after meeting Duquesne, her husband broadened his activities and "visited all the important airplane factories" in the United States. She said that "his sole reason for going to the United States was to visit the agents planted in such factories."[19]

In what Ritter later described as a "cold" letter of instruction, Canaris gave him a more specific mission: he was to secure the details of the Norden bombsight. Carl Norden was a Dutch immigrant who had worked for the Sperry Gyroscope Company and then launched his own Norden Company. Sperry and Norden had competed to produce an improved bombsight. Norden won the race to produce a marketable device equipped with a gyroscopic stabilization mechanism that promised to deliver aerial bombs to their targets with unprecedented accuracy.

Ritter operated through the German American network. His prior list of contacts included not only Duquesne but also Gudenberg, who by this time had inherited Lonkowski's responsibilities.[20] Exploiting such contacts, Ritter met a man who was in a position to help him.

Hermann W. Lang had long-standing fascist sympathies and in 1923 had participated in the Munich Putsch, an early Hitler-led attempt to overthrow the democratically elected government of Germany. He had immigrated to the United States in 1927. Acquiring US citizenship two years later, he worked at the Manhattan factory that produced the sought-after bombsight. Ritter arranged to meet Lang, whom he described as tall, blond, and trustworthy. (Ritter habitually praised men with Aryan characteristics.) Lang was so dedicated to the Nazi cause that he refused payment for his services. After a trial run, the engineer gave Ritter a partial blueprint for the Norden bombsight.[21]

The rather large blueprint would not fit into a normal briefcase or small package, so Ritter arranged for it to be rolled up inside a customized umbrella that he had brought with him to the States. On November 30, 1937, a spy courier with a fake limp boarded the SS *Reliance* of the Hamburg American Line, his hobble giving him the appearance of someone who needed to lean on the (loaded) umbrella for support. It contained the first of several Norden consignments.

By 1941 the German Air Force, the Luftwaffe, had its own gyroscopic device. Ernst Heinkel, the German airplane designer, said that the Norden acquisition had been pivotal in the development of its German equivalent. German bombsight engineers, however, denied it. Whether the German version was a copy of the American prototype or not, knowledge of the US capability in the 1930s was of interest to Berlin, whose armed forces might one day have to face more accurate bombing. The Norden theft impressed Germany's spymasters and helped Ritter further his career.[22]

The Ritter-Lang story shows how Willy Lonkowski's network was not all embracing; nevertheless, it was the principal German intelligence operation in the United States. Berlin valued Lonkowski's services and had plans to reward him with a sinecure in its Air Force Ministry. However, he did not stay in the country long enough to witness the full fruits of his clandestine labors. For this, he blamed a woman.

It had all begun with a sortie by his wife. Gunny drank heavily. One day in March 1935, she ventured out into the Hempstead community to buy wine and gin. She fell into conversation with Senta de Wanger, the proprietor of Clinton Wine Shop. In the course of subsequent purchasing trips and chats, she told Senta the false news that Gunny's husband, William Lonkowski, was terminally ill. Knowing that Senta had a large house and lived alone, Gunny suggested it would be mutually advantageous if she and Willy moved in with her.

Senta agreed, charging a rental of $20 a month. The benefits included the use of an additional space that served as a photographer's darkroom. The Lonkowskis installed a telephone in Senta de Wanger's name and operated a 1929 Nash sedan under someone else's name. Willy told Senta he was a piano tuner, but the Lonkowskis' lavish expenditures suggested otherwise. The three inhabitants of 83 Lincoln Boulevard threw wild parties with US Navy and Army personnel among the guests. Her tongue loosened by alcohol, Gunny eventually confided to Senta that Willy received money from the German government.[23]

The woman in whom Gunny confided had been born in 1907 in the southern German city of Ulm, and her parents, Paul and Dina Dirlewanger, still lived in nearby Stuttgart, where Paul was a banker. She was a slender five foot nine, with dark brown hair, blue eyes, and a slight German accent. To her friends, she was *die wilde* (the wild) Senta, a reference to her willful personality. Bored by the tedium of being a banker's daughter in provincial Stuttgart, Senta Dirlewanger had immigrated to New York, where, to mark her new start in life, she chose a new name. Now Senta de Wanger, she worked as a secretary and later set up an interior decorating store at Seven Park Avenue on Manhattan with undisclosed, but possibly parental, funds before moving out to run her liquor store on Long Island. In September 1935 she became a US citizen.[24]

Meanwhile, according to a statement Senta later signed for the FBI, the Lonkowskis had turned nasty. They told her that if she did not cooperate with them, financial measures would be taken against her parents, who were already in dire straits because of the Depression. So it came to pass that in late August 1935, Senta was to deliver a package. It had arrived from Buffalo, where Lonkowski was spending a few days, and contained materials supplied by Gudenberg, who at the time worked at

Buffalo's Curtiss-Wright Corporation aircraft manufacturing plant. The item for delivery had been wrapped inside a larger package with a note telling Wanger what to do. The note stipulated that she should give the interior missive to a courier aboard the SS *Europa* berthed on the Hudson River. The courier was nowhere to be found when she arrived at Pier 86, however; so she gave the package to the ship's purser instead.[25]

The combustible Willy was furious that Senta had trusted the purser, and he shouted that he would kill her if the package went astray. He calmed down only when a receipt arrived confirming that the package had reached its intended destination. Thereafter, operations continued smoothly until the night of September 27. That evening, Willy left the house on Lincoln Boulevard to deliver a package personally to his contact on the steamship *Europa*.

He did not return. When the new day broke, Gunny feared the worst and expected federal agents to appear any minute. She fled to her nearby sister's place. In an attempt to raise immediate funds, she tried to sell her sister the Nash sedan.

Gunny's fears were well founded. Lonkowski had fallen victim to his own tradecraft. When he had failed to locate his courier, he would not trust any other recipient. Instead, he came back onshore with his spy bundle. The package that Customs Service Officer Josephs found on Gunny's husband was rather obviously marked "Für Berlin" (for Berlin). Josephs saw at a glance that it contained rolls of film and materials relating to aviation. He handed it over to his superiors, who called in Maj. Stanley Grogan of US Military Intelligence. Grogan found a diagram of machine gun sights for navy airplanes and notes on the army's Langley Field in Virginia. There was a memorandum, signed "Sex," about tenders for a new "flying fortress" bomber being submitted to the army by Boeing and by Douglas Aircraft Company of Santa Monica, California. Another note indicated that von Papen was commissioning military intelligence from Lonkowski.

In spite of all this information, Lonkowski half convinced his interrogators that he was a journalist writing an article for the German aviation magazine *Die Luftreisen*. Perhaps because military intelligence was at a low point at the time—with only 69 headquarters personnel compared with 1,441 in 1918—the package received only perfunctory and local analysis. The interrogation team provisionally concluded that none of "this material was considered 'Confidential.'" The authorities remained suspicious of Lonkowski but decided to release him the following morning with the warning that they would want to question him again in three days' time.[26]

Scarcely able to believe his luck, Lonkowski planned an immediate evacuation. He sped out to Hempstead, where he destroyed documents and gathered his personal belongings. Afterward he returned to New York and, in the dead of night, drove to a summer residence in the Peekskill area. An Abwehr colleague lent him $100 to assist his escape, and Ulrich Hausmann, a German World War I pilot, appeared two days later. He drove Lonkowski to Canada at speeds of eighty-five to ninety miles per hour. They had no problems at the border. The German consul in Montreal arranged for Lonkowski to be smuggled onto the *Hagen*, a small, homebound freighter.

Aboard ship he wrote to his sister-in-law, saying all was well except for a shortage of underwear, and he expected to reach the fatherland on October 22. He asked her to dispatch the articles he had left behind to an address in Berlin and made a special plea: on no account was the "booze hound" Senta de Wanger to be allowed to take possession of his car. It was worth at least $100, and she wanted it for her lover, who was driving around in an automobile that was "only a wreck."[27]

Sex fled the United States before enjoying the full fruits of his spying activities and left behind agents such as Voss and Gudenberg, who continued to operate effectively. Back in Germany, Lonkowski joined a party organization as an affirmation of loyalty and was duly rewarded with a job as a technical adviser with the Luftwaffe.[28] His road would not be smooth. He declined to accept the rigors of further military training. After creating a stir by dismissing two of his colleagues on charges of incompetence, he was transferred to the Engineering Corps at a lower salary. His reputation for partying continued, and in 1940 the Gestapo investigated him because on one festive occasion he and Gunny supplied

their guests with a feast that defied his means and the rationing regula-
tions then in force in wartime Germany. Rumors about his US connections did not help. His spying escapade was such a well-kept secret that
these connections were open to misinterpretation until the Abwehr had
a discreet word with the Gestapo.[29]

A prickly individual, Lonkowski remained bitter about the circumstances that had led to his departure from the United States. He accused
Senta de Wanger of betraying him and, from his German base, sent her
threatening letters. She lived in fear of the Gestapo. Senta declared herself
baffled by what her former tenant meant by betrayal and was at a loss to
explain his anger. According to FBI speculation, Lonkowski's spite may
have stemmed from her amatory rebuttal, and Eitel recalled there had
been jealousy between Gunny and Senta.[30]

In the event, Wanger resisted Lonkowski's bullying just as she had
his putative seduction. In a statement to the FBI, she declared, "I have
no connection whatsoever with any organization of the German government and I am not a member of any political party in Germany and
consider myself nothing other than a good American citizen. My sole
interest in Germany are my parents and sister who reside there." Perhaps
her betrayal was that although she did Lonkowski's bidding under duress,
she never became a willing member of his team and had failed to develop enthusiasm for his enterprise. Die wilde Senta. Her independence
of mind was dangerous to the German spy ring.[31]

After Lonkowski's arrest on Pier 86, his questioners did not include an
agent from the FBI. At the time the bureau did not have any responsibilities in the area of counterespionage. In 1935 it was gathering strength
as a crime-fighting agency, but neither it nor any other US agency had
the remit of combating foreign spies in peacetime.[32] No one followed up
on the Pier 86 incident that, for the time being, joined history's list of
forgotten events. Lonkowski remained an unknown entity. The bureau
did not even begin to figure him out and had no inkling of his legacy, a
web of spies who were out to steal US secrets.

All this stood ready to change when the curtain rose on a further act in
the drama and revealed Jessie Jordan, a minor spy with major consequences.

2
JESSIE JORDAN

Her mother was Scottish, but the grown-ups decreed that Marga should be a patriotic German. In a nod to Kaiser Wilhelm II, they christened her Margaretha Frieda Wilhelmina. World War I broke out two months later, and Marga's parents were proud of their acquaintance-ship with one of its military heroes. Referring to Field Marshal Paul von Hindenburg, who had at the outset of the war crushed a Russian army at the Battle of Tannenberg, a British newspaper recorded how "Little Marga Jordan sat on the knee of the victor of Tannenberg and pulled his long mustache. Von Hindenburg laughed and murmured, '*Liebchen*' (darling)."[1]

The years passed. Von Hindenburg became president of Germany, and Marga started a career as a teenage actress and singer. In 1931 she married Hermann Wobrock, a Hamburg merchant, and three years later gave birth to little Jessie.

The enchantment in Marga's life now began to fade. Marga's mother, also called Jessie, was an immigrant of humble birth and fluctuating for-tunes who had invested in Wobrock's business. In the Depression, the Wobrock enterprise collapsed. Marga contributed to the family's woes by having a fling with a Greek hypnotist. The Wobrocks separated in 1935.

It was the foretaste of a grim scenario. Von Hindenburg had appointed Adolf Hitler as chancellor in 1933. Anti-Semitism now asserted its can-cerous hold on German society. Scottish-born Jessie had married not just one Jew but two in succession. Though the husbands had departed the scene, the clientele at her Hamburg hairdressing salon remained largely Jewish. Under the pall of persecution, these customers now faded away just when Jessie needed the money. As if that were not enough, the authorities told Marga to forget about resurrecting her stage career unless she could prove she had Aryan ancestry on her mother's side.[2]

At this point, a stroke of luck seemed to intervene. Jessie received an offer of employment in her native Scotland. She decided to gift her Hamburg business to Marga and to accept the post, taking this opportunity to certify her ancestry and thus her daughter's. She booked a berth on a vessel bound for the port of Leith, adjacent to Scotland's capital city, Edinburgh. The boat was scheduled to depart on February 2, 1937, and on that day Jessie left the family home to catch it.

To Marga's dismay, her mother disappeared for several days. Unbeknownst to the daughter, her mother had acceded to a change of plan. She missed the boat and became a spy.

The Scottish German spy Jessie Jordan would play an instrumental role in events that created a great stir in the far-off United States. She had experienced a less than privileged life. Her maternal grandparents came from humble Protestant origins in County Down, Ireland. Grandfather John Wallace worked as a laborer after arriving in Scotland. John's Irish-born daughter Lizzie Wallace gave birth to Jessie in Glasgow in 1887. The name of Jessie's father, William Ferguson, did not appear on her birth certificate, as he had escaped to the States and left Lizzie to fend for herself.[3]

After Jessie's birth, her mother married John Haddow, a widower who worked as a railroad locomotive engineer (an "engine driver" in British parlance). Jessie Wallace became Jessie Haddow as she grew up, and by 1907 she was a chambermaid in the east coast manufacturing city of Dundee. There, she met a German waiter who was a couple of years her junior. When her eyes first fell upon him, his brother had just died in London, and Karl Friedrich Jordan was in tears. Jessie put a comforting arm around Karl, and, as they say, one thing led to another. The young suitor had to return to Germany to do his compulsory military service, but he asked Jessie to join him and married her in 1912.

On July 29, 1918, Karl died in Hamburg. His death certificate stated lung collapse as the cause of his death; he may well have been a victim, therefore, of mustard gas poisoning on the western front. In the meantime, Jessie had become a German citizen, and she continued to live in Karl's native land until 1937. Marga later asserted, "My mother has always said, I am German. I love Germany. I would die for Germany and I would like to be buried in Germany."[4]

One might be tempted to believe that Jessie pined for Karl and that it was his death in the cause of the fatherland that prompted his widow to spy for Germany nearly twenty years later. If such an emotional tug existed, it must have been weakened when Jessie discovered a cache of letters her husband had sent from the front, as they were addressed to another woman.[5] Jessie just had no luck with men. In 1920 she married Karl's cousin Baur Baumgarten. He, too, had a roving eye. The marriage did not work out, and the Baumgartens divorced in 1923. Jessie became Frau Jordan once again.[6]

Jessie responded by becoming a successful Hamburg businesswoman. The city epitomized Germany's determination to overcome the economic disaster of World War I. Its shipyards built great oceangoing liners that rivaled those of Scotland's Clydeside. The Hamburg American Line was the world's largest shipping company, challenged only by the North German Lloyd Line in the nearby city of Bremen.[7] The resultant prosperity created opportunities, and Jessie saw one in the cosmetic industry. Her chance for success arose from the introduction of machinery, such as the hair dryer, and the rise of the cheap "perm." Jessie acquired hairdressing skills and, at a shop she opened in 1923, specialized in a setting known as the Viennese wave. As affluence returned to her Hoheluftstrasse quarter of Hamburg, customers, especially from the Jewish sector of the city's population, flocked to her salon, and she opened a new branch to accommodate them.

In spite of this success, or perhaps because of it in a nation riven by racial jealousies, Jessie Jordan was susceptible to intimidation by the 1930s. Quite apart from the vulnerability of her daughter and granddaughter, her son, Werner, was in military training in Germany and in a position to be victimized. These factors, as well as economic necessity, lay behind her decision to reconnect with her native Scotland.

So what did happen to Jessie Jordan on that February day when she set out with her baggage for Hamburg's harbor? Marga recalled the sequence of events: "When my mother missed the boat she did not come home. Later I found she stayed with friends called Ostjes. Herr Ostjes is a member of the Gestapo, the German secret police, and it was he who made the suggestion to my mother that she should confirm information of military importance when she came to Scotland and which was already known to Germany."[8] Ostjes—an acquaintance of a friend rather than an actual friend, as Marga was led to believe—had learned of Jessie's predicament and plans, and arranged for her to be intercepted on her way to the docks. Over the next few days, officials persuaded Jessie Jordan to spy for Germany's foreign intelligence service, the Abwehr.

The officials offered a carrot as well as a stick: Jessie would be paid for her services. However, there was more than fear and finances behind her decision to spy. She had split loyalties, even fragmented and destroyed identities, because of her background—her family's migration from the factional northern counties of Ireland to Scotland and her marriage into German society. On a more positive note, Jessie Jordan loved the "Great Game" of international espionage. She was a voracious reader of crime stories and spy thrillers. Explaining her espionage later on, she wrote, "Excitement and change . . . were life's blood to me." Those who commented on her appearance did not see the slouched form of a victim but a woman of proud and charismatic deportment. Her character helps to explain why she was not just a spy but also an enthusiastic one.[9]

Jessie's new spy friends detained her for eight days before dispatching her to catch her boat. When finally she contacted Marga to tell her that all was well, Jessie did not mention what happened at the gray, forbidding building that housed the Abwehr offices in Hamburg's Harvestehude district. It was there, at 14 Sophienstrasse, that Jessie received her instructions and some rudimentary tuition on tradecraft. The new recruit learned that she was to address all correspondence to "Sanders" at post office box 629 in Hamburg.

The correspondent's name derived from a past alias of Hilmar Dierks, whom we encountered in chapter 1 as the tutor of Niki Ritter, the spy who delivered the Norden bombsight secret. Dierks was in charge of Luftwaffe intelligence in Hamburg until 1937. A professional soldier who fought in World War I and spied for Germany more or less continuously from 1914 until his death in 1940, Dierks had at one time used the cover name Richard Sanderson, which evolved into the code name Sanders. In the words of a postwar British intelligence report, "SANDERS . . . was almost certainly a generic name . . . as was the cover-address Post Box 629, Hamburg 1." Spy correspondence mailed to that post box was addressed to Sanders regardless of the identity of the intended recipient.[10]

Jessie Jordan was a mere agent, not a trained intelligence officer. Like Hermann Goertz and Otto Karl Ludwig, precursor German spies sent to the United Kingdom and exposed in November 1935 and April 1937, respectively, she was expendable. With little regard for her inexperience, she had been thrown in against MI5, a professional counterespionage agency.

One could argue, it is true, that there were limits to MI5's competence. Maxwell Knight, who took over as its director in 1931, was an ardent anti-communist who in the preceding decade had expressed fascist sympathies. His agency left itself open to the charge that it took the communist menace so seriously that it neglected the Hitler menace. Another charge, made in a later age, was that MI5 was blinkered on the subject of women. It did not employ female officers in the 1920s. When the Soviet trade delegation named the All-Russian Cooperative Society (ARCOS) began supplying cover for spies in the same decade, the MI5 leadership became obsessed with the number of women ARCOS employed but suspected their only being femmes fatales laying honey traps for British victims and not having general competence in matters of spying. In 1931 Knight did employ Olga Gray to penetrate a communist spy ring at the Woolwich Arsenal. When she proved effective, her chauvinist employers gave her scant reward, and she emigrated. Thus, in sending Jessie Jordan to spy in Britain, the Abwehr potentially played on a British weakness.

In the event, Jessie did not stand a chance. There has been some exaggeration of the degree to which she was under surveillance. We can disregard an account that appeared in the *Empire News*, claiming that an agent of the Secret Intelligence Service (MI6) personally witnessed a Gestapo agent's approach to Jessie: "Then, buttoning up his coat and pulling down his hat, he followed them." More reliably, because of its previous dealings with yet another German spy and double agent named Christopher Draper, MI5 had known about box 629 since early 1936. MI5 did not have blanket authority to intercept and read private correspondence, but it could do so on the authority of a Home Office Warrant (HOW). It used this procedure to keep tabs on what went to box 629; thus, MI5 would soon know about Jessie Jordan.[11]

The unsuspecting Jessie was a busy spy. Having arrived in Scotland, she at first lived with her half brother, William Haddow, in the Friarton district of the city of Perth. He was the one who had offered her employment; after his wife, Mary, died, he needed someone to keep house for him and his two children. It occurred to Jessie that Marga could perform the housekeeping and mothering roles, so she summoned her daughter to Scotland. Then Jessie was free to go on her travels. In England she visited the military town of Aldershot. Hairdressers make good listeners, and Jessie chatted with soldiers in the local bars, making notes and drawing sketches. She also visited Southampton and spoke to sailors in that strategic port.

She then traveled to Talgarth, a village nestling in the eastern foothills of the Brecon Beacons range of hills in South Wales. Once the seat of an ancient Celtic kingdom, by the 1930s Talgarth was a sleepy backwater with a half-decent rugby team and not much else, and Jessie could be forgiven for imagining that her activities there would arouse no suspicion. She had chosen the village for a family reason. Mary Jean Mackay Wallace, her mother's sister, co-owned a nearby country house, Felin Newydd. Mary for many years had earned a living looking after infirm clients and in 1925 had established Felin Newydd as a convalescent home.[12]

In June 1937 post office personnel acting on behalf of MI5 intercepted a letter sent to "SANDERS, Post Box 629, HAMBURG," the address that the security service had under surveillance. The postmark on the envelope was Talgarth, Brecon. The enclosed letter described the officers' mess and barracks at Aldershot. Lt. Col. William Edward Hinchley

Cooke of MI5 later reported, "As it appeared to be a very feeble effort at espionage I allowed it to go forward for delivery in due course to the addressee. It was obviously the effort of a beginner."[13]

Before June was out, an opportunity arose for the now-doomed Jessie to establish what she thought would be enduring cover when she spotted a notice in Dundee's newspaper *The Courier* offering for sale the goodwill and contents of Jolly's salon at 1 Kinloch Street. Jolly was an acronym for "Jesus Our Lord Loves us Yet," and the selling proprietor was a godly citizen by the name of James Curran. On September 7, 1937, Jessie Jordan purchased the going concern for £75. She then spent a reputed £300 refurbishing it as a hairdressing enterprise. When later questioned about the money, she told the Dundee police that it came from Mary Wallace. In espionage terms, however, Mary was a fictitious cover. When MI5 obtained a letter purportedly written by Mary to her niece Jessie offering financial support, its handwriting expert declared it a forgery. Perhaps guessing that she was being watched and needing an explanation for her expenditures should she be questioned, Jessie had written the letter herself.[14]

Back in her half-brother's house in Perth, Jessie continued her correspondence with her German controllers. One of her missives was a letter to Hamburg that MI5 intercepted as usual. It was in an envelope that enclosed another envelope containing a letter from Sanders dated July 16, 1937. Posted from the Central Station in Amsterdam, this returned letter asked her to travel to The Hague "for the purpose of discussion in detail all your business affairs which are still pending in Germany." MI5 personnel took note of the enclosed letter but found the inner envelope of greater interest. It bore the traces of writing that had been erased, and experts applying special methods were able to make out Jessie's address in Perth. Accordingly, Hinchley Cooke was able to obtain a further HOW authorizing the interception of all correspondence addressed to her in Perth, and from then on Jessie was under even closer surveillance.[15]

With her cover established, or so she thought, Jessie Jordan finally left Perth for Dundee, where the local post office took over the task of monitoring her correspondence. She acquired an apartment with a view of the Tay estuary. Her new abode was a stone's throw from her freshly painted salon. She joined a local Dundee library and indulged her taste for thrillers. She borrowed, for instance, E. Phillips Oppenheim's *The Evil Shepherd*, in which the character Francis Ledsam gets through whisky, champagne, and liqueur in the first twenty-eight pages and meets his friends in a "small white Georgian dining-room, with every appurtenance of almost Sybaritic luxury."[16]

In Scotland Jessie continued her spying activities. Forty miles south of Dundee lay a series of naval installations. The estuary on which they were situated, the Firth of Forth, was heavily fortified and crossed by a mighty rail bridge. Warships put in for repairs and sheltered under the guns of the "inches," or fortified islands strung along the approaches to the bridge and the dry docks beyond. The entire US Atlantic Fleet had dropped anchor in the shadow of the bridge in 1918, lined up as neatly as the targets were in Pearl Harbor twenty-three years later, and were captured in an oil painting by the artist Sir John Lavery. The area had been a target of German espionage in 1912, when Armgaard Karl Graves claimed to have been tasked by the Germans to blow up the rail bridge. He turned out to have been a double agent, and his book about the plot, much discussed in the US press, sold 100,000 copies on the eve of World War I. The Germans still considered the area to be important, and Sanders told Jordan to "confirm" certain details.[17]

Traveling by bus, Jessie made sketches, took photographs, and wrote notes; then she sent her reports to Hamburg. Although her efforts were amateurish and she could have conveyed to her German masters little that they did not already know, her work confirmed the existence of a plan to provide German bombers with useful coordinates. In the immediate wake of Jordan's efforts, the Luftwaffe's Colonel Theodor Rowehl organized overflights of the North Sea coast of Scotland and the north of England, ostensibly to check out new routes for the civilian airline Lufthansa but secretly photographing points of strategic interest. On October 16, 1939, Hitler's very first anti-British bombing mission targeted Jordan's spy area resulting in the Battle of the Firth of Forth. But in 1938, MI5 was not moved to precipitous action. Hinchley Cooke and his colleagues were the inheritors of counterespionage tradecraft and did not want to rush in and make an arrest that would have betrayed their knowledge of box 629 and German methodology. Furthermore, the British government, like its US counterpart, was averse to taking actions at the time that might provoke a deterioration in relations with Germany. The policy of appeasement, as critics called it, was headed to its apogee in Prime Minister Neville Chamberlain's agreement with Hitler in Munich in September 1938. MI5's policy, then, was wait and watch.

In pursuing this policy, Hinchley Cooke and his colleagues ran into two problems. The first was that the people of Dundee were on to Jessie Jordan. One story that gained currency was that the local "postie" (postman) became suspicious of the volume of foreign mail that arrived at 1 Kinloch Street and told his superiors that Jessie might be dangerous. In truth, his superiors already knew about Jessie Jordan. Whether because of the postie's vigilance or not, from December 10, 1937, at the latest, Alexander Jack, an officer in the General Post Office in Dundee who operated under the authority of an HOW, steamed open envelopes addressed to 1 Kinloch Street and photographed their contents.[18] That was necessarily kept a secret and not released to the newspapers. The reality of MI5 surveillance would not prevent the humble postie from becoming a hero of the press in 1938 when the story broke. Meanwhile, keeping a lid on patriotic posties was one of Hinchley Cooke's tasks, and with news suppression as well as the investigation in mind, he regularly visited from London to confer with the Dundee police and senior postal officials.

Mary Curran was another potential inconvenience. She had worked for her brother-in-law at Jolly's, and Jessie kept her on staff. She and her husband, John, a tram conductor, maintained the appearance of a friendship with Jessie, who spoke about politics with John and loaned him "a book on anti-Jewism in Germany" and a copy of one of Hitler's speeches. Mary's superficial cordiality masked her suspicions about Jessie's purchase of Jolly's, which was not a prime property as it was in a relatively poor district. The seemingly extravagant Jessie had paid for the premises in Bank of England five-pound notes. (Could her German paymasters have been unaware that Scottish banks issued their own bank notes and that "fivers," as hundred-pound notes would in a later day, stood out a mile?)

Mrs. Curran also wondered about the money Jessie lavished on the establishment and how she so easily imported from Germany specialist wave equipment. Her frequent travels to Hamburg and her inquiry as to the location of the nearest military barracks also increased the Currans' curiosity. Mary reported her suspicions to the Dundee police. The force was already tracking Jessie's every move and reporting to Col. Vernon Kell, the founding director of MI5. Sir Vernon was in semi-retirement but still on a working retainer, and as he had done in World War I, he took an active interest in counterintelligence.[19]

On December 7, 1937, Mary Curran spotted Jessie's handbag sitting on a table in the rear room of the salon's premises. No devotee of privacy, she opened the bag and discovered a map. Handwritten numbers on the map identified locations in Scotland and northern England. Mary showed the map to the police, who took photographs. Then she replaced it in the handbag.[20]

Eleven months later, Mrs. Curran and her husband, John, tried to obtain financial reward from the government for their services to the nation. MI5 was aghast at the open nature of their request and resisted it. The agency noted, disapprovingly, that the Currans had in May 1938 received £25 for a two-day spread in Glasgow's *Daily Record*, in which they claimed to have cracked the Jordan spy case virtually single-handedly.[21] Of course, they had not, as Jessie was already under surveillance. As Colonel Kell put it, "We were fully aware of Mrs. Jessie Jordan's unlawful activities as far back as July 1937, viz. over three months before the present claimants approached the police on 18 November, 1937."[22]

Kell was being overly dismissive, for Mrs. Curran's discovery of the map in November helped persuade MI5 to concentrate its vigilance on Jessie's Dundee business address instead of on her recent Perth address, which was already the subject of an HOW.[23] The Currans' enthusiasm for disclosure was, nevertheless, an embarrassment to an agency whose byword was secrecy.

As for Jessie Jordan, her espionage was amateurish and trifling yet also indicative. It signaled that in spite of its professed friendship with Britain, Hitler's regime had aggressive intentions, for Jessie did not aim to steal technological secrets to help Germany's defense. Rather, she supplied details about bombing targets that would facilitate a military attack.

MI5's response to Jessie Jordan's espionage was conservative. Its mission in the fall of 1937 was to track a traitor while keeping a lid on the case amid the blundering efforts of amateur sleuths. It succeeded in that task—until events in the United States forced its hand.

3
MURDER IN THE McALPIN

Situated on New York's Broadway and Thirty-Fourth Street, the McAlpin was the world's largest hotel. Run by more than a thousand staff, it boasted progressive facilities that included a floor solely devoted to female guests and a pioneering ship-to-shore radio system. From certain windows, one could gaze at the imposing structure of Macy's, the world's largest department store.

The McAlpin had been a favorite with German spies in World War I, and the hotel's reputation held into the 1930s.[1] It attracted operatives who were addicted to big-name attractions: grand hotels, state-of-the-art ocean liners, fast cars. Women met their Abwehr lovers in the McAlpin or its rival, the Taft Hotel. The size of the former establishment offered spies a special commodity that they sought—anonymity.

In the early weeks of 1938, four Abwehr agents hatched a secret plot that would center on the McAlpin. The conspirators took care to conceal their identities, and for the sake of convenience, we can call them Agents A, B, C, and D. Agent B, however, was just an assistant and withdrew from the scheme because of cold feet.

Agent A accepted his role, which was to induce Col. Henry W. T. Eglin to visit the McAlpin. Eglin was the commander of the military facility Fort Totten, on the East River approach to Long Island Sound. The plotters knew that the US Army officer was privy to the Americans' East Coast defense plans. The Abwehr agents' scheme was to get him into a McAlpin bedroom while bearing documents that outlined those plans, to relieve him of those documents, and to send them to the military command in Berlin.

The plot went further than earlier attempts by Lonkowski and his confederates to steal the secrets of US military technology. It was an aggressive scheme reminiscent of what the Spanish Secret Service had tried to achieve in the Spanish-American War of 1898. Upon the outbreak of that war, Ramon de Carranza, Spain's military attaché in Washington, DC, fled to Montreal, where he established a spy base and sent agents to obtain the secrets of US coastal defenses. The Spanish naval command aimed to send five cruisers up the Atlantic coast to bombard strategic targets that Carranza's agents had identified—for example, Philadelphia's financial district. Rear Adm. William T. Sampson's blockade of the Spanish fleet at Santiago de Cuba and the US Secret Service's arrest of Carranza's main agents defeated the Spanish plan.[2]

At least in 1898, Spain and the United States were already at war. There was no such excuse for the Abwehr agents' aggression in 1938. In that year, diplomats in Berlin and Washington were promoting the appearance of friendship between their respective nations. Contrary to that appearance, Agents A, C, and D acted in a spirit of bellicosity.

With the approval of Agent D, Agent A drafted a message for Colonel Eglin. Agent A would telephone the message, representing himself as an adjutant of the chief of the US Army Staff, Maj. Gen. Malin Craig:

A secret emergency staff meeting is scheduled to be held at the McAlpin Hotel, New York, NY, on Friday, January 28, 1938. Your attendance is requested, and you are called upon to observe the following details:

1. You will not divulge the nature or circumstances of the meeting to anyone.

2. You will appear in civilian clothes and arrive and leave unattended.

3. You will time your departure so as to arrive at the Hotel McAlpin at 12:20 p.m., Friday, January 28th.

4. You will sit yourself in the main lobby of the hotel and will await being paged as Mr. Thomas W.

Conway. After identifying yourself as such you will
be escorted to the meeting rooms.

5. You will bring with you all mobilization and coast
defense plans in your possession, also pertinent maps
and charts and a notebook for entries at the meeting.

6. It is repeated that the utmost discretion is expected of you in regard to this meeting, as no one is
informed except those directly concerned.[3]

Agent C, who possessed nubile qualities, was to be held in reserve, so
she could exercise her charm on the colonel if necessary. Agent D, who
had links with the Gestapo, would be an enforcer. In preparation for the
unsuspecting army officer's entry into the hotel room, Agent D would
be standing on a sill, dressed as a window cleaner. At the right moment,
he would spring into the room and assist Agent A in overpowering their
victim. Agent D would administer to Eglin the contents of a syringe
disguised as a fountain pen.

The US authorities learned of this plot in a roundabout way. Their enlightenment stemmed from the dual nature of Jessie Jordan's spy mission.
Jessie served not just as a spy but also as a poste restante. She received
letters and parcels from agents in foreign countries and forwarded them
to Germany. The Abwehr had added this mode of communication to
its system of shipborne couriers. It thought sending letters via Perth and
Dundee instead of directly to Hamburg might cause fewer suspicions.
The service had another rationale in using Jordan: if things came un-
stuck, there would be a scandal not in the targeted countries like the
United States but more conveniently in the United Kingdom. As MI5's
Guy Liddell later put it, the postbox was in Scotland "so as to throw the
onus on the British in the event of unpleasant revelations."[4]

A few of the letters that Jessie received and forwarded came from
Czechoslovakia, where Hitler was planning hostile incursions. Most of
the communications, however, came from the United States. One such
letter, translated into English from the original German by MI5's bi-
lingual lieutenant colonel Hinchley Cooke, was postmarked Warwick

Street Station, New York, 1 December 1937; signed "Rt"; and addressed to "Mr. S," no doubt referring to Sanders. It acknowledged that future letters would be sent through Jordan and emphasized the sender's security consciousness: "I have nothing in my possession which could lead to the conclusion that I am in any sort of contact with you or Germany. The copies which were enciphered some time ago have now been destroyed. The addresses I have memorized."[5]

In January 1938 Jessie Jordan began to receive letters from an agent who called himself Crown. They arrived at 1 Kinloch Street, Dundee. Possibly thanks in part to Mrs. Curran, who had communicated her suspicions to the police, MI5 intercepted them and made copies. The letters covered a range of subjects. Crown constantly craved money, recognition, and assets. In one letter, he asked for "a very small Zeiss precision camera." On January 19 he asked for a supply of forged White House writing paper to help him request plans for the USS *Enterprise* and USS *Yorktown* aircraft carriers. In February he complained about not having heard from his controller and said his brother in Prague had written, as promised, to "Berlin."[6]

MI5 copied these and other letters. They scrutinized the letter Crown's brother had written that was posted from Prague and signed Hansjorg Gustav Rumrich. Dated January 24, it offered Gustav's services as a spy and mentioned that his "brother G" was "active for the matter in the United States." If this was a clue to Crown's identity, MI5 either missed it or failed to alert the Americans for reasons of their own. British intelligence had a long-standing policy of keeping their methods secret and of telling the Americans only what they wanted them to know.[7]

Another letter set the alarm bells ringing and at last prompted the British to send an alert. This letter was dated January 17, 1938. Addressed as usual to Sanders via Jessie Jordan, it outlined Crown/Agent A's plot to obtain details of US defense operations on the East Coast.

The letter indicated the date of the apocryphal "emergency staff meeting" to be held at the McAlpin Hotel—by then postponed to either Monday, January 31, or Tuesday, February 1. It explained how Crown and his confederates would handle Colonel Eglin: "We shall attempt to overpower him and remove papers that he will have been ordered to fetch along. I shall leave clues that would point to communist perpetrators." Crown admitted, "The matter will probably stir up a little dirt, but I believe it will work out all right. The arrangements have been made with extreme care, every little detail has been reckoned with."[8]

MI5 had no further details with which to assess the seriousness of the plot, but it could not rule out the possibility that Crown and his associates would resort to murder. A memorandum in its files noted, "This plot might easily have led to loss of life."[9]

Still, it was not a foregone conclusion that MI5 would alert the American authorities. It was true that there was a presumption of transatlantic strategic cooperation, and for some time Britain had cultivated a special intelligence relationship with the United States. For example, in 1898 the British had expelled Carranza from Canada to assist the US Secret Service's counterespionage effort, and in World War I, the British had shared cryptographic and battlefield intelligence with the Americans.

But information is power, and the Admiralty code breakers in the war had refused to share their code-breaking methodology with their American counterparts. Moreover, there was a cultural difference between MI5 and the FBI. When the latter saw malfeasance that threatened national security, its instinct was to make an arrest, but MI5 did not share this preoccupation. Its instinct was to follow a suspect, with the object of obtaining further information. With this objective in mind, why not just let Jessie Jordan run?

There were also political problems. Did the British really want to alert the Americans in such a way as to aggravate relations with Germany at a time when the London government was intent on preserving harmonious relations with Berlin? Until the beginning of January, the civil servant Sir Robert Vansittart had overseen British intelligence and had been keen on cooperating with the United States in thwarting Hitler's plans, but he had been moved from his position as permanent undersecretary of state for foreign affairs to another post precisely because of his strong anti-appeasement stance. In the following month, Foreign Secretary Anthony Eden would resign over the appeasement issue. Prime Minister Chamberlain's government simply did not want to rock the boat.

For their part, the Americans were loath to receive potentially destabilizing news at a time when Washington, too, was intent on getting along with the German government. President Franklin D. Roosevelt (1933–45) had just appointed Joseph Kennedy as the ambassador to the United Kingdom. He conceded that Kennedy was a "very dangerous man." On account of his Irish American heritage, he might resort to the old Anglophobic tradition of "twisting the lion's tail." Some suspected Roosevelt did not really approve of Kennedy and that he simply wanted to get him away from US politics. But another factor played in the new appointee's favor: Kennedy was attuned to Prime Minister Chamberlain's policy of not confronting Hitler, and this suited Roosevelt's purposes in early 1938.

Yet the time was propitious in two ways for MI5 to depart from its customary caution. First, Joe Kennedy had not yet completed the arrangements for his move to London. He would not arrive to take his post until March 1. In the meantime, the US Embassy was in a state of interregnum.[10]

Second, although Vansittart had officially moved on, his interest and influence lingered in his old domain. In his newly invented post of "chief diplomatic adviser to the British government," he was meant to be a vaguely defined "roving ambassador," but after a few weeks the devoted peace advocate Lord (Arthur) Ponsonby expressed concern that Vansittart might be running a "duplicate foreign office."[11] His successor as permanent undersecretary, Alexander Cadogan, expected Vansittart to "make trouble." He was "annoying" and keeping up his contacts with the secret services. Later in the year, an *Evening Chronicle* journalist would observe that the permanent undersecretary was "the only man who knows the name of every member of Britain's secret service." Vansittart was not about to forget or neglect the advantage that knowledge conferred.[12]

For months after his supposed removal from the permanent secretaryship, Vansittart continued to discuss Anglo-American intelligence cooperation with MI5 personnel and continued to receive MI5 confidential reports. He obtained, for example, a copy of the January 17 McAlpin plot letter. He was not imprudent enough to interfere openly, but his continued tenure of high office and his intimacy with intelligence circles would have been an encouragement to those deciding on a tip-off.[13]

Crown's letter of January 17 arrived in Dundee on the twenty-eighth. MI5's post office interceptors immediately photographed it and put the film on the night train to London. It arrived at MI5 headquarters in London the next day, and in spite of the politically delicate situation, the decision was taken to send the Americans an urgent alert. After all, it was one thing to appease Germany and to keep the transatlantic cousins in the dark as part of the power struggle known as the Great Game, but it was quite another to risk the Americans finding out that the British had allowed one of its US Army officers to be terminated in cold blood without issuing any kind of a warning.

On January 29, 1938, Colonel Kell gave a copy of the letter to Lt. Col. Raymond E. Lee, the US military attaché in London. Lee sent an urgent alert to the US Army General Staff, which transmitted a warning to New York to safeguard Colonel Eglin's life. MI5 also gave Lee a memorandum that outlined the nature of the plot. It noted that its prospective "perpetrator is a German espionage agent (he may be of any nationality; he has a good knowledge of the English language) whose identity is unknown." In an attempt to furnish clues as to Crown's identity, MI5 added that the conspirator was knowledgeable about aircraft. For the US Army had listed as his "choice of station" three locations: two airfields in the United States and one in the Panama Canal Zone.[14]

Alerted to the situation, US Department of State officials were still reluctant to be caught up in a spy case that might impair relations with Germany. That Crown's identity was a mystery suggested a way out—that is, to delegate responsibility to an investigative branch of government. They thus urged the FBI to enter the fray. Director J. Edgar Hoover at first dragged his feet and for good reasons.[15] Several government agencies and the military were involved, raising the possibility of jurisdictional buck-passing and warfare. Hoover also explained that his initial reluctance sprang from the fact that the story was already in the press, and, as one FBI agent ruefully remarked in retrospect, "discretion is the very essence of an espionage investigation."[16] In spite of these difficulties, Hoover changed his mind. The United States faced a clear danger of foreign penetration that threatened its security interests. It would have reflected poorly on the FBI director if he took no action, and, in any case, Hoover was not one to shirk a task that, if allocated to others, might diminish his agency's standing.

MI5's tip-off memorandum insisted, "It is of the utmost importance that in any action which is taken on this information, no indication whatever should be given of the fact that it was obtained in Great Britain."[17] The counterintelligence agency here was being true to a tradition exemplified by the Zimmermann telegram affair. Sent in the spring of 1917, German foreign secretary Arthur Zimmermann's encoded, top secret telegram had promised Mexico the restoration of the territories the United States had wrested from it in 1846 in exchange for Mexico's loyalty to Berlin should America enter the war then raging in Europe. When exposed, the Zimmermann telegram had inflamed Americans' opinion and contributed to the United States' entry in World War I. At the time London, not wanting Berlin to know it had broken German codes, had insisted that the United States could not disclose that the telegram came from a British intercept. A similar principle applied in 1938, with MI5's wanting to keep secret its knowledge of how Germany's postbox system worked.

In its handling of the McAlpin plot, MI5 continued its policy of restraint. It did not arrest Jessie Jordan, choosing instead to follow and observe her, hoping for the Americans' discretion. Jessie continued to operate as a spy in ignorance of her watchers. She had no idea the proverbial can of worms was about to open in the United States. It was her misfortune that the clues supplied by MI5 were being turned over to the FBI's greatest detective.

4

ENTER LEON TURROU

On January 30, 1938, military intelligence told the FBI about Crown's plot to kidnap Col. Henry Eglin.[1] Needing a lead investigator, J. Edgar Hoover turned to one of his most gifted special agents Leon G. Turrou, whose mastery of seven languages had impressed the FBI boss as early as 1921. FBI director of personnel Clyde Tolson, reflecting Hoover's views, noted Turrou's reputation for having "an uncanny knack of securing information." Another manager observed that Turrou was simply the "best investigator of criminal violations in the Bureau."[2]

Turrou had to overcome a certain degree of prejudice directed against him. One of his promotion assessors said he was "not very impressive looking." Another scrutinizer remarked on his "somewhat foreign physiognomy." Still another noted the "foreign accent" that went with features that bore "the stamp of his foreign birth." Turrou's own observation was that he had a "Slavic cast of countenance" and the "typical high-cheekbones oval face of a Russian."[3]

An objective description of Turrou's physique came from Walter F. Stillger, MD, who performed a medical examination on behalf of the FBI. He described a man, standing five feet eight inches tall and weighing 143 pounds, whose teeth were "in good condition several gold-capped." His genitals were "negative," a reference to their good health. His left leg was also "negative," but in accounting for his slight limp, his right limb showed a "healed scar . . . due to shrapnel wound." Turrou's body may not have impressed his colleagues, but it had a history.[4]

The later Turrou-Hoover feud that broke out in July 1938 gave Turrou's detractors a renewed opportunity to air their views, and FBI opinion fell in line with the director's lead in turning against the agent. For example, Special Agent Louis Loebl's officially commissioned account of Turrou's life focused on his habit of exaggerating and on his unreliability. It began with Turrou's account of his childhood, which Loebl said was "a lot of hooey."[5]

Turrou's account of the first twenty-five years of his life is indeed erratic to the point of invention. He once told a breakfast club in Los Angeles that by the time he reached his first birthday, both of his parents were dead, so he had limited means of ascertaining what happened in his very early years.[6] In reality, his mother, Rebecca, survived and immigrated to the United States in 1916, and he had two surviving brothers who could have jogged his memory.[7] Rebecca was a wanderer in more than the geographic sense. As her granddaughter delicately put it, she was "evidently before her time," and there was considerable family debate about the identity of Leon's "real father."[8] In these circumstances, Leon appears to have invented certain facts about his past and to have allowed invention to develop into a habit, especially when it was to his advantage. His capacity for invention earned him a great deal of criticism, but it may also have been an asset in that it helped him recognize other people's mendacity.

Leon was born on September 14, 1895, in the town of Kobryn, which is today in the east European nation of Belarus. Historically, this community was located in Poland; however, at the time of his birth, it was under Russian control, as it had been since the partition of Poland by Russia, Prussia, and Austria in the 1790s. Turrou recalled in his Los Angeles talk that his father might have been a French musician. The name Turrou was a simplification of his mother's name, Turovsky.[9]

Turrou's descendants hold DNA evidence indicating that he was 75 percent Jewish.[10] Turrou denied this heritage: "I happen *not* to be a Jew, either by birth or faith."[11] How do we interpret this remark? Turrou was not brought up in the Jewish faith and was not very religious, but there was more to his denial. Fear and opportunity played their role—fear in Eastern Europe, a land of pogroms, and opportunity once he left home and wanted to pass himself off as a gentile to ease his career. Our story reveals, however, that his denial was a paradox: he claimed to be a gentile to strengthen his campaign to save Jews and the rest of humanity from the evils of Nazism.

Turrou told his Los Angeles audience about his childhood. On his mother's "death," her next-door neighbors adopted him, but Turrou did not supply their names. The husband was a musician and took his adopted son on a "tour of the world," visiting Australia, China, and Japan, to name just a few of the countries they visited. In Egypt, Turrou continued, his new father placed him in one of Cairo's two Jesuit schools, where he remained until he was eight years old. "Give me a child until he is seven and I will give you the man" is the reputed Jesuit maxim, and even if he developed an agnostic outlook, perhaps Leon did acquire his exceptional literacy skills at this early stage. A Catholic upbringing may have been a convenient myth for him in later years, and his command of the Malay language suggests he spent at least some time in Singapore, where his mother is known to have sojourned in the bosom of the well-established local Jewish community. When he was eleven, the young migrant found himself deposited in Berlin for further education, and he learned German. By the age of thirteen, he spoke five languages. At this point, Turrou recalled, "I was abandoned at Berlin by my foster parents and it was necessary for me, at that time, to make my own living."[12]

This point of the narrative takes us to 1908. Continuing his radio story, Turrou said he got by in Berlin by selling newspapers and in the meantime continued his education. Then he migrated to London. At the age of seventeen, he departed for the United States. Immigration records certainly show that he passed through the Ellis Island processing depot on March 12, 1913. Turrou told his Californian listeners that once he arrived, he "sold newspapers and did odd jobs."[13]

Leon fell in love with the United States. Along the way, he also fell for a girl called Olga. It did not work out. Joseph Davidowsky, Olga's brother, vetoed their engagement "because Olga was a Greek [i.e., Orthodox] Catholic and Turrou was a Jew." The hoped-for marriage did not take place.[14]

According to Davidowsky, Turrou was "in despair" when things fell through with Olga.[15] So what does a young man do when true love fails to run its course? As any reader of *Beau Geste* will tell you, he joins the French Foreign Legion. P. C. Wren's novel was published in 1924, and it may well have influenced Turrou to romance his World War I experiences when he related them in later years. The FBI's chronicler Louis Loebl accepted Turrou's Foreign Legion story, though Turrou gave various conflicting accounts of his military service, none of them verifiable. Loebl estimated that Turrou was with the French unit from August 1917 to November 1918, a period when the legion took heavy casualties on the western front.[16] Turrou never explained why he risked his life with the legion, but it might be surmised that the growing US support for Poland influenced him. President Woodrow Wilson befriended Ignacy Jan Paderewski, the Polish pianist and future prime minister. Further, in his "Peace without Victory" speech to the Senate on January 22, 1917, and in his eye-catching "Fourteen Points" address on January 8, 1918, the president singled out the partitioned nation for special treatment, demanding "a united, independent and autonomous Poland."[17]

When recovering from wounds in a Paris hospital, Leon met a girl called Teresa Zakrewski, the sister of another wounded Pole. Teresa was a Catholic. Given his experience with Olga and the intolerance of the times—an enduring reason for being discrete on the subject—Leon may not have revealed his Jewish origins to her parents. Teresa's mother and father lived in China, and Leon traveled there to marry her. Soon they had two boys, Edward (born on November 19, 1918) and Victor (December 9, 1919). The family took up residence in Siberia at the Russian terminus of Turrou's new employer, the Chinese Eastern Railway.[18]

Misfortune now struck. Following their triumph in the Revolution of 1917, the Bolsheviks sealed the border.

```
There was a civil war going on in Russia. My wife got
stranded on the other side of the gate, while I was
in China, and for two and one-half years I was unable
to communicate with her. My inquiries at the Ameri-
can Consul indicated everyone in that little village
where she was living was eventually massacred. I gave
```

```
them up as dead. It was then I decided to return to
the United States.¹⁹
```

Back in America, Turrou joined the US Marines in a noncombat capacity, serving in France and Belgium, and in 1921 he petitioned for naturalization. With that paperwork completed, he became officially Turrou and not Turovsky. A new opportunity now arose. In 1919 Congress had approved the funding for an American Relief Administration (ARA) with the aim of addressing some of the hardship in war-torn Europe. Two years later, famine struck in Russia, where civil war still raged four years after the Communists' takeover of 1917. The ARA sent a task force of three hundred Americans under the leadership of Col. William N. Haskell. Turrou served with the mission from September 1921 to February 1923 and was Haskell's interpreter and assistant in Moscow. Bertrand Patenaude, a historian of the relief expedition, has noted that Haskell "raved about Turrou's talents."[20]

A few years later, Turrou recalled how in 1922 urgently needed US wheat could not get through on the Soviet railway system. After five years of wartime neglect, "engines rusted at the sidetracks for lack of vital parts." More frustrating, Communist Party officials were not letting supplies through the vital junction at Balashov in the Lower Volga region. Hundreds of cereal-laden cars stood motionless in sidelines, some of them diverted there for personal gain by Soviet soldiers. Furious, Colonel Haskell demanded that the responsible officials appear at his office. When they arrived, their spokesman was Felix Dzerzhinsky, the Soviet commissar for transportation who doubled, more significantly, as the head of the State Political Directorate, or secret police (known as the GPU). In the ensuing discussion, Turrou, as the translator, took a risky line by making Haskell seem more aggressive than he was. The outcome was satisfactory. Dzerzhinsky turned to his comrades and gave an order "with not a trace of emotion on his deathmask face": "The trains will move,—and if you fail, the supreme punishment is waiting for you."[21]

In Russia an even more important outcome awaited Turrou. He discovered that his wife and boys were alive and well—even if little Edward had searing memories "of people hanging by the necks from telephone poles, killed by the communist revolutionaries."[22] Turrou took his family back to the United States, where Teresa's mother joined them. Joseph Davidowsky, who continued his turbulent relationship with Turrou, recalled, perhaps imperfectly, that "he always spoke Jewish to his mother-in-law."[23]

Turrou never articulated his reason for wanting to join the FBI. He came from a part of the world that had long experienced ambivalent identities, and the chance to assume different roles and guises in undercover work may have been an attraction. One can speculate that his difficulties in finding his long-lost family may have helped to persuade him of the need for an effective detective service. Here, the FBI was an attractive choice. It already had the reputation of being an all-American institution, and for a relatively new arrival in the United States, joining the bureau would be an affirmation of his patriotism and newfound identity. Turrou's shrapnel-pierced leg meant that active military service, another way of accomplishing that goal, was not an option, and the bureau offered a life of risk and adventure for which Turrou had developed a taste in his restless youth. The high profile of organized crime in the Prohibition era also may have helped make the attraction of a career in the FBI irresistible.

J. Edgar Hoover had always wanted to appoint Turrou a special agent. As deputy director he had recommended Turrou's appointment in 1921, only to be overruled on the grounds that he did not possess the usual requirement for a special agent—a law degree.[24] After further fruitless applications and a long delay, political events tipped the balance in Turrou's favor. In 1928 the Republican Party nominated as its presidential candidate Secretary of Commerce Herbert Hoover, who had directed the ARA. Turrou expressed his admiration for what Hoover had done for Russia and volunteered to work on his behalf in the Russian-speaking precincts of New York. He spoke in several languages at public meetings in support of his former employer. At the general election on November 6, Hoover gained an overwhelming victory against his Democratic rival, Al Smith.

It was time for Turrou to claim his reward, and his supporters petitioned Assistant Attorney General William J. "Wild Bill" Donovan. Soon after Hoover's inauguration on March 4, 1929, Donovan sent Turrou his letter of appointment, which arrived in the same envelope as a letter from J. Edgar Hoover containing the standard injunction that there should be "no publicity." On April 1 Turrou entered into active service as a special agent in the city of Chicago.[25]

Between this date and the start of his investigation into the Crown affair in February 1938, Turrou worked on around three thousand FBI cases. He gained experience that was not only extensive but also in some instances germane to the great investigation that would bring him fame.

Turrou's language skills gave him an operational advantage. The tale of his first case illustrates the point. Special Agent in Charge (SAC) Earl Connelley of Chicago asked him to track down Ignatz Skropinski, an immigrant from Cracow, Poland, who had escaped from Leavenworth Penitentiary while serving five years for his part in a violent US mail robbery. More experienced agents had already interrogated Mrs. Skropinski on several occasions, to no avail. Connelley told his new recruit to try once more. The rookie arrived at the Skropinski apartment in an old tenement on Cicero Street. She reluctantly admitted him to her home and stalled in a desultory conversation, during which, Turrou later recorded, she "suddenly rattled off a quick burst of Polish. She was staring directly at a big potato in her hand, but she was talking to her daughter." She told the girl to go to the barbershop and "tell Poppa not to come back for a while." It never occurred to Mrs. Skropinski that an FBI agent might understand Polish. Turrou exited the tenement, found a Chicago policeman to assist with the arrest, and stunned a deeply impressed Connelley by delivering the escaped convict to his office. This case won Turrou the first of many commendations for his detective work.[26]

Another of Turrou's early cases saw him working undercover on the completion of the USS *Akron*, otherwise known as ZRS-4. The *Akron*, a pet project of the US Navy's, was a helium-filled rigid construction airship designed to be a carrier that launched and recovered F9C Sparrowhawk fighter planes in midair. Like its sibling dirigible, the USS

Macon (ZRS-5), it measured well over two hundred meters in length and compared with the German hydrogen-filled airship the *Hindenburg*. The *Akron* crashed into the Atlantic Ocean during a gale off the coast of New Jersey, killing seventy-three of its seventy-six passengers. The *Macon* met a similar fate two years later, and the consensus was that the experimental craft were not airworthy. According to Turrou, the Soviets had planned to sabotage the *Akron* with faulty rivets installed by a communist worker who then disappeared. In his report on the matter, Vice Adm. Charles E. Rosendahl found that the six million rivets had been sound. Nevertheless, in July 1941, to a fanfare of press publicity, Turrou revealed his role in trying to prevent sabotage at the time of the airship's construction.[27]

The *Akron* met its fate in April 1933. In November of that same year, Turrou was personally involved in another crash, one that revealed to his colleagues the self-boosting side of his character. At the time, he was helping search for the Kansas City Massacre gunmen. On June 17 three men had tried to spring Frank Nash, an escaped federal convict who was being escorted by local police and the FBI to Leavenworth Penitentiary. Outside the Union Railway Station in Kansas City, Missouri, Vernon C. Miller, Adam C. Richetti, and Charles "Pretty Boy" Floyd shot dead three police officers, and Nash also died from bullet wounds. The case ushered in the FBI's fully armed war on crime (Turrou had just undergone machine gun training). Although the perpetrators were midwestern rural bandits rather than big-time urban gangsters, the investigation was important in the propaganda war on organized crime that was launched by Attorney General Homer Cummings and J. Edgar Hoover. Turrou was pursuing lines of inquiry on Vernon Miller when, early on the evening of November 14, he was driving his brand-new Rent-a-Car Chevrolet from Memphis, Tennessee, to Paragould, Arkansas. There are two versions of what happened next.

Investigating the accident, the FBI's D. Milton Ladd reported a conversation with a witness, B. R. Harris, at the Judd Hill Plantation near Truman, Arkansas. Harris said that Turrou's car overtook him "at about thirty-five miles per hour." Then it "cut back to the right hand side of the road, and in doing so slipped on the loose gravel on this highway and

. . . he noted the rear end of the car was swaying badly." Then "about one hundred feet in front of him it went over the embankment." Harris stopped his own vehicle and went to the FBI man's assistance, for the Chevy had turned over twice, landing on its wheels in the water. Harris flagged down another approaching car, whose driver took Turrou to the nearest hospital.

Turrou gave Ladd a different version of the incident. Stopping for gasoline and to ask advice on his route, he half noticed a black Buick or Cadillac lurking nearby. He left on Highway 63, heading toward Jonesboro and driving at about twenty-five miles an hour. About three miles east of Truman, "he heard a loud honking in the rear and at the same time a black Buick or Cadillac coach drove past him at about fifty miles an hour, cut in, and pushed him over an embankment."[28]

It was a good story. "Attempt [to] Take Life U.S. Officer Fails" ran the *Jonesboro Daily Tribune* headline. The next day, the paper reported J. Edgar Hoover's promise to pursue "every possible clue" to identify the "gangsters" in the assassination plot. With slightly more skepticism, the *Memphis Press-Scimitar* headline ran its account under the tag "U.S. Agent Blames Gang for Highway Death Plot."[29]

After agents had inspected skid marks at the scene of the accident and reviewed all the evidence, SAC R. H. Colvin at Oklahoma City concluded that "there were no facts developed to substantiate to the slightest degree the story told by Agent Turrou as to his having been forced off the highway by two men who had followed him from Memphis." He added that SAC Ladd of the St. Louis office believed "there was absolutely no merit in Agent Turrou's claim." He reported to FBI director Hoover that Turrou had entertained the press at his hospital bed and gave out the stories that appeared.[30]

The ambitious Turrou had been unwilling to accept culpability for the car crash and had summoned the press to massage and embellish the news. At this stage Hoover was willing to tolerate this and kept assigning his brilliant agent to major cases.

No case was bigger than that of the Lindbergh kidnapping. Charles A. Lindbergh was a twenty-five-year-old airmail pilot when in 1927 he flew the *Spirit of St Louis*, a monoplane he had personally configured, from Long Island to Paris. Completing the first solo nonstop crossing of the Atlantic had made him world famous—and a target. On the night of March 1, 1932, a kidnapper used a ladder to access a bedroom in the Lindbergh home near Hopewell, New Jersey, and kidnapped twenty-month-old Charles A. Lindbergh Jr. The Lindberghs agonized over a $50,000 ransom note left by the kidnapper and paid up through an intermediary. Two months later, the boy's body was discovered in a shallow grave.

Turrou later wrote, "Not since Paris abducted Helen and precipitated the Trojan War has a kidnapping had so many repercussions." When Roosevelt became president, he insisted that the bureau must find the killer. Accordingly, Hoover formed a "Lindbergh squad" that included Turrou. At first the squad made little headway, but a tip-off from a member of the public led to the arrest on September 20, 1934, of a suspect, Bruno Richard Hauptmann.

Turrou sat with Hauptmann for hours. On this occasion, as on others, he displayed his uncanny knack of winning the confidence of a suspect. Turrou was able not only to spot mendacity on the other side of an interview table but also to win the trust of persons who looked back at their interrogator and believed they saw someone with shared characteristics. Remarkably he caused those suspects he questioned to incriminate themselves, at times in a manner that amounted to a self-imposed death sentence. Turrou persuaded Hauptmann, against his better judgment, to transcribe long passages from the *Congressional Record* and the *Wall Street Journal*. The same quirks and spelling errors that appeared in the ransom note began to crop up. Hauptmann was convicted and died in the electric chair on April 3, 1936.[31]

By this time, a familiar alarm bell had rung in Washington. Hoover complained that "there appeared in the press considerable publicity concerning Special Agent L.G. Turrou."[32] The boss saw a continuing problem with Turrou's love of the limelight. However, he refrained from disciplining his agent partly because he empathized with the publicity instinct and partly because what made the FBI look good made Hoover look good. It helped that Turrou at every turn gave the impression that he was devoted to Hoover, sending the director frequent and well-received suggestions about how the FBI might improve its performance.

Hoover and his FBI colleagues agreed on their verdict: Leon Turrou was a truly gifted detective. The Crown case that Turrou began to address in February 1938 would test his gifts anew.

5

CROWN IDENTIFIED

At first, Turrou made little headway chasing down Crown's identity. When he asked for checks on Crown's military profile, the army drew a blank. Other lines of inquiry yielded only half clues. For example, Turrou noted that Crown had posted his letters from a location in the Bronx, New York. This identification of a particular area reminded him of the way in which he had helped track down Hauptmann, the killer of the Lindbergh toddler. Here, though, the trail ran cold.

Turrou surmised from Crown's relocation to a first-floor apartment (mentioned in a letter) that he might be married with small children. The text of the letters suggested a good education. The typing indicated that he was familiar with a keyboard but was self-taught; uneven digital pressure had caused some letters to be more pronounced than others, meaning the typist did not use all of his fingers. But that was clutching at straws. "Baffled," Turrou recalled, "we settled back to wait for a break."[1]

When that break came, it was the accidental result of a police operation. Late on the afternoon of February 15, 1938, Detectives John S. Murray and Arthur J. Silk of the New York Police Department (NYPD) hovered within sight of the King's Castle Tavern on Hudson Street. While they awaited the reappearance of a Western Union Telegraph Company messenger who had disappeared into the tavern, a boy entered the pub and emerged shortly afterward carrying a parcel. Watched by the detectives, the boy approached a street corner. Upon hearing an expected whistle, the boy paused, then moved toward the whistler and handed over his package. At this moment the detectives made their arrest.

The police officers took the whistler to a room at the Post Office Building on Thirty-Third Street and Eighth Avenue. The sibilant parcel receiver confessed to being the person who had pretended to be Secretary of State Cordell Hull and had called Ira F. Hoyt, the New York chief of the State Department's Passport Division, requesting that thirty-five passport application forms be delivered to a "Mr. Edward Weston, undersecretary of state." It had been a weak effort, not just because Hull had an inimitable Tennessee accent but also because the real name of the undersecretary of state was Sumner Welles. Seeing through the ruse, the Passport Division had alerted the NYPD.

The State Department's security staff had made a dummy package for the Western Union messenger to collect and take to the appointed rendezvous, and the arrested man had fallen into the trap. He now faced a battery of interrogators from the NYPD, the State Department, and military intelligence. He admitted that his real name was Guenther Gustave Maria "Gus" Rumrich.

For the next few days, the US Army held Rumrich prisoner at its facility on Governors Island, eight hundred yards off the southern tip of Manhattan. Maj. Joe Dalton, the US Army assistant chief of staff at G-2 (military intelligence) who had received the original MI5 tip-off about the McAlpin plot, was based there. For several days, along with State Department special agent T. F. Fitch and the NYPD detectives, he interrogated Rumrich. The interrogators were not unfeeling, and on February 17 and 18, they escorted Rumrich to his home so that he could see his wife and two-year-old son, Gerald.

A certain feature of the affair indicated it should not be considered an isolated incident. At the time of his arrest, Rumrich had been carrying a briefcase. He later explained that he always carried it when he left his home, lest his wife inspect its contents and discover what he was doing. The briefcase contained low-level, open-access intelligence, such as army and navy registers, and other odds and ends. Of particular interest among those odds and ends was a rough pencil draft of a telephone call Rumrich had been planning to make. It addressed Col. Henry W. T. Eglin, the commanding officer of Fort Totten: "A secret emergency staff meeting is scheduled to be held at the McAlpin Hotel, New York, N.Y." The text would have been familiar to anyone who had studied the Crown correspondence, and Dalton had been one of the first to know about the McAlpin conspiracy. Confronted with the scrap of paper, Rumrich confessed to the intelligence officers that he was connected to the plot against Colonel Eglin at the McAlpin Hotel.[2]

The State Department agents attempted to extract more details from Rumrich. In exchange for full disclosure, they asked, what guarantees would he want? Rumrich demanded promises of safety for himself and his wife and children. He did not want to be deported, as his fate back in his native Germany might be dire. He wanted all criminal charges against him to be dropped and asked for his personal indebtedness to be wiped out.[3]

The Department of State's officials refused to accept these conditions, but they faced a dilemma. They did not want to prosecute Rumrich over the theft of the passports because Secretary of State Cordell Hull would have to appear as a witness, and the case would strain relations with Germany. The military could prosecute Rumrich for deserting the US Army instead of for espionage, but that response seemed too benign in relation to the gravity of Rumrich's activities. In addition, it would not get to the bottom of what was going on. Like his State Department collaborators, Major Dalton was keen for the FBI to take over the case.

Leon Turrou learned of the arrest on the morning of February 17 from "badly garbled" accounts in the metropolitan newspapers. Though he had not yet seen the incriminating note, he suspected right away there was a McAlpin connection and wanted to be in on a case that might help him solve his own, more urgent inquiry. J. Edgar Hoover at first hesitated, but at 9 a.m. on Saturday, February 19, State Department agent Fitch and NYPD detectives Murray and Silk went to the Hotel New Yorker, where Rumrich was being held, and told him he was being handed over to the FBI. Rumrich protested to Fitch that "he did not appreciate being pushed around and turned over to another agency," but it was to no avail. At 10 a.m. he was in the hands of Leon Turrou, the FBI's top detective.[4]

Sensational and erratic accounts of the arrest continued to appear in the newspapers, apparently fed by an NYPD leak. Within days, details of the passport scam were public knowledge. Temporarily, the press observed the polite fiction that an unnamed foreign power was behind the plot. This allowed the *Hamburger Nachrichten* to publish on its front page, no doubt to the accompaniment of local mirth, an account indicating that "a large international spy ring" was responsible.

Although Turrou made no public comment, by the end of the month details of his widening inquiry had appeared in the American press. Reed E. Vetterli tried to calm the situation. As the special agent in charge in New York, Vetterli ran the local FBI office while Turrou ran the Rumrich investigation. When quizzed, Vetterli denied there was a threat to national security and declined to say which foreign power was involved. The American press had not really needed to ask that question as it had already deduced the source of the espionage. The *Washington Post* noted the "Teutonic appearance" of the arrested man, and Germany was unambiguously in the frame. In vain did Undersecretary of State Welles try to impress upon the British ambassador the US government's view that the "news had got into the press prematurely and that the authorities wanted its importance to be minimized."[5]

The leaks had reduced the chances of uncovering any wider spy ring that may have existed and of bringing the spies to justice. To Turrou's dismay, German intelligence diverted ships carrying spies, destroyed evidence, and told its agents to run for cover. There was a danger that the full working apparatus of Germany's US spy network would remain undetected and continue to operate.[6]

Contemporaries and historians wondered at the way in which Turrou nevertheless succeeded. The FBI special agent–turned-historian Raymond Batvinis wrote that "Turrou, with seemingly no effort, gained admissions from practically everyone he interviewed."[7]

As noted previously, Turrou had the gift of being able to make people talk. For illumination on this point, Turrou's book *The Nazi Spy Conspiracy in America* is a firsthand source.

In drawing on this book, we need to remember that Turrou spared no effort in trumpeting the role he played. "Who was this man before me?" he asks in his account of the passport scam interrogation. "Was this— could this be 'Crown'?"[8] By this stage, it must have been abundantly clear that Rumrich was Crown. His brother in Prague had referred to him in one of the intercepted letters included in the Crown batch, copies of which were by then in Turrou's possession. There was the penciled note Rumrich had so carelessly carried in his briefcase, and other interrogators had already connected Rumrich to the McAlpin plot.

Here, it should be interjected that in its US operations at least, German foreign intelligence displayed certain weaknesses. It allowed its agents to use the same hotel they had frequented in World War I; gave a pivotal role to the same shipping line, Hamburg American; and resorted to similar tactics, such as fraudulently acquiring US passports. Repetition made for predictability, and predictability is the enemy of security. Rumrich and his colleagues were asking to be found out, and it was only the historical amnesia resulting from the absence of a continuous US counterintelligence service that had afforded them a temporary reprieve.[9]

It was disingenuous of Turrou to suggest that he made the Crown-Rumrich discovery through his own brilliant analysis of the evidence. His book *The Nazi Spy Conspiracy* nevertheless provides an insight into the psychological tactics that Turrou used in extracting vital clues from the arrested agent about the German spy network. Rumrich was by this stage Prisoner 13 at the guard house on Governors Island. Each day, he would be delivered to the FBI's interrogation room in Manhattan, where Turrou would interview him in the presence of just one other FBI special agent. Turrou wanted no more leaks. So Rumrich suffered questioning in claustrophobic conditions, cut off from any sources of human support. The German authorities made no attempt to extricate him from his situation, leading him to believe he had been abandoned. This circumstance encouraged him to talk in order to procure a deal from the Americans.[10]

The room in which Turrou questioned his suspect was on the sixth floor of the US Courthouse on Foley Square. The twenty-foot square chamber had only one door. Yellow walls surrounded a floor covered with red linoleum. A gray rug gave some relief from the bright colors. A row of chairs along one wall gave Turrou's colleague a choice of viewing angles. A flat-topped desk at the other end of the room accommodated a chair for the interrogator, and opposite, slightly to one side, was a large and comfortable chair designed to make the suspect feel at ease. A few moments after Rumrich entered the yellow room for the first time, Turrou motioned to him to sit down and rang for coffee, sandwiches, and cigarettes. While Rumrich was still standing, he ran his eye over him and formed an impression of his character.

The detective saw a man with a military bearing and high forehead. Pulling himself to his full height of five foot eleven, the prisoner demanded to know why he was being dragged around from one place to another. His manner of speaking suggested to Turrou that he was proud to the point of weakness. He played on that and suggested to Rumrich that he was an intelligent man who had cleverly played the fool to keep the full story from the stupid NYPD detectives. He indicated that a conversation would now occur between equals. Revealing his credentials, he said he knew about the code words employed in the Crown letters; for example, they had used the word "furs" to indicate secret plans.[11]

Having played the pride card, Turrou deployed an empathy ace and arranged for Mrs. Rumrich, now pregnant with the prisoner's second child—the future Robert Rumrich—to visit together with toddler Gerald. Though showing emotion toward his weeping wife in a patriarchal sort of way, Rumrich fobbed her off with the story that he was being questioned about a minor fraud back in the Midwest. Softened by Turrou's approach, Rumrich talked that same day until 2 a.m. Sunday, February 20. On Monday, February 21, he signed a confession. Thereafter, he continued to talk and talk and talk. He lied and withheld information, but gradually a picture emerged about his life, his espionage activities, and his confederates.[12]

Rumrich's signed confession opened with his life story. He was born in 1911 in Chicago, where his father, Alphonse, served as the secretary of the Austro-Hungarian Consulate General. His paternal grandfather had been the mayor of the city of Turn, near the spa town Teplitz-Schoenau, in Bohemia. His maternal grandfather had an estate in the Hungarian township of Drávatamási and was a professor at the Royal Hungarian University in Budapest. Rumrich boasted he was able to trace his

Hungarian ancestry back a thousand years, yet his exalted ancestry was also a source of low self-esteem, given his high family expectations but his own indifferent achievement.[13]

The biographical portion of Rumrich's confession to the FBI charted a troubled life. In 1913 he and his younger sister Lillian moved from Chicago to the German city of Bremen, where their father took a new post. Upon the outbreak of war, there were further family disruptions, for Alphonse served as an artillery officer in Russia, then moved to Italy, and after that to Budapest. Another upheaval in the life of the young family occurred in 1918, with the Chrysanthemum Revolution, the short-lived social democratic overthrow of the Austro-Hungarian Empire. They sought refuge in the newly formed Republic of Czechoslovakia, settling in Teplitz-Schoenau and nearby Turn. Guenther attended school there but did not do as well as his younger brother, Gustav, who went on to study chemistry at the German University of Prague. Meanwhile, Alphonse suffered a business failure and had to fall back on his relatively modest imperial consular pension. In more peaceful times, the brothers Rumrich would have benefited from the rich cultural tapestry of Central European life. As things stood, they were casualties of war, revolution, and imperial collapse. Gustav became a fascist. Guenther found himself adrift in a sea of uncertain identities.

Aware that he qualified for US citizenship on account of his Chicago birth, Guenther Rumrich went through the necessary procedure and sailed for New York in 1929. Reaching the required age of eighteen, he joined the US Army. An Associated Press journalist observed that "although he had gained a brilliant technical education during his student days in Germany, he enlisted as a $30-a-month roughboy in the Medical Corps."[14] Within a few months he was in debt and went absent without leave (AWOL). After being court-martialed and serving a prison sentence, he resumed his military career, rose to the rank of sergeant, and spent some time on Governors Island, where he would later be held in custody. He moved west with the army and, in November 1935, married a girl from Missoula, Montana.

At sixteen years of age, Guiri Blomquist was almost nine years his junior. Rumrich's insecurity meant that he could only have married an innocent. Possibly knowing that she was already pregnant, her parents approved of her marriage to the army sergeant. Rumrich now took to drinking heavily and sank once more into debt. He told the FBI at that point there occurred "some irregularities with the hospital fund, which I administered." On January 3, 1936, he again went AWOL. He went to New York City, where he worked as a dishwasher and then as a German teacher at the Berlitz School of Languages before finding a job as a translator with the Denver Chemical Manufacturing Company at a salary of $22.50 per week. He sent for his wife and their baby, Gerald, who in the meantime was born June 22, 1936, in Missoula. He borrowed money to buy furniture and settled with his young family in the Bronx.[15]

In January 1936, while still washing dishes, Rumrich made his fateful move. He wrote to the official Nazi organ in Germany, *Völkischer Beobachter*, and enclosed a letter for Col. Walter Nicolai in which he offered to serve as a spy. Rumrich had read the colonel's memoir about his activities with German military intelligence in World War I. The prospective spy asked to be contacted under the name Theodore Koerner through a notice in the advertisement columns of the *New York Times*. That notice duly appeared on page 3 every day between April 6 and 10, 1936: "THEODORE KERNER—letter received, please send reply and address to Sanders, Hamburg 1, Postbox 629, Germany." The FBI later ascertained that the letter commissioning the ad was written on the stationary of the North German Lloyd Line.[16]

Once Rumrich had supplied his address, Nicolai's successors sent him a letter "in which a great deal was said about patriotism and in which stress was made of the fact that Germany was very glad to be in a position to be helped by foreigners who recognized the injustice being done to Germany."[17] The Abwehr continued, for a while, to receive Rumrich's communications through the Sanders post office box 629 in Hamburg and soon sent him $40 for information about artillery units in the Panama Canal Zone, where its newly recruited agent had spent time with the army. Late in 1937 the Abwehr instructed Rumrich to communicate in the English language, to use the name Crown, and to write via an intermediary in the United Kingdom. The address of his new "letter box" was Mrs. Jessie Jordan, 1 Kinloch Street, Dundee, Scotland.

Why did Guenther Rumrich spy for Germany against the land of his birth? It was not because of a pressing invitation or threats by the Gestapo. Unlike Jessie Jordan, he was a volunteer. Money was a factor, but there was more to it. A woman who knew him in later years observed, "He always tried to be a 'big shot.'"[18] Guenther Rumrich was the self-doubting product of an insecure upbringing who desperately wanted to take on a mission that increased his sense of worth and self-importance. Like other spies, he was capable of "splitting," or living two parallel lives, given his background of the ethnically divided Czechoslovakia that was reinforced by a life divided between two continents.[19]

In the course of his interrogation, Rumrich divulged some information on how the Nazi spy ring operated. For example, he explained how as a means of identification, he would receive one half of a torn postcard that would be reconciled with the other half carried by one of his fellow agents. He did not, however, reveal many names. Rumrich was a minor cog in a greater machine and knew less than his more senior colleagues. Furthermore, as he explained to Turrou, Germany's spies in the United States were kept in ignorance of one another—standard practice in a professional intelligence organization. This policy of compartmentalization meant that if any agent were captured, he or she could reveal only limited details to interrogators.[20]

Rumrich achieved the fame that he craved. The covert network that embraced him came to be widely known as the Rumrich spy ring. The FBI's case files almost without exception are headed "Rumrich," reflecting that Rumrich was the first to be exposed. Turrou's report of February 27, 1938, based on his questioning of Rumrich became the template for most of the later FBI reports on the spy case, and agents continued to head their memorandums "Rumrich" long after the investigation had widened and taken in more important spies. This heading was not just a matter of filing convenience; the more accurate title "Nazi spy ring" was too strong a label when American leaders were shying away from a confrontation with Hitler's Germany.

Guenther Rumrich's spying activities were limited and ineffective. In a first phase, ranging from the summer of 1936 to the end of 1937, the Abwehr tested his reliability. After sending information on Panama in June–July 1936, he sent further data on troop dispositions and other military matters that he obtained from open US Army and Navy sources and from newspapers. The intelligence was, as he later pleaded in an attempt to minimize his offense, "available to any one."[21]

Trusting him a little more, in a second phase the Abwehr provided him with what were meant to be the more secure addresses—that is, a new address in Hamburg and Jessie Jordan's. From November 1937, it paid him a monthly retainer of $30.

In December Karl Schlueter contacted Rumrich. Schlueter was a long-serving German spy. He had been the intended recipient of Lonkowski's ill-fated parcel on board the SS *Europa* in September 1935. More recently, Schlueter was the Abwehr's replacement for Karl Eitel, who had lost his post on the SS *Bremen* because of embezzlement. Schlueter asked Rumrich to find out about the latest US aircraft carrier designs. Finally he had asked for the passport application forms, explaining that the Abwehr wanted US passports to give its German secret agents false identities; they planned to pose as American sailors when attempting to penetrate the Soviet Union.[22] Another agent, code-named Ruth, would be in touch to arrange the collection of the passport forms, and the fee for this job would be $300.

On January 1, 1938, a certain N. Spielman sent Rumrich advice on how to be a spy. In a letter sent from Bordeaux, Spielman wrote in the guise of a businessman and issued various cautions about tradecraft. There were words of encouragement: "I believe that in time you will get acquainted with European business procedure." There were instructions on discretion followed by the injunction, "If you wish to become a good merchant you must pay heed to these little things and hints." Spielman also wrote that his representative, a person named Jenni, would soon be in touch about the price of "furs."[23]

An agent improbably called Schmidt next got in touch. The FBI never ascertained his first name, and evidence not available to the FBI at the time indicates that Schmidt was an alias that Schlueter used.[24] It was Schmidt who requested the East Coast defense plans and outlined the McAlpin Hotel kidnap scheme as a means of obtaining them. The Abwehr now began to pressure Rumrich, threatening to cut his funds if he did not produce results. It gave him further tasks, such as finding out about a US Army effort to synchronize antiaircraft fire with searchlights and stealing heat-detection technology that would help identify incoming aircraft. To pacify his employers, Rumrich used a false identity to obtain figures on venereal disease in the armed forces—figures that incidentally revealed how many troops there were and where they were stationed.

To help him with his tasks, Rumrich recruited another agent, Erich Glaser. Turrou described Glaser as "a strapping six-footer of about twenty-nine, rather handsome, with dark brown hair and dark, stupid eyes." A native of Leipzig, Germany, Glaser had served in the US Army in Panama, where he first met Rumrich. He was in awe of his fellow soldier, whom he admiringly described as "an intelligent young man with a good education and background."[25] When Glaser left the army, his former comrade invited him to New York, and in January 1938 he moved in with the Rumrichs, living rent free. At Rumrich's request, he reenlisted, serving with the US Army Air Corps at Mitchel Field in Long Island. He stole some minor codes and plans, and delivered them to the Abwehr via Rumrich. He also agreed to help with the kidnapping and passport plots.

In his confession, Rumrich supplied the sought-after details of the Schmidt-McAlpin plot. The honey trap element of the plan fell through at an early stage; in Turrou's words, Colonel Eglin "was not the type of man who could be lured to a hotel room by a woman." Rumrich was to impersonate General Craig's adjutant and make the phone call to summon Colonel Eglin. After booking the room to which the unsuspecting victim would be led, Glaser would hide in a closet ready to leap out and help overpower the army officer. Schmidt would assume his position on a window ledge, his pen-syringe at the ready. Once the deed was done, the three-man crew would exit the scene with the sought-after plans, leaving behind the crumpled body of Colonel Eglin and a copy of the *Daily Worker* to indicate that the communists were to blame.[26]

Turrou described Rumrich as "a minor figure in this vast spy plot" and as a "sap" hung out to dry by unscrupulous Nazi agents who creamed off the money due to him. He insisted that a Nazi espionage operation existed that was far more sinister than the limited maneuvers of a lowly pawn.[27] It was indeed true that except for the McAlpin Hotel–coastal defenses plot, Rumrich posed no real threat to the United States. Even the McAlpin plot would come to nothing. The British tip-off that had risked exposing the secrets of MI5 turned out to have been unnecessary, for the Abwehr never authorized the scheme.

Turrou was right, then, to dismiss Rumrich as a minor character. Yet Rumrich/Crown still had real significance, for Rumrich's confession led to further arrests and revelations—beginning with the unintended apprehension of a redheaded beautician.

6
TALES OF HOFMANN

Another ship, another German spy. The SS *Europa* was due to berth at Pier 86, Hudson River, on Thursday, February 24, 1938, and Rumrich had said that the Abwehr's Karl Schlueter would be on it. Turrou decided to intercept the steamer before it docked. He requisitioned a US Coast Guard cutter and waited. At last, the great ocean liner approached its destination. Entering the world's busiest port, it slowly maneuvered into quarantine, at which point Turrou and two colleagues drew alongside and clambered aboard. By prior arrangement with the authorities, they represented themselves as immigration officers.

When the FBI men examined the ship's passenger list, they seemed to be out of luck. There was no passenger named Schlueter, nor was there any sign of another person Rumrich had told them to expect, "Jenni Hofmann, flirtatious *aide* to the wily Schlueter." Turrou now wondered whether the spies were disguising themselves as crew members. He inspected the ship's manifest, and the words leaped out at him: "Karl Schluter . . . steward" ("Schlueter" was variously spelled Schluter and Schlüter). The detective's elation was short lived, for there was a line through the name and, alongside, a handwritten note: "Did not sail." Schlueter had boarded the ship at Bremerhaven but heard about the FBI probe in the States and disembarked before the vessel went to sea. According to Turrou, the Abwehr put him on a battleship for his own protection.

Deflated at first, Turrou continued to inspect the ship's manifest and found his reward, the entry for "Johanna Hofmann . . . hairdresser." Turrou and his fellow special agents decided not to rush in and make an immediate arrest but to ascertain what Hofmann looked like and then follow her. By arranging a parade for the inspection of boarding passes, the detectives were able to see each member of the ship's crew. And there she was. Either Turrou was greatly taken by Hofmann's appearance or he decided to dwell on it to give greater impact to his later account of the event. He wrote about how she stood: in her trim white uniform, "an attractive girl, poised and sure of herself, but with a carriage and glance which revealed, even in these impersonal circumstances, that she was quite sensitive to, and aware of, men." Standing five foot six, she had a mass of wavy auburn hair, fair skin, deep blue eyes, and a trim figure, wearing dress size 14 or 16.

Turrou already had a man posted on the dock, and once the hulking vessel nudged its way to its allotted berth and tied up at around 5 p.m., he and his colleagues joined him. Together they watched the human cargo from a dictatorship disgorge itself into the Land of the Free. They waited in the hope that Hofmann would lead them to other German agents. At 7 p.m. she disembarked, wearing just a light coat against the winter evening's chill. She walked a few paces toward the steps at the end of the pier and stared beyond. She frowned. Her anticipated lover or spy, or "combination of both," had not appeared. She made as if to return on board.[1]

Turrou and two other agents approached her. The FBI's crack detective asked her if she knew Schlueter and Rumrich. She denied all knowledge of them. The agents arrested her and took her to the US Courthouse in Foley Square. According to Hofmann in a statement she made at her later criminal trial, Turrou told her at this stage that "if I would sign for him a direction to the first officer of the S.S. *Europa* to deliver to him, Turrou, certain articles, namely a brown suitcase, and a light-brown leather handbag, I would be allowed to depart for Germany upon the sailing of the S.S. *Europa* the following night."[2]

Equipped with his note, Turrou boarded the *Europa* and, in company with Heinrich Lorenz, the ship's captain, visited what he recalled was Jenni's cabin on D deck (according to Jenni, it was cabin 67, A deck). It later emerged that Lorenz had cooperated with the Abwehr and had helped establish its original links with Rumrich. He must have been filled with trepidation when the FBI man boarded his ship and made his request. There was, however, another side to this story.

Though penetrated and controlled by the Nazis, the German shipping lines did retain traces of their original pedigrees; the person who built the Hamburg American Line into the world's largest shipping enterprise had been, after all, a self-made Jewish businessman, Albert Ballin.[3] Bullied as they were by the Nazis, senior officers serving on the North Atlantic run were in some cases lukewarm, if not antagonistic, toward Hitler, and Turrou was able to build friendly relations with a few of them. In her autobiography of 2017, Captain Lorenz's daughter Marita painted a sympathetic portrait of her father. While he liked to wear a sword on ceremonial occasions, he was not a militaristic expansionist. He married an American with a distinctly anti-Nazi inclination; born Alice June Lofland, Mrs. Lorenz had acted on Broadway under the stage name June Paget. Both she and her daughter Marita would later spend time in a Nazi concentration camp. (Alice was held on suspicion of helping the anti-Nazi underground.)

Marita maintained that in 1938 her father was apolitical but against Hitler. She furthermore claimed that he became a double agent, acting for Turrou and the FBI, and thus he was allowed to continue to sail after being interrogated in New York. In the interest of balance, it should be noted that Marita had a traumatic and colorful life that potentially affected her judgment. A US Army sergeant raped her when she was just seven years old. Later in life she fell in love with Fidel Castro. She claimed the Central Intelligence Agency recruited her when she was Fidel's mistress, but she declined the agency's commission to poison the Cuban dictator. Marita's recollections may have been tinged with melodrama, and her memories of her father's politics are secondhand, for she was not born until 1939, the year after the Nazi spy scandal. However, she was very close to her father, and when she wrote about his views, it is reasonable to suppose that she knew his opinions.[4]

Meanwhile, Turrou found a brown leather bag under Jenni's bunk and, in the left-hand drawer of her bureau, a key that fit its lock. He decided not to open it there and then but to maximize the psychological effect by doing so in Jenni Hofmann's presence. Returning to his office and finding her in the same chair where he had left her, he asked her to confirm that the bag was hers and then opened it. It contained $70 and a package. As he opened the package, Jenni gave him a "Mona Lisa look." It contained letters, all in code. She said she had no idea how to decode them. Just as she uttered that disclaimer, Turrou's colleague discovered in a recess of the leather bag a scrap of paper with the key to the code. Jenni later said she was supposed to have learned the code by heart and then destroy the paper on which the key was written, but she had neglected to do so. It was not the finest moment in the history of the German secret service.

The letters in Jenni's package were all from Schlueter, and they revealed some new names. One letter addressed to a Miss Moog explained that Schlueter was "on vacation" and that Jenni was standing in for him. It indicated Schlueter had made a premeditated decision to send the expendable Jenni to meet her fate in lieu of him, her treacherous lover. Another letter was for Rumrich. It said the $70 was for him, indicated another $1,000 would be forthcoming for the aircraft carrier plans, gave various instructions, and asked for a progress report. Further missives of a more cryptic nature were addressed to Martin Schade and Dr. Ignatz Theodor Griebl, both of New York City. The FBI would investigate these names.

Turrou prided himself on his interview technique. He prized from Jenni the secret of an unhappy love affair she had had when very young. She was sensitive on the subject of unhappy romances, as her younger sister had killed herself when a German naval officer jilted her. Turrou tried to take advantage of her emotional state, but at first it did not work. Claiming to be an unwitting courier, Jenni denied knowing about the contents of the letters. She also repeated her claim of ignorance about Rumrich, so Turrou tried one of his trademarked tricks. After one of her more vehement professions of ignorance, Turrou signaled to an agent standing at the back of the interview room, near the door. Following his gaze, Jenni turned to look at the door. As the door opened, she heard

Rumrich's voice saying, "Hello, Jenni." Then the man himself walked in. Jenni screamed and went sheet white.

Although Jenni later retracted the confession she made on February 25, it was useful to the FBI investigation at the time. It was a succinct admission of the role she had played. The next day, Rumrich, Glaser, and Hofmann appeared in court and were charged under the terms of the Espionage Act. Bail in each case was set at $25,000. As none of the defendants were able to pay this amount, they were all remanded in custody, pending the convening of a federal grand jury.[5]

A widening circle of officials and journalists, and indeed the general public, clearly saw that the German spy ring extended beyond Rumrich and his immediate confederates. German officials began to panic. Dr. Richard Bottler had just arrived in New York to be the counselor at the German Consulate General's Office. Turrou described him as "a pompous, officious man with red cheeks," adding that he was "typically Nazi." Immediately after Jenni's arrest, the consulate had received a report on the event from Capt. Wilhelm Drechsel, who was in charge at the German shipping line piers. Reacting to the report, Bottler took on the task of damage limitation.

The FBI allowed Bottler to visit Jenni on the condition that Turrou would be present. Not realizing that Turrou spoke German, the counselor raged at Jenni for revealing too much in her confession and told her to divulge nothing more. Calming down, he arranged for Jenni to receive a weekly stipend so she could buy what she needed and supplement the prison's dietary rations. She would also have legal representation in court. Not long after Bottler's visit, George C. Dix assumed the task of being Jenni's defense counsel. Dix was a combative lawyer, and his relationship with Turrou would be, as the detective put it with rare understatement, "personal."[6]

Higher up the diplomatic chain, the German Embassy in Washington reacted the day after Jenni's arrest. Baron von Ginan, Ambassador Hans H. Dieckhoff's secretary, was in New York at the time. He arranged to meet Captain Drechsel and told him that the ambassador was acutely worried about the spate of publicity that had followed the Pier 86 arrest. Drechsel replied that the New York executive officers of the Hamburg American and North German Lloyd Lines shared the embassy's concern about the impact of the case on German-American relations and were worried about their companies' potential business losses. This last point was a serious one. By 1938 French and British ships had taken the Blue Riband for the fastest transatlantic crossings, and commercial competition was intensifying just when passengers were finding the atmosphere on board the German ships distasteful. A high-profile spy scandal was the last thing the German shipping lines needed.[7]

Drechsel, like Lorenz, was a man in a quandary. At fifty-eight years old, he was about to receive his pension, wanted to settle in the United States, and was expecting his naturalization papers to arrive soon. He was afraid that the German authorities would cancel his pension rights if he did not cooperate with their fascist designs. He confided these concerns to Turrou. He enlightened the investigator about the nature of the Nazis' grip on the German shipping lines. He explained how the Berlin government dictated who should be given jobs on German ships and how it designated a member of the National Socialist Party as the political officer on each ship, stipulating that he should have superior authority over the ship's captain. Drechsel had been subjected to all kinds of intimidation and threats, and he had been forced to expedite the work of Karl Friedrich Wilhelm "Willy" Herrmann, who was in charge of the Gestapo in New York. He worried about the future of his company and made the rather unlikely claim that he was going to lobby his company's bosses to limit the reputational damage by refusing to facilitate Nazi spy operations.[8]

The Germans were right to worry about the arrests' repercussions. The day after Jenni's detention, J. Edgar Hoover issued a press release. He said he had "unearthed" a "widespread plot" and promised further arrests. The nation's journalists wrote stories that sparked international coverage. An informed account of the affair appeared in London's *Daily Mirror*, which claimed, "G-man Hoover and his lieutenants have now turned their backs on crime investigation to search for more alleged spies who have gravely jeopardized America's safety." The *Mirror* reported that a top-level emergency meeting of US Army officers was addressing the security issue. The paper also hinted at sympathy for the "red-haired German girl" who now languished in solitary confinement, where she received no friends and no messages. In the United States, *Time* was distinctly less sympathetic toward the "spy Hofmann, who spoke no English and whose orange-colored hair showed traces of dye." The magazine reported that "plump" Jenni had been part of the plan to "lure" Colonel Eglin to the McAlpin Hotel.[9]

Actually Jenni Hofmann was more a victim than a seductress and was, like Rumrich, a minor cog in the Nazi spy ring. But her story did throw further light on the workings of that ring. Born in Dresden in 1911, she was the middle of five siblings. She attended a local trade school, where she learned the art of hairdressing. Unlike Rumrich she seems to have had no bad habits, and the FBI found no evidence of a criminal record in her history. Yet she was adventurous and left her inland city for a life on the high seas. She joined the North German Lloyd Line in 1931 and again, after a lengthy spell back home, in 1936.

Jenni first met Schlueter on a Far Eastern voyage on the SS *Gneisenau* and later sailed with him on the *Europa*. She had the potential to be a useful courier, but there was more to their relationship. With Jenni, Schlueter talked of getting a divorce. No doubt he engaged in a similar discourse with the tall young blonde from Queens whom he also dated.[10] Jenni was at first attracted to him. Both were of similar height, and the Abwehr operative had a long scar across the top of his head, which was made more visible by his closely cropped hair. He was a few years older, with a son in the Hitler Youth. Possibly Jenni was more drawn to him ideologically than physically; historians write of Nazism's appeal for some women who fell prey to the romanticization of an idyllic German past, now under threat from a toxic mix of industrialization and communism.[11]

Schlueter's lifestyle helped to entice Jenni. He took her to a Japanese restaurant near Times Square and promised her a date at the cabaret. Once she was roped in to his schemes, there was no turning back. When he wanted her to undertake a riskier enterprise and she balked, he turned nasty. He told her that if she did not cooperate, her father's pension would be at risk.[12]

Although the US press told lurid tales of how Germany's redhead had assisted in the nefarious Nazi plot, Jenni's activities had been mostly mundane. She had promised Schlueter she would carry letters, and he undertook to enroll her as "a member of the German Military Intelligence." In company with Schlueter at first, she delivered missives to German spies in New York, including Ignatz Griebl, Martin Schade, Katherina "Kate" Moog, and Guenther Rumrich. On one occasion, she played with Rumrich's little boy and listened to the men discussing a number of espionage plans and objectives, which she later was able to pass to the FBI, giving it some additional leads. She played her espionage game under Schlueter's supervision until that fateful day when he told her he was taking a vacation and that she would have to act as a courier alone.[13]

Perhaps wishing to inflate the importance of every arrest he made, Leon Turrou argued that Jenni was much more than a courier. He referred both to the letters she received from the "mysterious spy chief in Bremen," who signed himself "N. Spielman" and who referred to Jenni as "my agent" in a manner that indicated implicit trust, and to the fact that "Jennie was far from a blind dupe." Making his claim for Jenni's importance, Turrou noted that she "was entrusted with the task of looking over and signing up a Nazi spy in Czechoslovakia while Hitler was 'softening up' that country for conquest."[14]

The spy in question was Gustav Rumrich, a chemistry student at the prestigious German University in Prague. On December 20, 1937, Gustav wrote to his brother in New York, saying he needed money and was looking for a job. He was thinking of signing up to fight for the fascists in the Spanish Civil War. Guenther said no. Though it is unlikely he knew that Admiral Canaris was flooding the Sudetenland with secret agents, he told his brother he should instead spy for Germany in Prague. He should mail a typewritten letter—addressed to Jessie Jordan at 1 Kinloch Street, Dundee, and opening with the words "very esteemed Mr. S." (i.e., Sanders)—and include his particulars. Guenther enlisted the support of Schlueter and Hofmann, and gave them photographs of Gustav.

In January Guenther wrote to Hamburg via Jessie Jordan, saying his brother would be in touch, and Gustav duly wrote to the same address on the twenty-fourth. Guenther explained the urgency of his request: his brother was due to be conscripted into the Czechoslovak Army later in the year. MI5, of course, intercepted and read the letters.

On February 15 (the very day of Guenther's arrest in New York), Schlueter and Hofmann visited Gustav in Prague. Representing themselves as Mr. and Mrs. Schlueter and as good friends of Guenther's, they agreed to meet the next day at the Hotel de Saxe in Teplitz (now Teplice) near the German border. Schlueter checked into the hotel showing a German passport that indicated he was born in Bremerhaven in 1905 and gave his profession as businessman.

At the de Saxe on the sixteenth, the pseudo-married couple gave Gustav a letter from his brother advising him to be "sensible." Jenni and her "husband" then confessed they were fellow agents, not a married couple, and proceeded to brief their new recruit. Gustav would receive expenses and payment for his spying services. Jenni would be his minder and paymaster, but he would receive written instructions from the Irish capital, Dublin. Though he had been writing to Dundee, he would in the future communicate with the Irish poste restante, Mrs. G. Brandy of 14 Willow Terrace, Dublin. He was to pose as a philatelist so that instructions could be sent to him concealed in stamp collections. Schlueter gave him a cipher on a small piece of paper concealed in a cigarette.

Gustav was soon arrested on suspicion of espionage, and the Czech police found the cipher when they raided his house. In his confession, Gustav Rumrich explained his mission. In the words of an MI5 translation, he was to obtain "information regarding the Czech Communist Party, and the relationship between Czechoslovakia and the U.S.S.R." Hofmann confirmed that the recruiting duo had persuaded Gustav to join the Communist Party in Czechoslovakia. Undoubtedly, the Abwehr had an anti-communist mission; however, her description of the mission was also designed to please, for the Americans, the British, and the Czech government were all opposed to communism. Moreover, Gustav admitted to being tasked in a further way: "If found suitable, it was proposed to use him for military espionage against Czechoslovakia." As Turrou noted, he was one more weapon in Hitler's annexation armory.[15]

Turrou depicted Jenni Hofmann as a dangerous spy. Potentially, perhaps she was. In the event, the efforts of the UK and US counterintelligence services stopped her in her tracks. For this reason, she was less important for what she did than for the consequences of being caught and of telling what she knew. She was an asset to the FBI in that she revealed more about Germany's spies and about the workings of the shipborne courier system. Her arrest and those of Rumrich and Glaser were steps toward exposing the wider Nazi spy ring.

However, because the US press was on to the story, the arrests and ensuing confessions were also problematic. As chapter 7 reveals, they proved acutely so for the British.

7

AVOIDING A
HIGH COURT TRIAL

The arrests in the United States presented the British authorities with a dilemma: What were they to do with Jessie Jordan? Three factors had hitherto dictated that they should do precisely nothing. One had to do with tradecraft. Barring an imminent threat to national security, they felt it was so much better to follow a suspected spy and find out what she was up to without alerting the Abwehr to the extent of MI5's knowledge about its operations. The second factor in promoting nil action was the perceived advantage of not offending Hitler's Germany. A third factor, at least according to one contemporary newspaper, was the desire to give Leon Turrou time to do his job without creating publicity that would alert the Abwehr to too many clues.[1] The overall challenge then was how to avoid a sensational trial of Jessie Jordan in Scotland.

The arrests of Rumrich, Glaser, and Hofmann and their New York court appearance on February 26 meant that MI5's knowledge of Jessie Jordan's activities could no longer be completely concealed. There was indeed a distinct possibility, as later events would confirm, that Jessie Jordan would be required to testify in the upcoming US espionage trials. This prospect sharpened MI5's dilemma. While the Anglo-American special intelligence relationship was important, it was also subject to limitations: Jessie was MI5's intelligence responsibility and not to be trusted to the vagaries of the US court system. All this pointed in one direction: the British would have to arrest the Dundee hairdresser to keep her out of the US justice system, but an open trial was to be avoided at all costs. The traitor would have to be silenced.

Responsibility for the hushing up fell to Lieutenant Colonel Hinchley Cooke, whom MI5 dispatched to Dundee for the arrest. Hinchley Cooke had overseen Jessie's surveillance and had already made several trips to Edinburgh. He was an experienced officer. In World War I, he had questioned German women who passed through British ports, sometimes passing himself off as a German, and operated with sufficient effectiveness to be awarded the Order of the British Empire while still in his twenties.[2]

Hinchley Cooke traveled to Scotland to handle the fallout from the Americans' revelations. City of Dundee chief constable Joseph Neilans prepared the ground by obtaining search warrants for Jessie's business premises at 1 Kinloch Street and for the house of her half-brother, Frank Haddow, at 26 Strathmore Avenue, Coupar Angus, Perthshire. Haddow's daughter Patricia, who worked at Jessie's shop, also lived there. On the morning of March 2, two police cars bore Hinchley Cooke, Neilans, Detective Inspector Thomas Nicholson, and Policewoman Annie Ross to Kinloch Street. Their guide was Detective Lt. John Carstairs, who had started a dossier on the Jordan case in November 1937.

At the street corner, the approaching officers saw a double-fronted salon; one window was painted over with black lacquer, while the other was used to promote beauty products. A sign above the shop announced "J. Jordan, Hair Specialist." The five-strong raiding party entered the salon and found Jessie, whom they detained, and fourteen-year-old Patricia. The police searched for evidence. They dug up the drains, raised the floorboards, and inspected Jessie's former apartment at 23 Stirling Street. The evidence they found, however, lay unconcealed in a cubicle-cum-bedroom, off the beauty salon, where Jessie was currently spending her nights.[3]

According to one version of events, the cubicle contained a see-through bag containing airmail letters. In his report on the raid, Joe Neilans did not mention them; from the outset, the Americans' dimension of the case received discreet handling. The police officers did record their discovery of Jessie's passport, her military sketches, a road map of Scotland,

Admiralty handbooks, and Ordnance Survey maps of areas of possible strategic interest. MI5 and the police were intent on uncovering evidence to confirm what was in fact easy to prove: Jessie had personally spied on the British defense establishment.[4]

At noon the officers placed Jessie under detention in the policewomen's section of their Dundee headquarters. They then departed to inspect the residences of her two half brothers. Before proceeding to Frank and Patricia's home in Coupar Angus, where a number of other officers had already assembled, they had another call to make. They visited William Haddow's establishment at 16 Breadalbane Terrace, Perth, where Jessie's daughter, Marga Wobrock, was doing the housekeeping and caring for his children. By the time they arrived at 1:25 p.m., the local police were there too.

The Breadalbane Terrace raid was the lead story on the front page of the *Daily Express*. Though Jessie was the spy, she received only a small, separate paragraph. The main spread was about her photogenic daughter. Marga told the paper's staff reporter, "Two men and a policewoman came to my flat. The policewoman took me into the bedroom while the men went through all drawers and cabinets and examined all my papers. The woman searched the bedroom, looked into the pockets of my clothes— even the pockets of the dressing gown I was wearing. I had just come out of the bath." Neilans reported that his men found no additional evidence in either Perth or Coupar Angus.

The *Express*'s reporting was sympathetic. It ran a head-and-shoulder photograph of Marga, suggesting a woman of beauty and sensitivity; mentioned her singing career; and made a heart-tugging reference to her little girl. All this reflected the fact that the proprietor of the *Express*, Lord Beaverbrook, was a supporter of Prime Minister Neville Chamberlain's determination not to provoke Hitler. (The editor of the *Express*, Arthur Christiansen, later in the year would authorize the infamous headline, "There will be no European war.") With its unrivaled circulation running into the millions, the *Express* not only helped shape public opinion but also reflected British opinion, which had not yet turned decisively against Nazi Germany.[5]

The next day, while crowds gaped at the suddenly infamous salon at 1 Kinloch Street, Jessie Jordan made a one-minute appearance in court, where she was charged with offenses under the Official Secrets Act. Facing blanket secrecy, the *Courier* reporter on court duty had little to go on, so the story simply recorded that Jordan, "attired in a smart black coat with fur collar and a little green hat adorned with a feather," looked "pale and anxious."[6] A few days later, Jessie made a four-minute court appearance in a sealed-off courtroom. As a backstop, she was further indicted under a 1920 law for having failed to register with the post office as a forwarder of mail. At the same hearing, her solicitor John R. Bond successfully pleaded for her to be kept not in Perth but in Dundee, where her defense could be better prepared.[7]

The day after her first court appearance, Jessie went on a journey. That morning, she left Dundee Police Station in a large automobile. It rolled on to the Firth of Tay ferry (there was no bridge in those days) and, once across the mile-wide estuary, traversed the county of Fife. The police car wound its way past the sodden fields and green hills of an ending winter. It growled through sullen mining villages ravaged by the unemployment of the Great Depression.

The driver headed for another great sea inlet, the Firth of Forth. From that firth's northern shore, Fifers could gaze across the water at Scotland's capital city, Edinburgh, shimmering in power and rectitude in the rays of the low-slung southerly sun.

Jessie was one of six occupants of the vehicle. The driver was a police sergeant. Next to him in the left front seat was the knowledgeable detective lieutenant Carstairs. Immediately behind Carstairs and the driver were two backward-facing folding seats. On the left-hand folding seat sat policewoman Annie Ross; Jessie occupied the right-hand seat. On the left side of the car's back seat was Chief Constable Neilans. Although the senior police officer in the car, on this occasion he occupied little more than a ceremonial role, for sitting at the right rear, directly facing the woman he was questioning, was a man who had traveled from London.[8]

Lt. Col. William Edward Hinchley Cooke, the son of a British father and German mother, retained a hint of a German accent when speaking

English. Contemporary photographs reveal he was a portly man squint-
ing at life through a pair of heavy glasses. This description was not good
enough for the spy-crazy press corps. Hinchley Cooke impressed a journalist from the *Evening Standard* as a "tall, middle-aged Englishman" of
"benevolent" appearance with "twinkling eyes" who had "the knack of
turning up in odd places during interesting political and semi-political
events." He worked for "the mysterious MI5," an organization based
in a nondescript London house, but the journalist was "not allowed to
say where" (actually the top floor of Thames House, Millbank).[9] A local
Dundee newspaperman thought Hinchley Cooke "looks as though he
might treat spies on the 'Hardly cricket, my dear fellow,' principle."[10] More
recently, MI5 historian Nigel West described "Cookie" as a "sweetie."[11]

Colonel Hinchley Cooke worried that Jessie might become famous.
Starved of more substantial information, the national and local press had
so far commented only on her appearance. The *Empire News* was a popular Sunday paper that did not like traitors, and accordingly it had her
down as a "51-year-old ash blonde" who on the occasion of her court
appearance donned the same "shabby, old-fashioned plumed hat" she had
been seen wearing at the time of her arrest.[12] Dundee's *Courier* stood up
for its local lass, its "small and full-figured blonde." Whether the press-
men were pro or con, they would be sure to demand more and preferably
sensational details. MI5's plan was to suppress the story.[13]

The driver of the Dundee police car followed a route based on the
cross-marked map found in Jessie's premises. What went through her
mind with all this evidence against her? She did appear to have been
affected by a confessional urge. Perhaps she was hoping her interrogators
might believe one of her two stories: she was settling an argument with a
Hamburg friend about the state of Scottish coastal defenses, and she had
been sending the men in Hamburg merely corroboration of what they
already knew. At the same time, she likely entertained the hope that her
cooperation would result in leniency.

Hinchley Cooke knew that he was pushing on an open door. He engaged in no bullying. He did not call upon the Dundee coppers to be the
hard men to his Mr. Nice Guy. The gentler approach reflected Hinchley

Cooke's personality, his experience as a long-serving officer, and his appraisal of the situation. It still made for a bizarre scene, with a traitor who was willing to talk and a questioner who had a keen interest in finding the truth but a matching hope that he could conceal it from the wider world.

As the car wound its way south, Jessie turned over recent events in her mind. What would happen to Marga now, she wondered, and to the little granddaughter who bore her own name, Jessie? And how had she been discovered? She had no idea that MI5 had kept her under surveillance for months. Perhaps she wondered about the postie, the one who had alerted the Dundee police to her strange correspondence, and her suspicions must have fallen on false friends, such as John Curran and his wife, who had taken such a close interest in her affairs.

Hinchley Cooke's mind in the meantime focused on the task of detailing the evidence of Jessie Jordan's guilt in terms of her personal espionage, apart from her facilitation of the Crown correspondence. He was interested in questions as well as answers. To know what questions the Abwehr was asking was to gain an insight into what the Abwehr knew. So in spite of already possessing overwhelming evidence, Hinchley Cooke continued to probe for further information, exhibiting a disarming and confidence-building curiosity about Jessie's background and feelings.

As he faced his traveling companion, Colonel Hinchley Cooke found himself sympathizing with a person whose life had been a catalog of misfortune, a woman who, in spite of her proactive personality, had been as much a victim of the Nazis as their servant. Being half German himself, he knew what prejudices one could encounter in the United Kingdom.

As the police car visited locations along the Forth coastline, Jessie identified the places she had spied on. At Crombie, just beyond Rosyth, she had illegally photographed the Admiralty Pier at the Royal Naval Armament Depot.[14] Cooke asked her why she had written "3 Castles" against Fife Ness and concluded that she had mistaken some derelict aircraft hangers for fortresses.[15] Cooke summed up her spying as "obviously the effort of a beginner." Her data-collection efforts were paltry.[16]

By the time the police limousine turned north and headed back to Dundee, the conversation had become desultory, for Hinchley Cooke had other things on his mind. How could the whole affair be hushed up? More than four decades would pass before the British government would even admit the existence of MI5; thus, it wanted to conceal details of its modus operandi and the extent of its knowledge of the Abwehr. Would it perhaps be possible, in spite of pending US court cases, to prosecute Jessie Jordan on the basis only of her own espionage and without reference to the Crown affair? It was a tall order, but the less the Abwehr learned about what MI5 knew, the better. When the car finally returned to the Dundee Police Station, after an absence that the *Daily Herald*'s reporter described as "mysterious," MI5's challenge was only just beginning.[17]

The service had options available for tricking the Abwehr into believing that MI5 was less competent than it was. One was to point to accidental disclosure, such as the curious postman's discovery of letters from abroad arriving at 1 Kinloch Street. Another was the Zimmermann option. As noted in chapter 3, in 1917 the British had pretended the Americans discovered the Zimmermann telegram with its fateful contents. Now, in 1938, information appeared in the press suggesting that the FBI had tipped off MI5 about the Nazi spy ring, not vice versa. Newspapers on both sides of the Atlantic reported that evidence unearthed by the FBI was helping the British realize what German spies were doing in their own backyard—for example, stealing the design secrets of revolving gun turrets under development at Parnall Aircraft in Tolworth, Surrey. The story placed the FBI in a good light, which was never a bad thing from J. Edgar Hoover's perspective, and potentially removed MI5 from dreaded scrutiny. If only the Americans could be seen as kissed with genius, then MI5 could languish in obscurity.[18]

A couple of weeks after her arrest, Jessie Jordan released a little bombshell that threatened to unravel any such plans for blanket secrecy. She wrote a letter to the secretary of state for Scotland from His Majesty's Prison at Perth, requesting permission to write her memoir. No doubt wishing to ensure his client's ability to pay his fee, her solicitor John Bond had arranged a publishing contract for her despite prison rules that restricted the free speech rights of inmates. Bond entered a plea on Jessie's behalf that said as she was pleading not guilty, she should be considered in the meantime innocent and free to write. The opposed parties reached a compromise: Jessie undertook not to publish until after the trial. "Mr. Bond my Law Agent would take care of this artickle untill I am tryed."[19]

Here was a conundrum that would foreshadow events in the United States: in a free country, could the state suppress a story on the grounds that the teller's freedom of speech would injure the public interest? It was a pressing matter from Jessie's viewpoint. She needed to fulfill her publishing contract to pay her lawyers. The governor of Perth Prison supported her case, saying the interest in her story would be widespread. He added that she was poorly educated and unlikely to use her opportunity to send out coded messages; however, he suggested MI5 should approve the texts before sending them for publication. On April 27 her solicitors, saying the matter was urgent as the trial was imminent and they could not instruct counsel without promise of payment, agreed to honor an arrangement whereby "the biography would be carefully scrutinized." The Scottish *Sunday Mail* did in due course publish a sanitized version of Jessie Jordan's life story; it appeared in serialized format between May 22 and June 19.[20]

The sanitization of the memoir was just one aspect of the concealment effort. The British authorities still had to contend with the problem of publicity arising from the legal proceedings. The Edinburgh High Court trial promised to be a drama. Mrs. Curran relished the thought and is reputed to have bought a new dress for the occasion.[21]

MI5 had other ideas and prevailed. Mrs. Curran's first disappointment came when the authorities decided to try the case in camera. Just a hand-picked few, such as MI5's director Vernon Kell, would be allowed into the public gallery, and certainly no newspaper sleuths or photographers would be admitted. A heavy police presence would restrict access to the courtroom area, including the lobby, and admission to the proceedings would be strictly rationed.[22]

The Crown prepared a formidable case, with forty-two witnesses and a mound of evidence ready for the High Court Trial. A portion of the effort came to naught when Jessie's legal team challenged the relevancy of the charges preferred against their client. As some of the offenses had taken place outside Scotland, could they be tried under Scots law?[23] The prosecution responded by removing the English, Welsh, Czech, and US dimensions from the indictment. The relevancy objection was then withdrawn. At the same time—no doubt because of plea bargaining and an intercession by the Security Service—the prosecution made a further amendment to the charges and struck the following clause from the indictment: "having between 1st November 1937 and 2nd March 1938 acted as the intermediary for forwarding correspondence and information to . . . foreign agents from persons in America and Czechoslovakia." Thus, the alterations to the indictment removed all references to Jordan's activities as a forwarder of spy mail. The case against her would focus solely on her well-documented personal espionage activities.[24]

Solicitor General for Scotland and Member of Parliament James C. S. Reid accepted a revised indictment that focused on Jessie's gathering of military information in Scotland between February 14 and November 17, 1937—prior to the Crown affair. The *Empire News* recorded how the accused now pleaded guilty "in a voice made harsh by long years of talking German." The newspaper reported that she had accepted a secret deal and entered a guilty plea "on the understanding that the indictment would be amended to exclude a number of particulars—none of which was made public." In a similar vein across the Atlantic, the *New York Times* noted that "no hint of the connection between the [UK and US] cases had been allowed to appear in British newspapers."[25]

The arrangement meant gains and losses for the parties involved. On the one hand, a certain amount of information was kept from the Abwehr, though its officials must have deduced that MI5 knew more than it admitted. From the diplomatic standpoint, the danger of an inflamed British public opinion leading to friction with Germany had been avoided—an outcome that pleased UK government officials at the time.

On the other hand, Jessie Jordan faced prison. She had expected some leniency because of her guilty plea, and her advocate had an opportunity to strengthen that plea. Jessie's courtroom lawyer was the aspiring Conservative politician Arthur P. Duffes, King's Counsel. He was not and could not have been a specialist advocate, for spy cases were rare in Scotland; thus, no one had accumulated such courtroom experience. Duffes was making a name for himself in a very different sphere while serving as an automobile accident compensation specialist. In later years, the *Scotsman* marveled at the logic of the accident specialist's claim that he had never traveled in a motorcar himself. Duffes claimed to be "the last of the pedestrians."[26]

There was nothing pedestrian, however, about Duffes's plea in mitigation: "Having started as an unwanted child 51 years ago, she finds herself . . . once again an unwanted child as regards her native country and the country in which she has spent the greater part of her life."[27] In another country at another time, Jessie might have been shot, but she had been defended by a competent advocate in a civilized democracy that was, so far, at peace with the world. She received a less than draconian sentence of four years in prison.

Though confined in a Scottish prison, Jessie Jordan remained on the FBI's wanted list. The British authorities would take further steps to keep her out of what was by now a rapidly unfolding American drama.

8

WHAT GRIEBL KNEW

The FBI men who arrested Jenni Hofmann on February 25, 1938, seized the letters in her possession. Written by her manipulative lover Karl Schlueter, they addressed Guenther Rumrich and two others. In his letter to "Miss Moog," Schlueter asked for news of Moog's impending divorce and urged her to trust his stand-in courier Jenni, "since she is a good little skate." The second letter haggled over the price of "furs." It was addressed to Dr. Ignatz T. Griebl of New York City.[1]

As soon as they had decoded that letter, Leon Turrou and other FBI agents descended on Dr. Griebl's medical practice in Yorkville, a neighborhood on the Upper East Side of Manhattan. Members of the team posted themselves at all exits to the premises, and Turrou stepped into the waiting room. A crisply dressed and just as crisply mannered nurse told him to leave, as it was after office hours. Turrou informed her to tell Griebl he was from the Justice Department. The nurse squared her shoulders and went to get her employer. It gave the G-man time to peruse the waiting room's decor. On its walls were French etchings and a parchment of Griebl's commission in the US Army Reserve.

A bespectacled thirty-nine-year-old emerged from his office. He nervously fumbled to undo the buttons of his white physician's garb, which he discarded in favor of a double-breasted coat that was too tight for his portly frame. His ashen complexion indicated that he was in the grip of fear. Turrou told Dr. Griebl he was to come along with him to answer a few questions.[2]

In the course of many days of interrogation, Griebl at first held firm. He denied all knowledge of Jenni Hofmann and said there was an "innocent" explanation for his use of Schlueter as a courier. He stated that he had given Schlueter materials about communism and Judaism that he wanted people in Germany to see. Some of them concerned the Protocols of the Elders of Zion, which purported to show that in the previous century international Jewish leaders had met to hatch a conspiracy to dominate the world. A London *Times* report in 1921 had shown the protocols were a 1903 forgery by Russian fraudsters, yet Griebl claimed he had given Schlueter items that proved they were genuine. Another item he entrusted to Schlueter was *Salute the Jew*, an anti-Semitic book Griebl had written under the pseudonym William Hamilton. He added that on his behalf Schlueter had delivered correspondence regarding a real estate deal with a "Hebrew" in Germany. (Indeed it turned out that Griebl was in cahoots with the Nazi authorities to swindle the Jewish family in question.)[3]

His defense was sufficiently vile to have the ring of truth. When the G-men searched Griebl's office, they found voluminous anti-Semitic materials. Griebl had files on virtually all prominent American Jews, detailing their ancestry, wealth, and activities. His observations on individuals contained defamatory and obscene remarks. Among those featured were Roosevelt's treasury secretary Henry Morgenthau Jr., US House Committee on Un-American Activities founder Rep. Samuel Dickstein (D-NY), New York governor Herbert H. Lehman, New York City's Republican mayor Fiorello LaGuardia (1934–45), and the social reformer and Zionist rabbi Stephen Wise. "You are not a Jew," Griebl told Turrou, "so you will not be offended by what you find." He could not have been more mistaken. However, as the files had nothing to do with espionage, Turrou could not use them to advance the FBI's investigation.[4]

From his interviews with Jenni Hofmann, Turrou knew that Griebl was a spy. What he lacked was proof and a confession. The FBI man tried one of his stock tactics to break the suspect's resistance. Speaking loudly to drown the sound of an opening door, he said, surely the physician would remember an attractive, auburn-haired girl with blue eyes calling herself Jenni? Of course, he would remember such a person, said Griebl, but he could not, as he had never met her. At that moment, he heard behind him the voice of Jenni, who had just entered the room. The voice stated that he had given her spy packages for transmission to Bremen. Shaken out of his aplomb by the courier's sudden appearance, Griebl flew into a rage and told Jenni she would be shot. But he still held out and denied his complicity.

It was time to play dirty. How, Turrou inquired, did he get along with Mrs. Griebl? Ignatz replied that she was an admirable if sometimes difficult woman. Turrou asked him whether she was five years older than he and wealthy, and whether she had recently departed on a trip to Germany. When Griebl said that was correct, the detective fumbled in his pocket for a scrap of paper on which he had written some dates. "Dr. Griebl, would it be too indiscreet for you to tell me about that tall woman who registered with you at the Taft Hotel about four times in the last month?"

Thus blackmailed, Griebl began to talk. He remained circumspect, objected to notes being taken, constantly demanded confirmation there was no hidden microphone in the room, and, like every spy, told lies. But he squealed at length. Dr. Griebl made Turrou, and ultimately all Americans, aware for the first time not only that Germany's US spy network was extensive but also that it had functioned without impediment for a considerable time.[5]

Griebl's background and history were now of considerable interest to the FBI, and Turrou and his colleagues gradually pieced together the story. Born on April 30, 1898, Griebl was similar to more than one spy, as he was the product of a region with a split identity. In his case, he was from Strasbourg, the Alsatian city coveted by both France and Germany. Little emerged about his boyhood, but in the First World War, Griebl was an artillery officer in the forces of Imperial Germany. An Austrian nurse called Maria helped him recover from a wound sustained fighting Italian forces. Thereafter, Maria traveled to the United States and worked to pay his expenses while he trained to be a doctor, first in Munich and, once they had married, at Long Island University, where he graduated in 1927. In a tearful session with Turrou later, Maria complained, "I slaved for him and worked my fingers to the bone for him, and then he ran after other women."[6]

A few years after arriving in the States, Griebl established his practice in the German American community of Yorkville. He specialized in women's problems but was a danger to them. The FBI dug out information on his troubles. It found that in 1933, a client threatened to sue him for "serious and severe personal injury sustained by her as a result of an assault." She did not go through with the suit, but her attorney denounced Griebl as an abortionist.[7] Then in 1935 he had a messy affair with Antoinette Heim, an independent businesswoman in her forties. Heim sued Griebl in the Commercial Claims Court, saying that after he made love to her, she paid him $300 a month to help him get a divorce. After receiving thousands of dollars, which allowed him to build a summer cottage in Westchester County, New York, he dumped her. Maria testified to discredit the plaintiff, saying Antoinette had offered to pay *her* to initiate a divorce. Ignatz tried another story. He swore that the monthly $300 had been to pay for the brokerage rights in connection with the sale of a $15,000 painting. The court disbelieved the Griebls, and Antoinette Heim won the case.[8]

The Griebls had no children on whom to spend their dollars, but Ignatz spent money on his lavish lifestyle. Avoiding trouble was not one of his strong points. To augment his income, he became an ambulance-chasing doctor, testifying in court on behalf of injury claimants; however, he was accident-prone himself. His automobile crashes of 1930 and 1936 left him open to lawsuits and out of pocket to such a degree that Griebl contrived a legal fiction that he owned no property to guard against the damages that might arise from a compensation case.[9]

All this information was potentially relevant in showing that Griebl needed the money he made from espionage. He never explained his disloyalty to the Stars and Stripes he was fond of displaying, but his devotion to the Nazi cause and his thirst for financial gain played their part. Griebl was connected to the Nazi hierarchy through his brother, who had been close to Paul Joseph Goebbels, the minister for public enlightenment and propaganda in the Hitler regime. In the wake of Hitler's confirmation as chancellor, Griebl became the leader of the US pro-Nazi group Friends of the New Germany. The Nazi leadership in Berlin wanted to recruit German American supporters. Griebl, a flag-waving, English-speaking first lieutenant in the US Army Reserve Medical Corps, seemed a perfect choice for the group's leadership job. And it suited him commercially. He was already well known for his activities in German American social and cultural circles, and the new post seemed to promise ever-more lucrative medical work in the German American community.

At this point, however, Hitler's deputy Rudolph Hess stepped in, saying Griebl would be too difficult to manage. Friends of the New Germany gave way to the German American Bund (association) movement, which was still a Nazi front but less abrasive and more "American." Moreover, Griebl's local Nazi rivals started a smear campaign, claiming that Maria was Jewish (she was actually a gentile and anti-Semitic) and that Griebl was a communist. Griebl lost his leadership position and, with it, some earning capacity. One historian has suggested the Reich's sacking of Griebl was a ruse, for it made him available to spy.[10]

Griebl never ceased to agitate for the realization of Nazi goals, and that was anathema to Turrou. Yet in one sense Griebl's contemptible mentality was a side issue, for Turrou's task was to find out how the Abwehr worked so that he could hunt down its spies. Interrogating Griebl, he made a breakthrough that was to shape his thinking:

```
T: When did spy activities in this country start?

G: In 1933, soon after Hitler came to power.

T: Who was responsible for organizing the ring?

G: A man by the name of Wilhelm Lonkowski.11
```

Thus, Turrou, hitherto unaware of Lonkowski and of the time line and architecture of the Germans' spying in the United States, began to arrive at greater wisdom. To learn more about this mysterious character called Lonkowski, he decided to contact Joe Dalton, the military intelligence officer who had been privy to the MI5 tip-off about the McAlpin plot and had conducted Rumrich's original interrogation when the spy was later arrested over the passport scam. What interested Turrou was that the major had also been at his desk at the time of an earlier episode. Turrou was thinking of the debacle of October 1935, when Lonkowski had been caught seeking to deliver a spy package to Karl Schlueter aboard the *Europa* but was released after being interrogated by Dalton's colleague Major Grogan.

Dalton now showed Turrou the military intelligence file on the Lonkowski case. He defended his failure to have Lonkowski arrested by saying that with one exception (design details of an aircraft carrier detention hook), the materials contained in the spy package were in the public domain and harmless.[12] Turrou may have thought that Lonkowski's sudden flight afterward suggested otherwise, but he was too tactful to suggest that.

Griebl told the FBI that Lonkowski had approached him in 1933 and asked him to spy for Germany, but he had refused this invitation.[13] Be that as it may, Griebl was certainly involved by 1935. In the spring of that year, the Abwehr chief Wilhelm Canaris ordered a handpicked officer to establish a new substation in Bremen, a unit with the specified mission of spying on the United States. The officer's name was Erich Pfeiffer.

Griebl heard about Pfeiffer's special role and asked Schlueter to give him a letter in which the doctor offered to spy for Germany. Pfeiffer took him on and wrote to him via the courier Karl Eitel. The Bremen spymaster's letter arrived at 56 East Eighty-Seventh Street, adjacent to Yorkville on the Upper East Side of Manhattan, and gave Griebl his general intelligence targets—technical data on US Navy destroyers and on military aircraft.[14]

Pfeiffer subsequently sent Griebl more specific questionnaires via both Eitel and Schlueter. According to Pfeiffer, he received expenses and, on one occasion when he delivered blueprints of US warships and planes, a bonus of $200. According to MI5, however, Griebl received a handsome retainer of $500 a month plus bonuses. Griebl's spy data came directly from Otto Voss at the Seversky plant and sometimes from Lonkowski. Pfeiffer considered the latter to be improper "poaching" because Lonkowski was supposed to report directly to Berlin, but he went along with it and may have privately welcomed the procedure. German agents constantly vied with each other for the best intelligence coups.[15]

When asked about Lonkowski's escape, Griebl responded with his customary evasiveness. First, he said he had no knowledge of the event. Then he maintained that he had sheltered the fugitive only for the night, whereupon Lonkowski departed alone for the airport—whence the German aviator Ulrich Hausmann flew him to Montreal for $800. Gradually, though, Griebl admitted to full complicity. Lonkowski stayed the night with him in Yorkville, and Griebl then drove him to his summer home in Larchmont, Westchester County. There, he gave Lonkowski $100 for expenses and loaned him his car, with Hausmann acting as chauffeur. Thirty-six hours later, the car had reappeared in Griebl's garage.[16]

The Lonkowski story was truly a revelation for Turrou, yet there were things that Griebl did not know. He was not in contact with Nicholas Ritter, the spy who obtained the details of the Norden bombsight, nor was he aware of German intelligence operations on the West Coast.

Griebl, though, did provide Turrou with his arch villain. Turrou would find in Erich Pfeiffer not just an antagonist in the spy wars but also a potent propaganda tool. The FBI detective rolled into one the identities behind the code names Spielman and Sanders, making for a simple, understandable message about a German master spy. Turrou's aims—not at the outset but as the case rolled on—were threefold: he wanted to unmask the spies and arrest them, to identify who dispatched them, and to tie that person to the hierarchy in Berlin in such a way as to demonstrate the iniquity of the Nazi regime.

Oversimplified though it may have been, the image of Pfeiffer as the schemer at the center of a joined-up evil web would strike home with the American public. Turrou would inflate Pfeiffer's image for publicity reasons, but he hardly needed to, for the Abwehr officer was a formidable opponent. Pfeiffer was the product of both privilege and hardship. Born in the Rhineland-Palatinate town of Altenkirchen in 1897, he was the son of a mining director and received a Catholic education in local colleges. With the advent of war, he joined the navy and in 1916 was a junior officer on the SMS *König* when the battleship led the German line in the Battle of Jutland. That stalemate confrontation between the German and British fleets took the lives of almost ten thousand men. If the patriotism of Erich Pfeiffer had ever been a half-built construct, the thud of heavy artillery and the screams of dying countrymen finished the job.

At the war's end, Pfeiffer married into his own social class. Elisabeth Helene Charlotte (Lotte, née Weimann) was the daughter of a university professor, a high-status job in 1920s Germany. Erich took a doctorate in national economy from the University of Freiburg and worked in the Essen chemicals industry. He stood as a parliamentary candidate for the center-right and strongly anti-communist Deutsche Volkspartei (German People's Party) and hoped for a political career.

Building his electoral power base, in 1925 Pfeiffer accepted labor union administrative posts in Altenkirchen and Koblenz. The contemporary political scientist Selig Perlman noted that by this time the German labor movement had "shelved, perhaps for good, its former radical anti-capitalism."[17] However, a labor union background was still anathema to the Nazis, who consolidated their power with the rise of Adolf Hitler. With an eye to his future preferment, Pfeiffer reenlisted with the navy at half the salary he had earned as a labor union administrator.

In 1933 the newly installed Hitler regime signaled naval expansion, and Pfeiffer accepted an invitation to take on an intelligence role. The regional intelligence hub was in Hamburg, a major port with strong international connections. Pfeiffer was dispatched to a coastal subbranch, the Wilhelmshaven naval base, where he first built up the Customs Service as a counterespionage force of around sixty men. Then he spread his wings. In May 1934 he established a spy network in the Low Countries with the intention of using it as a springboard for the planned penetration of Britain.

An old-style naval officer and royalist who looked upon Hitler with distaste, Captain Canaris took note of Pfeiffer's talents and genteel background. He decided to pull him out of Wilhelmshaven, which he regarded as too much of a naval enclave for an enterprising spymaster, and installed him in a new substation around thirty-five miles inland in the ancient port and industrial city of Bremen.

Like his contemporary Ritter, Pfeiffer remarked on Canaris's frigid personality, relating how the Abwehr chief "coldly" crushed a Wilhelmshaven naval commander who was opposed to the Bremen transfer.[18] Yet Pfeiffer was Canaris's blue-eyed boy. In Bremen Pfeiffer established an anti-American spy ring that was his pride and joy, and whose competence he never ceased to defend. His office was on the third floor of a side-street building off Bahnhofstrasse that housed a US shipping company on the first floor. His unit had its own identity, and he could stamp his correspondence with its own seal—the legend "Abwehrneben stelle Bremen" surmounted by the German imperial eagle and the Nazi symbol, the swastika.[19]

Pfeiffer took a house for Lotte and their pre-teenage sons, Dietmar and Manfred, at Friedrich Misslerstrasse, a military facility next to a forced labor camp. (Thus, he undoubtedly knew the nature of the Hitler regime.) He appears also to have had a residence at Kronprinzenstrasse, possibly in association with his secretary and long-term mistress, Hilde Gersdorf.[20]

In Bremen Pfeiffer developed his ideas on the espionage profession. He was a disciple of Maximilian Ronge, a renowned Austrian intelligence officer. Ronge had first won attention in 1913, when he exposed his boss, Alfred Redl, as a double agent acting for the Russian Empire. (Opinion is divided on whether the Russians blackmailed Redl, who was gay, or whether they just paid him a great deal of money.) Ronge succeeded Redl as the director of Vienna's Evidenzbureau and served through World War I. In 1930 he published *Kriegs -und Industriespionage*, a memoir that expounded his philosophy. He presented espionage as, ideally, a way of preventing war. He deplored the demobilization of intelligence after the last war and the way in which spies who had done their patriotic duty were sometimes vilified. Having little time for amateurs or for espionage veterans who glorified their spy days by publishing colorful accounts, he placed great emphasis on the protection of operational secrecy.

Building on his study of Ronge, Pfeiffer began instructing his own students. Abwehr officers traveled from far and wide to attend his spycraft courses.[21]

Pfeiffer's espionage against the United States played against a complex background that made it hard for Turrou to identify the lines of command. Bremen had no monopoly on the American show. Hamburg, the more senior spy station, sent agents to the United States with Canaris's backing and not always with Pfeiffer's full knowledge, as Canaris cleaved to the intelligence doctrine that you only get to know what you need to know. Other spies took their orders from the Nazi hierarchy. Again, information is power, and Hitler's confederates Reinhard Heydrich and Heinrich Himmler attempted to infiltrate the Abwehr and pressure it to further the party's objectives. Canaris tried to resist this, having strong reservations about Hitler's militaristic policy, but he had to play a cunning game to survive. He was in no position to take an openly anti-Nazi stance, and his failure to do so sent mixed messages to his subordinates. Pfeiffer was in step both with Nazi Party members and with Canaris in the years 1935–37. Whether out of moral pliability or from a disposition to obey orders, he facilitated the ambitions of his superiors regarding the United States.

Hitler's views on and plans regarding the United States were a work in progress with a distinctly downward trajectory. In the 1920s, Hitler had admired America's "Nordic" ethnicity and was in awe of Henry Ford and the US automobile industry. A close student of the United States, he viewed the country as blessed with plenty of "free" land (lebensraum) resulting from the extermination of the native population, and he sought space for Germany at the expense of the Slavs to the east. He also sought a sphere of influence for Germany in Europe that would match the advantages conferred on the United States by its generous land mass. Hitler was determined to brook no US opposition to that idea and saw the German American population as an asset that could help him influence and control the United States. In the early years of Hitler's regime, his Nazis aimed to spread their doctrines by exploiting people such as Griebl and others in America's substantial population of German descent. In theory, this would be done without engaging in provocative behavior. It was not until 1938 that Hitler declared the United States to be a "Jewish rubbish heap."[22]

Canaris also was convinced of the importance of conducting espionage against the United States. Giving a pep talk to Abwehr personnel early in his tenure, he told them that the United States was a "key target" but not for aggression. The Abwehr chief understood that in the 1930s having survived the crash and the Great Depression, the United States had strategic strength. He said, "The USA must be regarded as the decisive factor in any future war. The capacity of its industrial power is such as to ensure victory, not only for the USA itself, but also for any country with which it may be associated."[23] He wanted to steal its military technology but without making the United States an enemy of Germany's.

Briefing one of his agents, Pfeiffer insisted that in relation to the United States, the Abwehr engaged only in military espionage. A true pupil of Ronge and Canaris, he wanted to avoid war and persuaded himself that Hitler was of like mind:

> There was no question of war between Germany and America, and a situation such as had arisen in the first World War, where the USA came into the war against Germany, need never occur again. That was not just talk with me, but was my firm conviction; I think that at the time it was also HITLER's. . . . As regards rearmament, it was for us to see that Germany caught up as quickly as possible with the progress in the development of arms in the past 14 years by making use of the experience of others.

In practice, though, Pfeiffer admitted that he found it was impolitic to "curb the enthusiasm of Party members" in the United States, and some of his agents would cooperate with the Gestapo and engage in extreme methods.[24]

Griebl was too prejudiced and ignorant to convey such nuances to his FBI inquisitors—nuances that would have weakened Turrou's propaganda campaign. Propaganda depends on a simple message for its effectiveness. Thus, Turrou latched enthusiastically onto one of Griebl's tales that spoke of a simple perfidiousness on Pfeiffer's part. The awful tale had a further advantage in that it led straight to Berlin, allowing Turrou to point an accusing finger at the Nazi center. Griebl's poisonous fable was about the propositioning of Miss Moog.

9

MISS MOOG SAYS NO

In May 1937 Griebl wrote to Pfeiffer asking for help with his proposed Jewish property deal. Pfeiffer replied that if Griebl wanted to hasten the Jewish property transfer, he would have to come to Germany. At the time, the physician had several patients nearing confinement. He decided to shunt them to a colleague and made a reservation to sail on the *Europa* on June 1.[1]

Maria observed his preparations to leave home and head for the ship. She put on her hat and went to carry one of his bags. He told her to stay at home as he hated shipside sentimentality and would see himself off. As soon as he had left, Maria's worries began to crowd in on her. It was not just Ignatz's philandering history or the hints and half-averted gazes from his clients. His secretary had told her there was someone, in particular, who was always on the phone to him. Maria had a premonition of finality.

Mrs. Griebl had no maternal duties to inhibit sudden choices. She took a taxi to Hudson River's Pier 86, arriving an hour before the ship's departure. She stood on the pier, wondering how to proceed. Suddenly she saw them, high on an upper deck, her husband and an attractive woman whose waist he fondled. She stormed onto the ship. Confronted, Ignatz tried to fob off Maria with an unconvincing story, and his wife left the boat unhappier than she had been for years. It was more than Griebl's being, as Maria put it, a "born skirt-chaser." The problem, she later explained, was the double-strength spell that Miss Kate Moog seemed to cast on him. Maria felt that it was she who had ruined their lives and got Griebl into his ultimate predicament with the US authorities.[2]

Turrou described Katherina "Kate" Moog as tall, merry, and flirtatious, with a girlish voice. Another FBI agent said she was "temperamental" and "hysterical." British intelligence noted that she was "well shaped."[3] To elements in German intelligence, she had potential as a honey trap, while to the FBI and Turrou, in particular, she was a key witness whose background invited scrutiny.

Kate's parents had been affluent enough in Germany to send her to the United States to train as a nurse. In the 1920s, according to an account credited by the FBI, she had attended to the needs of Franklin Roosevelt when the future president was struggling against the onset of polio.[4] She told the FBI that she then accepted an invitation to marry John Warwick Halsey, whose brother, Edwin, was secretary of the US Senate, and had met a range of senior politicians including Sen. Claude Augustus Swanson (D-VA), who served as secretary of the navy under President Roosevelt (1933–39).[5] When John Halsey died, she moved to New York and married a fellow German immigrant, Emil Busch (sometimes spelled as Bush), from whom she subsequently separated. Putting the failed marriage behind her, Kate Busch became Miss Moog once again. She set up a nursing home business in New York, and several of her elderly clients were Jewish. She proved to be a capable businesswoman, and on the basis of her earnings, she was able to rent a fourteen-room apartment on Riverside Drive and to pay the salaries of several servants.

In New York Kate also met Ignatz Griebl. She dazzled him with her looks, with her charm, and not least with her gilded account of high-flying days in Washington, DC. Ignatz embarked on his customary seductive trajectory, but this time it was not a fleeting relationship. The FBI documented the occurrence of regular trysts in the Taft Hotel from January through December 1937. Following her separation from her husband, Kate had obtained a Mexican divorce, but worried about its force in US law and with new expectations in mind, she now filed in the courts of New York. (The decree nisi would be granted on June 27, 1938.)[6]

Kate and Ignatz sailed together on the *Europa* on June 1, 1937, distancing themselves mile upon nautical mile from the bereft Maria. On board, the steward/courier/spy Schlueter took them aside and said he would make the arrangements for their meeting with Pfeiffer. Five days

later, Erich Pfeiffer met them as they alighted from the liner at Bremerhaven. They had more meetings, some of them held at locations that
were meant to impress Kate. On one occasion, for example, all three
dined at the Hotel Columbus in Bremen, where they remained drinking
until three o'clock the next morning. Pfeiffer confirmed in the wee hours
that in return for their spy services rendered, he would help Griebl with
the real estate deal and get him a post in the Air Defense Ministry. Another time, Pfeiffer held forth in the Café Bremen on the subject of his
omniscience about US naval technology. According to Pfeiffer, the new
generation of destroyers under construction for the US Navy was built by
overpaid workers at too high a cost. The destroyers were "suicide craft"
because of their thin hulls.[7]

In spite of this professed scorn, Pfeiffer exhibited a thirst for US naval
technology. Reflecting the stated needs of the German navy, he wanted
details of the two aircraft carriers under construction—the USS *Yorktown*
and USS *Enterprise*. His agent Karl Eitel had outlined to him a new arrangement on their flight decks with the use of "arrester" equipment to
slow down landing aircraft, and he wanted details.[8]

Pfeiffer later recalled that in the course of their discussion, Griebl
offered him an asset—Kate Moog. His mistress might do useful work
but not in the manner of a male secret agent. Griebl asserted that she
had high social standing in Washington and good connections with the
White House, right up to her former patient, the president of the United
States. She would be able to provide timely information about meetings
between President Roosevelt and Secretary of the Navy Swanson, and
about their deliberations over forthcoming shipbuilding contracts. Were
Pfeiffer to visit the United States, she could arrange his introduction to
the "best circles at Washington."[9]

When quizzed in later years, the Bremen spy chief claimed that he had
harbored doubts about Kate's utility as a spy. In his meetings with Griebl,
he diplomatically refrained from mentioning these doubts. Instead, he
indicated the Abwehr never sent its officers on visits to those countries
on which they were spying, so he could not possibly travel to Washington
to meet Kate's contacts.

Pfeiffer valued written items and blueprints more than human contacts, and he asked Kate if she could smuggle documents out of the White House. Kate could offer no reassurance on this point. The spymaster said he was not interested in political intelligence. While he appreciated any suggestions for future projects, he was really in the hunt for more concrete evidence about the capabilities of the US Navy. When seeking to exculpate himself under interrogation later, he hinted that in espionage women could be of value only up to a point.[10]

Pfeiffer told Griebl there was no "central agency" for organizing the flow of intelligence to Germany via New York City.[11] Apparently he wanted to hold the strings in his own hand and control Griebl's access to the Abwehr's Berlin hierarchy. Then he discovered that Griebl was about to achieve that access on his own.[12] This had made Pfeiffer "very angry." The spy chief rationalized his ire, saying that it stemmed from a security concern: he was "very much opposed to agents getting to know too many officers and vice-versa."[13]

After their few days in Bremen, the gynecologist whisked Kate to Berlin by express train, and the couple took up residence in a suite at the Hotel Adlon. The grand frontage of this establishment imposed itself on the famous avenue Unter den Linden, dwarfing the adjacent eighteenth-century Brandenburg Gate. The Adlon's luxurious rooms had accommodated guests ranging from Kaiser Wilhelm II to Albert Einstein.

Within an hour of the couple's arrival, two men strutted past the baroque fountain in the hotel's lobby and ascended to their suite. A round-faced, balding man in his early fifties, Hermann Menzel was the Abwehr's director of naval intelligence. Canaris had entrusted him with sensitive tasks, such as brokering a deal with the arms manufacturer Krupp to exchange intelligence on foreign armaments industries.[14] Forty-one-year-old Udo Wilhelm Bogislav von Bonin was Menzel's deputy, entrusted with the duty of writing up intelligence reports for the high command. The Breslau-born Lutheran was more debonair than military in his deportment, but he was a ruthless man who had recently served in Spain as part of the Abwehr's mission to help Gen. Francisco Franco's Falangists install a fascistic dictatorship in that country. Since receiving intelligence training in November 1935, von Bonin, a convinced Nazi, had risen rapidly through the naval ranks.[15]

After a few minutes, the officers escorted the New Yorkers on a short journey. Skirting the Tiergarten, the woodland park so essential to Hitler's plans for an imperial remodeling of Berlin, soon they arrived at 76–78 Tirpitzuferstrasse (today's Reichpietschufer). This was the site of the Bendlerblock building complex, an extensive military office facility. The foursome walked between Doric pillars onto the polished tiles of the entrance hall and braved the unreliable elevator to an upper floor, where chunky oak doors guarded the Abwehr offices. They finally arrived at the "Fox's Lair." Canaris sat at a desk on which sat a model of his former command, the battle cruiser SMS *Dresden*. Behind him were tall windows and a French door leading to a balcony overlooking the Landwehr Canal. Only three photos were in the sparsely decorated room: one of the admiral's dog, another of an obscure Hungarian hussar, and a portrait of General Franco, whose campaign against Spanish democracy Canaris had materially assisted.

Canaris spoke to his visitors under the assumed name of "Colonel Busch." The admiral asked Griebl and Moog to spy for Germany in New York and Washington. The FBI summarized Griebl's version of what ensued in Canaris's office:

```
VON BONIN offered a plan whereby Miss MOOG would es-
tablish herself in a large, luxuriously furnished
apartment in Washington. She would then cultivate the
acquaintance of low-salaried members of the Army and
Navy stationed in Washington, particularly junior
officers assigned to the Army and Navy Departments.
She would then entertain these officers lavishly, gain
their confidence, and then notify Berlin. A suitable
agent would be sent who would be introduced to these
officers by her, and the Agent would thereafter at-
tempt to get the information desired by the German
intelligence service from them. VON BONIN emphasized
that money was no object and could be spent fully to
make the plan successful.[16]
```

The next day on the opposite side of the Tiergarten, as all accounts agree, von Bonin and Menzel continued the briefing over lunch at the Hotel Eden's rooftop garden. Griebl described an occasion that opened with a charm offensive on Kate. The Abwehr officers then started to quiz her about her Washington social circle. Von Bonin cut to the point: They knew all about her and had done considerable research on US Army and Navy officers who lived in Washington. They knew who was embittered about a lack of promotion and who had fallen into debt through one indiscretion or another. Such individuals might be induced to sell information to Germany. What they needed was a suitable vehicle for approaching such men, and fine wine and beautiful women could be the key. How did Kate feel about the idea of running a luxury salon in America's capital? There was a cautionary note: all of Kate's expenses would be paid but not those of her girls, for they would receive their money from clients. The proposal was for an industrial-scale honey trap.[17]

There are different versions of who mooted the brothel idea. At the end of World War II—when Nazis were running for cover and trying to exculpate themselves to escape punishment—many officials blotted out such episodes and invented convenient versions of the past. Von Bonin said he became involved in the Griebl-Moog visit for the sole reason that he spoke English and covered for the usual desk officer who was away. He learned in the foreign press about his and Menzel's alleged involvement in the brothel plot. Not only did he flatly deny they had made the proposal but he also claimed that Griebl invented the story to cover up his own complicity and to escape prosecution in the United States. Von Bonin had seen that Griebl was a swindler and had advised Menzel to reject the honey trap salon proposal.[18]

Miss Moog offered her own version of what transpired at the Hotel Eden's roof garden. Her account can be taken with a slight dose of salt, as she said that she and Griebl had found themselves fellow passengers on the *Europa* "by coincidence"; yet in important respects her narrative has the ring of truth. She said von Bonin did offer to set her up in Washington, where she would entertain her old friends and "young underpaid officers." She confirmed that Menzel and von Bonin reiterated Pfeiffer's offer to help secure the Jewish-owned home in Giesen in Lower Saxony. She added that they promised to give Griebl, on the conclusion of his period of service as a spy, another home in Bavaria and a medical sinecure. She stated that she and Griebl left for Bremen on June 27 as they were embarking for the United States two days later, and on that day Pfeiffer took them to the Astoria Club. In a four-hour conversation he pushed the brothel idea, having been briefed by Menzel and von Bonin in the meantime. According to Moog, Pfeiffer now said that he would be the follow-up agent and would visit the States to approach the pre-identified military traitors.[19]

Kate Moog said, "We did not give [Pfeiffer] any affirmative answer but indicated to him that we would consider this matter and let him know later."[20] Perhaps realizing she was being exploited, she kept her counsel. Karl Schlueter made further approaches when she was back in the States, and, she asserted, Pfeiffer kept up the pressure.

Pfeiffer later contradicted the Griebl and Moog version of events. He claimed, "I certainly never told Moog she should become a second Mata Hari." Loyal to his superiors, he added, "Nor would Kapitane Menzel have. Bonin would never have made such a stupid statement."[21]

What seems to undermine Pfeiffer's assertion is that the German authorities stuck to their side of the bargain with Griebl. On July 19, 1937, the Jewish couple Isidor and Helena Berliner had to give up their house in Giesen, worth $50,000, in exchange for the $20,000 house in Peekskill, the staging post in Lonkowski's flight to Canada two years earlier.[22] Even that did not save them. The Berliners stayed on in Germany and died in the Auschwitz concentration camp in 1942, victims of the Holocaust like several of Isidor's siblings.[23]

The honey trap salon never materialized. Miss Moog in all probability said no. Yet the aborted plot had both consequences and significance. Turrou either believed the Griebl-Moog version of events or pretended that he did to give further impetus to his anti-Nazi crusade. Whichever, it was a good tactic, as the American press loved the story.

The Moog brothel story suggested the existence of a German Mata Hari mentality. "Mata Hari" was the assumed name of an exotic dancer of

Dutch heritage who mixed with high military and political circles in both Germany and France during World War I. A practitioner of *la grande horizontale* style of intelligence gathering (prostitution crossed with pillow talk), she faced a French firing squad in October 1917 after having been convicted of spying for the Germans. The prosecution's claim that she was responsible for the deaths of fifty thousand French soldiers testified to the contemporary belief in her espionage potency. That death toll was improbable, but so was Abwehr chief Friedrich Gempp's claim that Mata Hari "never did anything for German intelligence."[24]

Mythology held that Mata Hari had offered to pose naked for the execution squad and blew them a final kiss before meeting the final hail of bullets. Cultural media exploited the legend. The German silent movie of 1927 *Mata Hari* was an example, as was the identically titled American talkie of 1931 starring Greta Garbo. The celebrated Austrian director Fritz Lang in the meantime created the silent film *Spione* (*Spies*, 1928) about a glamorous Russian spy called Sonya Baranilkowa. Such celluloid heroines rarely had agency; they simply performed pillow talk duties.

Griebl may have concocted the brothel plan, thinking that the German intelligence officers would succumb to the seductive mythology. The cautionary memoir of one German intelligence officer hints at such a weakness. Oscar Reile, who was with the Abwehr from 1934 and worked for West German intelligence after World War II, cautioned that women such as Mata Hari were too unstable to be effective agents. Invisibility was a better attribute for female spies than the glamor and fame preferred by fiction writers. Reile considered it an opportunity lost that most of the Abwehr's women had been secretaries; he argued that the service had generally underestimated the capabilities of women. He even claimed that women had superior instincts and intuition when it came to spotting "fishy" behavior.[25]

Anathema though they may have been to Reile, femmes fatales were ingrained in 1930s culture. The Mata Hari mystique gripped the American public as well as the German naval officers. Sex scandal stories appeal not only because of the scandal itself but also because of the subliminal sexual gratification experienced by the reader. When the *New York Times* decorously reported that Moog "played a glamorous role" in the Nazi spy case, it might as well have added, "read on . . . "[26] The Moog story fizzled out as a spy plot, yet its significance was considerable. It could have been spun, of course, as a feminist parable. But for Turrou, the Moog story was a gift because of its titillation and because of the poor light in which it placed his main opponents, especially as it purported to show the line of command leading directly from the Abwehr spies in United States to the Nazi high command in Germany.

The brothel episode can hardly have enhanced the relationship between Kate and Ignatz. By the time Turrou interviewed the pair in the spring of 1938, the relationship was showing signs of strain. In May Ignatz told Kate that his wife was seeking a divorce in Reno, but Kate suspected he was spinning her a line. When she expressed doubt, Ignatz "became very excited, slammed the door and left the apartment."[27]

Turrou's questioning of Kate Moog in March 1938 enlightened him about her visit to Germany the previous year, but she was never charged. If she had accepted the Washington assignment, she might have become another Belle Boyd, the "Siren of Shenandoah" who charmed her way into the confidence of Union soldiers in Washington during the Civil War and passed their secrets to the Confederate leadership. But, at most, Kate was a minor spy courier. She was an insignificant figure—except as a witness.

As a witness to what happened in Germany and to the activities of Ignatz Griebl, she was, of course, invaluable. Listening to Kate and to Ignatz as he "sang" (and lied) about his own exploits, Turrou formed his views about German espionage. He was convinced it was essentially Nazi in character and had become a problem with the advent of Adolf Hitler.

The other lesson Turrou drew was that Eric Pfeiffer was at the nerve center of German espionage against the United States. Pfeiffer would have liked to believe that, too, but in truth he did not preside over a single, centralized operation. Pfeiffer complained that sometimes even his own agents would work for Hamburg or take their orders directly from Berlin, as Canaris launched initiatives independently of Pfeiffer. As noted in chapter 1, on Canaris's instructions in 1937 Nikolaus Ritter had obtained the Norden bombsight details in an operation that was connected only informally to the Lonkowski-Gudenberg network.

Right under Turrou's nose, even as he interrogated Griebl and other suspects, Ritter's brother was setting up another operation that was all but independent of the Gudenberg-Pfeiffer chain of command. Hans Walter Ritter lived in the United States from 1936 until his departure in early 1941. Charged with robbery in his first year in the States, he was a rough type. He intimidated his American "wife"/companion of five years by claiming that his brother Niki was a "Gestapo agent." The FBI later deduced that Hans directed his brother's spy ring in the United States after Niki departed to take further espionage roles in Europe.[28]

Hans Ritter helped maintain communications with a San Francisco outpost of Niki Ritter's network. In World War I, Germany had used Indian nationalists on the US West Coast in an attempt to run guns to the Indian subcontinent and undermine British rule. In the 1930s California figured once again in Germany's strategic thinking, and the consulate general in San Francisco developed secret service links with Canada, Mexico, Brazil, and Argentina. Although Germany had direct intelligence communications with South American nations, San Francisco was a significant lateral thread in its espionage web.

In June 1937 Baron Manfred Freiherr von Killinger, an ardent Nazi Party man and confidant of Hitler's, had arrived as the new consul general with the mission of stepping up espionage activity. San Francisco–controlled Abwehr agents attempted to force local businessman Weston G. "Pop" Frome, who was of German descent, to yield the technical secrets of his multinational corporation Atlas Powder, a spin-off from the chemicals conglomerate DuPont that Frome and his confederates had established. When he refused, the agents kidnapped Frome's wife, Hazel, and one of his daughters. The evidence suggests that Hazel and Nancy held out and refused to pressure Pop into making concessions to secure their release. In March 1938 the near-nude bodies of the two women were found in the Chihuahua Desert not far from El Paso. This botched and minor operation serves to illustrate the point that while the biggest, Pfeiffer's was not the only Abwehr operation in the United States.[29]

Turrou was unaware of the Ritter brothers' operations, but his interrogation of Kate Moog and Ignatz Griebl did make him wiser about the main Abwehr operation run by Erich Pfeiffer. It would give him a trump card in future prosecutions and propaganda, yet he was still aware of the gaps in his knowledge of the Pfeiffer network. He wanted to know about its full extent and about the damage it inflicted. Griebl had given him a number of leads. Now Turrou needed more evidence.

10

A SEASON OF INQUIRY

In March 1938 the FBI inquiry into the Abwehr spy ring gathered pace. By the beginning of April, its agents had extracted confessions and witness statements that enabled them to justify the convening of a grand jury. The jurors met on May 16, held hearings over the next month, and issued indictments that promised a political impact. The *Washington Post*'s Leland Stowe predicted that the "Mata Hari racket" would be a "major problem" for the government in the event of "a second great war."[1]

The role of German shipping personnel came in for scrutiny. Ignatz Griebl told of a conversation with Erich Pfeiffer regarding Capt. Wilhelm Drechsel. The captain was the chief marine superintendent for the Hamburg American and North German Lloyd lines, with responsibility for all German steamers docking in New York. Griebl alleged that Drechsel used his position to organize the secret transportation of spies and spy materials. He added that the official safeguarded German spies and couriers, and liaised with Wilhelm Herrmann, the New York Gestapo chief.[2]

Leon Turrou wanted to confront his suspect with a key witness but decided to proceed with circumspection. Instead of pulling Drechsel in for questioning straight away, he arranged for Griebl to visit the captain at his Pier 86 office on a pretext. Ignatz would say he wanted to arrange a cheap passage to Germany for Maria Griebl, who was still working on the formalities of the Jewish property transaction. Griebl protested he was nervous about the plan. What if Drechsel realized he was cooperating with the FBI and had him kidnapped?

Turrou agreed to supply protection. When Griebl and Drechsel met on the morning of March 20, Special Agent J. A. Berry lurked nearby. He kept Pier 86 under observation and was under orders to call for reinforcements immediately should Griebl not emerge from his meeting within half an hour. Griebl emerged unscathed after twenty-five minutes, and the next morning he visited the FBI office to give an account of his conversation with the maritime supervisor.

DRECHSEL: A cigarette, Doctor?

GRIEBL: Yes, please; why do you tremble so much, Captain?

D: You do not know the trouble I am [in], Doctor.

G: You speak of trouble? What should I say, Captain? I am under FBI surveillance for three weeks and I don't know if I am coming or going. They are trying to break me down mentally and that is the reason why I have come to you today. I want your advice.

D: Tell me who is involved up to this time and whose names have been mentioned?

G: Well, first of all, Dr. PFEIFFER in Bremen.

D: What, Dr. PFEIFFER? How in hell did they get his name?

G: That is not all. They also mentioned Col. BUSCH [Canaris's alias], Captain Lt. MENZEL and Captain Lt. von BONIN of the War Department in Berlin.

D: My God, my God, how is this possible? Have they been warned?

G: No, of course not.

D: Well, then I will take care of it immediately.

Whether Turrou scored an own goal by letting Drechsel deduce from Griebl's questions how much the FBI knew is difficult to determine. But Turrou concluded that at least he now had enough on the shipping manager to pull him in for questioning.[3]

Reed Vetterli joined Turrou in quizzing Drechsel. An able detective who had been promoted to special agent in charge (New York) following his work on the Lindbergh case and a subsequent kidnapping inquiry,

Vetterli was supportive of Turrou's early investigative efforts.[4] Drechsel explained to the two detectives his responsibilities at Piers 84 and 86, and freely admitted to partial responsibility in the matters Turrou and Vetterli were investigating. For example, he had facilitated the placing of the April 1936 advertisement in the *New York Times* that led to the recruitment of Rumrich.

Drechsel confessed to having supplied a free pass to Willy Herrmann, allowing the Gestapo man to board all German vessels berthing in New York. He took orders from high officials in the National Socialist Party in Germany. One of them, whom he called La Salle, was a director of the Hamburg American Line and served as a liaison between the shipping company and the Nazis. Seeking to exculpate himself, Drechsel insisted that he and his company were victims of the Nazi machine. After meeting Griebl on March 20, he claimed to have sent a secret handwritten letter to his company's headquarters in Bremen detailing the pressures being brought on him; however, he had no copy he could show the FBI. Drechsel confirmed that after Hofmann's arrest, no spies were allowed "to touch any American ports for the time being." The FBI suspected the reason was that Drechsel himself had tipped them off.[5]

Under further interrogation by Turrou, Drechsel admitted that he had personally transmitted messages to Griebl but had not kept copies of these communications. Turrou's reports noted discrepancies between Griebl's account of the radiograms received and Drechsel's account. By now, though, Drechsel was mounting his defense. In spite of his remark about La Salle, he claimed his employers were deeply upset that their ships were used for espionage and feared a loss of business because of current revelations. He added that "a vigorous investigation [was] now afoot by company officials at Bremen with the view of ascertaining the reason why Pfeiffer was permitted to utilize the confidential steamship company code for purposes other than those intended by the company." Drechsel improbably claimed that the president of the now state-administered Hamburg American and North German Lloyd firms had left for Berlin to launch a vigorous protest.[6]

Drechsel complained party enforcers were on every ship. He said he lived in fear of the consequences of displeasing the Nazis who controlled the liners.[7] Drechsel claimed to have resisted pressure to bar a Jewish firm run by Simon Sarashon from operating on the piers he controlled, but he insisted he was in a difficult position. He had worked for Hamburg American for thirty-five years, expected his US citizenship papers to arrive soon, and hinted he wanted to live in the States when his pension matured in one year's time. He was terrified the party might cancel his pension rights and was no doubt nervous that the FBI might stymie his citizenship application. Drechsel was clearly a fellow traveler who had facilitated Nazi espionage in significant ways, but he was sufficiently persuasive about his predicament to escape prosecution. He had contributed another piece to the jigsaw, and that, for Turrou, was enough.[8]

That the shipping lines facilitated a crucial link between the top echelon in German intelligence and its lower levels was becoming abundantly clear. The FBI deployed its panoply of methods to uncover the truth. Its agents interviewed, requisitioned telephone records, and used the already disputed technology of polygraphy. Senior FBI official Edward "Ed" Tamm reported on other approaches: "The mail of each alleged German agent is being covered, bank accounts are being reviewed, credit ratings established, associates determined, and their income tax returns are being requested."[9]

Abwehr officers—commissioned officers in the German armed forces—sat behind desks in Berlin and in the Hamburg and Bremen branch offices. There, the middle-class men with dueling scars nursed the grievances of a lost war and directed the activities of their operatives through shipborne communications on vessels bound for the United States. The FBI's investigation left the Abwehr hierarchy relatively unscathed. The operatives were a different matter. These more exposed assets fell into four sometimes-overlapping categories: couriers, enforcers, agents, and informants. The last group consisted typically of German Americans with technical expertise who worked on US defense contracts. Apparently the Abwehr did not try to recruit Americans of non-German extraction. They did not need to, as a sufficient supply of German Americans with the right expertise were willing to oblige.

Otto Voss was a leading example. He had been a colleague of Willy Lonkowski's, and it was by investigating the Voss case that the FBI realized the German secret service had been stealing US military technology for at least three years. After Griebl fingered him, Voss was questioned on March 10 and charged the next day, eventually confessing to his role on March 14. The FBI dossier on him noted that he had extensively trained as a mechanic in Hamburg, had fought in Finland and France with the Imperial German Army, and had immigrated to the United States in 1928. His wife, Anna, was a domestic servant who opposed his involvement in espionage, but he ignored her objections and was an enthusiastic agent. According to one FBI report, "It should be noted that as far as the investigation of this [New York City] office is concerned, the information furnished by VOSS to agents in Germany was by far the most damaging, inasmuch as he furnished confidential construction details of Army pursuit planes which are at the present time the most advanced type in this country."[10]

Not every interviewee interrogated by the FBI was a spy, but, innocently or otherwise, those questioned shed light on different aspects of the inquiry. German-born Johannes K. Steuer was a case in point. Steuer was a mechanic who had moved to the United States before World War I. In 1917 with fears of sabotage running high, he had been interned at Ellis Island along with all other Germans who worked within a mile of the Brooklyn Navy Yard. He and the others were released without charge, and at the war's conclusion he returned to work for his former employer, the Sperry Gyroscope Company. He became an America citizen.

By the 1930s, Steuer was a principal inspector at Sperry, the Anglo-American concern that designed and manufactured military equipment. One of its projects was a bombsight. The Sperry device would see only limited service, as in the battle for major contracts the firm lost out to Norden, whose plans were being betrayed to the German authorities even as Turrou launched his investigation into Sperry. These outcomes could not have been foreseen at the time, and the penetration of Sperry would have been cause for serious concern. Turrou questioned Steuer all day on March 11 and 12, while two of his colleagues searched the Steuer residence on Hudson Boulevard, North Bergen, New Jersey, "with negative results."

Turrou worried that Abwehr agents were grooming German Americans with skills at the level of Steuer's either to use them as agents in situ or to induce them to return to work in Germany, where their know-how would be utilized. He cited the example of another Sperry employee named Irwin Backhaus, who had worked on government contracts in his native Germany as well as in the United States. Backhaus was internationally respected for his work on automatic pilot planes, an antecedent to present-day drones. One day an engineer from Germany met him at the St. George Hotel in Brooklyn and offered him a contract in the old country. The money on offer was suspiciously generous, and Backhaus realized he was being asked not just to work but also to supply Sperry blueprints.

In a parallel case, Griebl, with backing from North German Lloyd, offered a lucrative two-year deal to the naval engineer Christian F. Danielsen, whose three daughters were still in Germany despite his thirty years' living in the United States. When the North German Lloyd return ticket came through, it was for a one-month stay only, the idea being that Danielsen would pass on the secrets and then be let go.

In the event, the FBI could not pin anything on Steuer, but the principal inspector did shed light on security arrangements. US military intelligence had to give clearances to any foreign dignitaries who wanted to inspect the Sperry plant in Brooklyn. Steuer told a story that illuminated the weakness of the arrangement. Sperry's president had visited Germany, and a German delegation subsequently arrived to see how the three-thousand-part bombsight was produced. The delegates were not given access to sensitive assembly points, and evidently there was some compliance with the demand for security. However, potentially even these precautions were rendered futile by the company's ambition to export for profit sensitive equipment that Germany's arms industry could have disassembled and imitated.[11]

All this occurred against a hot political background. A significant number of Americans were convinced that arms manufacturers, the so-called merchants of death, had conspired to drag the United States into World War I to swell their profits. These Americans believed that the GIs' ensuing sacrifices had been for nothing. They also held that the peace settlement on the conclusion of World War I had been deficient, causing the sort of growing discontent that resulted in the rise of fascism in an embittered Germany. In a high-profile US Senate investigation between 1934 and 1936 chaired by Gerald P. Nye (R-ND), the US arms industry came under a distinctly hostile gaze. Amid the widespread conviction that self-serving profiteers had dragged the United States into a war that was inhumane and against the national interest, Congress passed a series of Neutrality Acts, with the first signed on August 31, 1935, that imposed a general embargo on trading in arms and war materials.

All this was at odds with Secretary of State Cordell Hull's efforts to liberalize trade and pull the United States and the rest of the world out of the ongoing economic depression. US shipyards were already making money and jobs by building warships for Brazil and communist Russia.[12] However, any revelations that the weapons manufacturers were trading by the back door or allowing a potential aggressor access to their secrets, whether through negligence or not, would be politically explosive. The country was divided, and feelings ran deep on both sides of the debate.

Yet another Griebl tip-off led to the March 15, 1938, raid on the Brooklyn home of Johannes Kögel on Wythe Avenue. A former German soldier, he had served a mechanics apprenticeship in Darmstadt and had become an American citizen in 1931. Kögel was a skilled designer who worked for the Kollmorgen Optical Corporation, for whom he developed a pistol-drive periscope and other optical devices for use in naval warfare. When FBI agents found blueprints in his house, they took him in for questioning.

Defending himself, Kögel said he often brought work home. Nowadays it was doubly convenient, as he had to work in the evenings. In the depressed 1930s, his firm had laid off men, and he had to labor for longer hours to compensate and help his employers complete contracts on time.

Asked to comment on the security risk of taking confidential materials away from the workplace, he tartly commented that they were making better periscopes abroad; Germany would learn little from US technology. Kögel withstood the questions of five FBI interrogators, who must have felt they were up against a brick wall. Perhaps Griebl was inventing Abwehr informers to throw Turrou off the scent. Just as likely, though, is the possibility that Griebl had a list of German American mechanics regarded as *potential* informers. For such individuals, the FBI inquiries may have been a deterrent.[13]

Turrou was keen to show that the German spy ring was uniformly Nazi and that it reflected the totalitarian character of Hitler's regime. The FBI did not have the means to investigate how the Gestapo might have intimidated individuals in Germany, forcing them to become spies; however, it looked for examples of intimidation within the United States. For example, Turrou ascertained that Lonkowski had sent Senta de Wanger threatening letters after his flight to Germany, and in the winter of 1937–38 while using the pseudonym Frederick von Klotz, Guenther Rumrich had attempted to terrorize Senta by making appointments to see her and then not turning up.[14]

In pursuing evidence on intimidation, the FBI took an interest in the Gestapo's Willy Herrmann. Special Agent G. A. Callahan spoke to Herrmann at Griebl's house, confronting a man of medium height with aquiline features and greased-back black hair. The Gestapo man lived at a 75 West Eighty-Ninth Street apartment with Margaret Stevenson. She was a Works Progress Administration actor who innocently believed that her lover's job as a waiter in Brooklyn was his true vocation. Recalling what Pfeiffer had told him, Griebl had informed Turrou that "Herrmann is charged with the enforcement and execution of orders sent to him from headquarters directly from Berlin and sometimes relayed from Berlin to Pfeiffer and in turn relayed to Herrmann in New York City." He said that Herrmann's job was to ensure the "trustworthiness" of German agents in the States and to organize protection for the spy-couriers plying their trade on the Atlantic liners.[15] In an eight-page statement witnessed by Callahan on March 28, Herrmann proclaimed himself a proud Nazi, acknowledged his Gestapo mission, and confessed to knowing most of the spies identified by the FBI. He insisted he was doing political work, however, and not conducting espionage.[16]

Herrmann tried to ingratiate himself with his interrogators by saying he was trying to stop communist murderers and bullies on the water-front. Ewald Fritz Rossberg, one of his henchmen, told a more revealing story. He and Heinrich Bischoff, the party enforcer on the SS *Europa*, went in pursuit of "a German woman flyer" who "had betrayed Germany." He was referring to the actor and athlete–turned–test pilot Antonie Strassmann, a strikingly beautiful woman who had become a focus of adulation in the Weimar Republic for promoting German airplanes in the United States. By the 1930s she had given up her involvement with Crown Prince Wilhelm of the House of Hohenzollern; had taken up instead with Robert L. Hague, senior vice president at Standard Oil; and was a permanent resident in the United States.

In 1937 Antonie, who was of Jewish descent, took business parties onto both the *Europa* and *Bremen*, where she evidently befriended crew members. Especially after one of them visited her hotel in a chauffeur-driven limousine, Herrmann suspected that "the Strassmann woman" was trying to "turn" members of the crew. Rossberg and Bischoff were supposed to keep Antonie under observation and sabotage her anti-Nazi efforts. Like most of Herrmann's operations, this one was misconceived and ham-fisted. Antonie Strassmann continued unimpeded with her multiple business and later Red Cross activities until she died in New York in 1952. Yet, with this episode, Herrmann had brought to the States a little whiff of the Nazi surveillance state.[17]

By the beginning of April, Turrou and his colleagues had gathered enough evidence to allow them to write the reports on which the grand jury hearings would be predicated. However, much work remained to be done. There would be more testimonies as the story unraveled, in the words of a London *Daily Telegraph* reporter, "piecemeal like a detective tale." For example, Christian Danielsen, the naval engineer who had turned down the Abwehr's money, would be arrested as a material witness in time for the grand jury hearings. Yet only four spies were in custody, many of the interviewees told lies, and all were reluctant to confess to criminal behavior.[18]

Moreover, the FBI knew the senior spies—von Bonin, Menzel, and Pfeiffer—were beyond its reach in Germany. It continued to believe in the delusion that it should be hunting down the mythical Sanders and Schmidt. And the bureau had another problem. The FBI knew of spies who had been operating in the States but had not yet helped the bureau with its inquiries. The reason was that they were gone.

11
THE FLIGHT OF THE SPIES

The problem had begun in mid-February, when Karl Schlueter failed to board the SS *Europa* and allowed the besotted Jenni Hofmann to travel to America instead. Turrou now would have no chance of interviewing Schlueter.

The Abwehr had realized that the FBI was on to the case and set out to protect not just Schlueter but also as many of its key agents as possible. One of them was Theodore Schuetz, alias Karl Weigand, whom Turrou described as being "a tremendously important Nazi spy contact man, ranking almost with Karl Schlueter."[1]

Schuetz's day job was that of a steward aboard Hamburg American Line's SS *New York*. When Berlin executed its protective plan, the *New York* was on a Caribbean cruise. The order came through to the vessel's commodore, Fritz Kruse. Schuetz was to return to Germany by any route, provided he did not set foot in the United States. The agent accordingly left the ship on March 2, 1938, when it docked at Havana.

The Abwehr top brass feared that the FBI would arrest Schuetz when the *New York* put in at its namesake's port. Its fears were well founded, for Turrou immediately boarded the vessel upon its arrival in the United States. When he found a line drawn through Schuetz's name on the ship's manifest, the FBI's lead detective realized that a full-scale escape-and-evasion plan was in operation.

The Miami branch of the FBI laid plans to have Schuetz arrested in Havana, but he left for Mexico, leading to potential diplomatic difficulties. Turrou pursued the case as best he could. Following his visit to the Schuetz-less SS *New York*, the detective asked to see the radiogram that had instructed Kruse to disembark his steward, but the "lofty" commodore refused to produce it even when pressured to do so by the worried waterfront boss Wilhelm Drechsel. Commodore Kruse declared, "I have got nothing to do with any of the activities of the personnel onboard the ship." It was a wretched admission by the chief officer of a passenger ship. So was his afterthought: "I am not involved in anything."[2]

Later that month, Captain Drechsel met Consul General Bottler, members of his staff, and two attorneys Bottler had retained to assist with Jenni Hofmann's defense—William J. Topken and Reimer Koch-Weser. The attorneys were interim Reich-approved appointments who served until supplanted by George C. Dix, who saw his main duty as the defense of his client. Drechsel proposed a damage limitation plan. Three wanted agents—Karl Schlueter, Karl Herbert Janichen (a recent Pfeiffer recruit on the *Bremen*), and Theodore Schuetz—would return voluntarily to the United States and "face the music." They, together with Hofmann, would plead guilty.

Advocating a tactic that paralleled that of the British authorities in the Jessie Jordan affair, Drechsel's "unquestionable" view was that "the matter could be perfunctorily disposed of in the United States District Court without giving the case the amount of publicity which would arise if the case should go to trial." Drechsel argued, "Germany would benefit considerably by sacrificing three or four persons rather than revealing at the trial in detail" the full extent of German espionage and the names of other agents. Topken and Koch-Weser gave their "tentative" assent, and the intention was that the plan would be promoted in Berlin via Ambassador Hans Heinrich Dieckhoff in Washington. Hinting at a double-agent role, Drechsel promised the FBI he would secretly inform it of the outcome.[3]

For the time being, Berlin ignored the proposal. It persisted with a policy of discontinuing agents' voyages to the United States, defending those under arrest, denying everything—and extricating agents who were currently in the States and not yet under arrest.

The most prominent example of such extrication was Ignatz Griebl. One day when the swindler was sitting in Turrou's office and spinning him a line about how Germany was exchanging intelligence with Japan about the strengths and weaknesses of the US Navy, he suddenly sighed, "Ach, Gott!" Then he covered his face with his hands. "What is it?" Turrou asked. He received a bitterly intoned reply: "Don't you realize, Mr. Turrou, that what I am doing is signing my death warrant in Germany? If they ever found out what I had told you—the secrets entrusted to me by von Bonin, Menzel, Pfeiffer, and others . . ."[4] Griebl made a chopping gesture aimed at his own neck.

The gesture helped explain why Turrou never arrested or charged Griebl. He just wanted him to keep talking, and the best way to do that was to let him run free. This strategy was a tactical departure for the FBI, with its ingrained "arrest culture," and an indication that the bureau was preparing for a new age with new challenges. At the same time, Turrou was acting in the apparently secure knowledge that Griebl would be too terrified to flee to Germany. This was before the scales dropped from his eyes.

On the evening of May 10, Ignatz was unusually attentive to Maria and asked her to accompany him to Greenwich Village to see a patient. Afterward he said he had business on board the SS *Bremen*. They arrived at the waterfront at 10 p.m., and Maria could see the glittering lights of the SS *Bremen* and SS *Hansa* berthed at Pier 86. Ignatz excused himself to use the men's room in a nearby saloon; then Maria saw her husband walk in the direction of the *Bremen*. He never returned.

Another place to which he might have deviated at short notice was the Riverside apartment of Kate Moog. But at 6 a.m. on May 11, Ignatz's other woman phoned Turrou in a panic: "Ignatz—Dr. Griebl—he has disappeared! . . . He has been kidnapped! They have taken him on a ship! They will kill him in Germany!"[5]

Griebl had left his physician's bag in the car and boarded the ship with no belongings, no passport, and no ticket, which made him a stowaway. He did have as means of identification a driver's license and a gun permit, together with the sum of $180. He told Capt. Adolf Ahrens he was fleeing the United States because of the espionage case. Ahrens allowed him to buy a tourist class ticket for $156. So it came to pass that the *Bremen* slipped through the Narrows past the unseeing gaze of the Statue of Liberty and headed out into the Atlantic bearing a man who would have been Leon Turrou's leading trial witness. On his first day at sea, Griebl penned letters to his wife, complaining about his treatment on board, and to his mistress, claiming he was departing to conclude the Jewish land deal. He reassured Maria he would be back in time for the spy trial. He spent the rest of the voyage largely confined to cabin 656, emerging only to dine at a table for one.

When the *Bremen* put in at Cherbourg, the US ambassador in Paris William Bullitt failed in his efforts to have Griebl taken off the ship. Ambassador Joe Kennedy never really tried when the *Bremen* docked in Southampton; a person of Kennedy's political persuasion would not have wanted to offend Germany by engaging in such a provocative action. From Southampton, Griebl cabled Reed Vetterli in impudent style: "Stop trying to interfere will be back in due time arrange passport facilities for return through France with American Consulate Berlin."[6]

Arriving in Bremerhaven, Griebl tipped his table waiter $5 (around $90 in today's values). He then went ashore, and there to greet him was not a vengeful posse from the Gestapo but Eric Pfeiffer. We have Pfeiffer's account of the course of events:

```
There were no mutual recriminations: GRIEBL boasted
that he had served Germany well to the last, surviv-
ing the most searching interrogations, "the only rock
on the shifting sands of German-American espionage;"
and then he enquired urgently for monetary compensa-
tion. . . . GRIEBL later went off to his home in Wurz-
burg, whence he bombarded PHEIFFER with new demands
and threats, so that eventually a sum of between 50
and 100,000 Rmk. [between $350,000 and $700,000 to-
day] was paid to him and arrangements were completed
for satisfaction of his long-standing plans to ex-
change his property in New York for that of a Jew
living in Giessen, with the latter's agreement.
```

That was the last Pfeiffer saw of him. Griebl then decamped to Vienna, where he sought to practice from the conveniently vacated premises of a departed Jewish gynecologist.[7]

Compared with Griebl's flight, that of Werner Georg Gudenberg seemed less damaging to the FBI's prosecution case. Griebl—a middle class, anti-Semitic, and consummate confidence man—had extracted major compensation from his Abwehr employers and made a similarly deep impression in America. Gudenberg's escape, while lower profile, was nevertheless significant. He had enjoyed the confidence of premium defense contractors and not just at Ireland Aircraft. By this time a US citizen, in September 1932 he had married Veronica Karp, a pretty girl from Bristol, Pennsylvania, who soon bore him a son. Gudenberg was the epitome of upwardly mobile respectability. Between 1932 and 1936, he was a foreman in charge of thirty men in the cowl and patternmaking departments at the military-contracted Curtiss Wright Corporation in Buffalo, New York. The couple then moved to Bristol, Pennsylvania, where Werner ran the sheet metal department at the seaplane designer Hall Aluminum Aircraft Company.

Lonkowski visited Gudenberg in Buffalo in the summer of 1935. They had a few beers, and Gudenberg boasted about his technical expertise. When Lonkowski said that Germany needed him, the newly minted American citizen agreed to become a German spy. Gudenberg thereafter either supplied blueprints for Lonkowski to photograph or used his own Leica camera, though it resulted in blurrier prints. He passed on information about Curtiss planes, such as their armament specifications and cruising range, and about a prototype "scout bomber" being built in Buffalo. Some of the Curtiss blueprint reproductions were in Lonkowski's possession at the time US Customs Service officers detained him on September 27, 1935.

Turrou regarded Gudenberg as guilty but an innocent, thinking that Lonkowski had led him astray. This was a lenient view, or perhaps it was a rationalization in light of Gudenberg's later escape. As noted in chapter 1, Gudenberg lured technicians to Germany, where they could pass on the secrets of US military technology. According to Pfeiffer, Gudenberg's mission was no fleeting venture, for Gudenberg took over Lonkowski's functions when the latter escaped to Germany. In further evidence against him, Nikolaus Ritter would later explain that when he operated through local contacts to steal the Norden bombsight plans during his New York visit in November–December 1937, Gudenberg had been one of those contacts. Turrou had underestimated Gudenberg.[8]

To the distress of his wife, Veronica, who was thrown into penury by his action, Gudenberg suddenly disappeared. He had already testified to the grand jury and was about to make a second appearance on May 27, a day when jurors were scheduled to hear evidence about Griebl's defection. Turrou was grooming witnesses in the court's anteroom when Drechsel burst in and announced that he had received a message from Theodore Koch, captain of the SS *Hamburg*. At 4 a.m. the previous day, a steward had discovered, fast asleep in the third-class lobby, a penniless stowaway who could not produce a passport or other means of identification except for a Social Security card. His description, radio-telegrammed to Drechsel, indicated he was Gudenberg. Koch said he had Gudenberg thrown into the ship's brig and indicated he would turn him over to the Gestapo to be disciplined upon the liner's arrival in Hamburg. The German authorities telegrammed him fake instructions, which were later produced in an attempt to deceive American officials: Gudenberg was to be kept under lock and key for the whole voyage unless the French authorities demanded his disembarkation in Cherbourg.

In the event, neither the French nor the British authorities put the ship's captain to that inconvenience. American officials had requested Gudenberg's detention, the State Department had briefed Ambassadors Bullitt and Kennedy about the warrant for his arrest, and District Attorney Lamar Hardy of the Southern District of New York made some urgent transatlantic phone calls. However, the *Hamburg's* captain responded by moving Gudenberg to the ship's sickbay and asserting that he was too ill to be moved ashore in either Cherbourg or Southampton. The Abwehr's repatriation plan had worked once again. Veronica, whose penniless predicament had worried Turrou, was soon able to join her husband in Germany.[9]

To what extent did the German escape plan work? When the federal grand jury issued its indictments on June 20, it named eighteen defendants. As stated in the indictments, they were Udo von Bonin, Hermann

Menzel, Ernst Mueller, Erich Pfeiffer, Schmidt (first name unknown), Sanders (first name also unknown), Mrs. Jessie Jordan, William Lonkowski, Karl Schlueter, Theodore Schuetz, Karl Herbert Janichen, Karl Eitel, Johanna Hofmann, Ignatz Theodor Griebl, Otto Herrmann Voss, Werner Georg Gudenberg, Erich Glaser, and Guenther Gustave Rumrich. A review of this list indicates that the FBI was not as lax as many have supposed.

By way of prelude, it is of interest that the American authorities did not indict the person more responsible than anyone else for launching the spy ring, Admiral Canaris. He may have been too big a fish to fry for diplomatic reasons. Furthermore, Turrou and his entourage had only a hazy concept of the German espionage hierarchy. The word "Abwehr" rarely, if ever, made its way into FBI reports of the late 1930s, and Canaris's name never did, though Turrou did know the admiral by one of his aliases, Busch. In this ignorance, the FBI did not lag behind its approximate British counterpart. Authorized historians with full access to MI5 files for the 1930s note a similar deficiency on the part of the British counterintelligence agency.[10]

Nine of the indicted were out of reach because they were abroad. Udo von Bonin, Hermann Menzel, and Ernst Mueller were thought to have tasked the American spies from Berlin; Erich Pfeiffer worked out of Bremen; and Willy Lonkowski was safely tucked away behind an air force desk in Germany's capital. To indict such men with no chance of arrests being made demonstrated the breadth of the FBI's investigation yet invited a reputation for failure.

A sixth indictee, Karl Eitel, had been caught embezzling and had been deployed to other duties in Europe beyond the FBI's reach. A seventh, Janichen, had been a Pfeiffer courier when working as a waiter on the SS *Bremen* and had been questioned by Turrou, but he was also in Europe, far from the arm of American justice. An eighth, Schlueter, had been kept in Germany, allowing Hofmann to be arrested in his stead. A ninth, Schuetz, had been diverted from US ports and made it back to the fatherland.

Two more can be eliminated from the list. Schmidt, whose first name was unknown, was never properly identified. Rumrich used the name interchangeably with that of Schleuter, but Schmidt did not exist as an independent entity. Sanders was a generic alias. Being fictitious, Schmidt and Sanders can thus be stricken from the list of those who eluded the FBI. Five were under arrest in the United States or Britain: Hofmann, Voss, Glaser, Rumrich, and Jordan. That brings the total to sixteen. Of the last two, Gudenberg escaped when he was a witness and before he was indicted. Had he been more fully investigated, he might have yielded information about Lang and the Ritter brothers. Apart from that notable lacuna, it may be concluded that Turrou made just one serious error with his decision to trust Griebl.

Turrou's critics would claim that in the words of historian Tim Weiner, he made the bureau "a laughingstock."[11] They charged that he was responsible for self-serving, publicity-driven leaks that allowed mass escapes. It is closer to the truth that the leaks, for which Turrou was not responsible, had alerted the Abwehr and kept its spies from US shores.

The German escape plan did damage the US counterespionage effort. Griebl's evidence, if only he could be made to tell the truth, would have been an asset for the prosecution. Furthermore, one can add to the absentees' roster a number of material witnesses, several of them shipboard couriers, who either decided to return to Germany or were persuaded to do so. For whatever reason, these potential witnesses smuggled themselves onto boats undetected. They included Ewald Fritz Rossberg, Wilhelm Boehnke, Walter Otto, Lutz Leiswitz, and Johann Hart. Heinrich Lorenz and Franz Friske, two ship's captains who were arrested as material witnesses and posted bail of $2,500 each, had absconded on a midnight sailing of the SS *Europa*.[12]

The *Los Angeles Times* attempted to make a political evaluation of the spy affair. It observed that the grand jury indictments had created a "ticklish diplomatic situation." In support of its view, the *Times* referred to what it described as the German press's indictment of "American spy hysteria."[13]

This was a misperception. One German newspaper poured scorn on the American press: the *Hamburger Nachrichten* focused on US newspaper reports of the false arrest of an innocent German citizen in West Virginia, whose wife had been mistaken for a latter-day Mata Hari. Yet the *Hamburger Nachrichten* account, though it was on the front page, was not a lead story. The official German response was a know-nothing silence. *Völkischer Beobachter*, the voice of the National Socialist Party, appears to have mentioned the American spy affair not once.[14]

Public reaction at home to the spy case developments was one of shock at the extent of German espionage and at the way it appeared to have been orchestrated from the top levels of the government in Berlin. It also involved finger-pointing at the failings of Turrou and his colleagues. On Capitol Hill, pro-FBI legislators sprang to the bureau's defense. To defuse potential criticism of its record, they trumpeted the FBI's success in fighting organized crime. Rep. Fred Crawford (R-MI) protested that the FBI was underfunded, giving license "to the yellow, lily-livered vipers of the underworld." Sen. Henry F. Ashurst (D-AZ), chairman of the Senate's Judiciary Committee, reiterated his support for Attorney General Homer Cummings's anti-crime campaign. Another prominent contributor to the debate was Rep. Samuel Dickstein, who was the son of a Lithuanian rabbi and, we now know, in the pay of the Soviet intelligence agency the People's Commissariat for Internal Affairs (Narodnyi komissariat vnutrennykh del, or NKVD). Destined to become famous for his opposition to both fascism and communism, Dickstein fulminated against Griebl and other spies, and welcomed the recent creation of the House Un-American Activities Committee.[15]

Turrou recalled the feeling among his FBI team that the bureau's efforts had been "checkmated." But he cited the response of District Attorney Lamar Hardy: "The important point is that the American public must be made aware of the existence of this spy plot, and impressed with the dangers. Our Government and citizens must be awakened to the fact that it is imperative that we have an efficient counter-espionage service, to protect us against such vicious spy rings as this. We will go ahead with the case." Hardy articulated goals that Turrou fervently espoused.

Propaganda had always been important to the FBI detective. Speaking to the American people about the dangers of fascism was for him a primary, perhaps *the* primary, aim.[16]

As we have seen, strictly defined, only two spies managed to escape— Gudenberg and Griebl. But should they have been able to leave, and should the FBI have undertaken a more immediate security clampdown to prevent the departure of other suspects and witnesses? Effective counterintelligence was not without precedent in US history. In the Spanish-American War of 1898 and in World War I, the Secret Service and other government agencies had arrested spies and saboteurs, and held them in custody until they went on trial. Since then federal enforcers had acquired stronger powers that were meant to make them even more effective. The Espionage Act of 1917 articulated that the spy was a public enemy, and it spelled out stiff penalties, including death, for those found guilty under its provisions. In 1934 Attorney General Cummings promoted a reform package that gave FBI special agents the right to carry guns and the power to make arrests for the first time.[17]

But Turrou's efforts still faced impediments, not the least important of which was that the German spying operations of the mid-1930s took place in peacetime when the regard for the civil liberties of a suspect is higher than exists during war. Also, the Espionage Act was in disrepute because during World War I and the ensuing Red Scare (1919–20), it had been misapplied to persecute dissenting minorities within the United States. Another obstacle to effective detention was the US Constitution, which, in peacetime especially, gives citizens protection against arbitrary arrest and guarantees their right to free speech. Those who leaked information about the FBI's counterespionage investigation may have done so for personal gain, but they did so secure in the knowledge that the right of free speech was enshrined in the First Amendment.

In further exoneration of Turrou, the leaks and open statements that alerted German spies and witnesses to remain abroad or to flee originated with others. The disclosures went through three phases. Publicity about the original arrest, that of Guenther Rumrich on February 15, had been so great that Director Hoover was initially reluctant to take the case.

District Attorney Hardy and the police said they were incensed at the "premature and about 75 per cent wrong" leak to the press, though keeping the matter under wraps indefinitely was unlikely in an open society like the United States.[18]

The second blast of the publicity trumpet occurred on February 27, when Hoover and Vetterli supplied the *New York Times* with a detailed account of the arrests of Rumrich, Hofmann, and Rumrich's sidekick, Glaser.[19] Hoover, who favored publicity when it placed the FBI and its leader in an advantageous light, was on a promotional high. Earlier that month his name appeared on a book based on FBI case files, *Persons in Hiding*. (Ghostwritten by Courtney Ryley Cooper, the book gave rise to four movies, including a February 1939 Paramount Pictures release also called *Persons in Hiding*.) Perhaps Hoover reasoned that as the story was already out, the FBI had nothing to lose in promoting the idea that it was making headway on a major case. But there can be no doubt about the consequences. Nobody associated with the German spy ring could have failed to realize the arrests signaled the need to make stay-away and getaway plans.

Against this background, Turrou embarked on a third course of action that put Germany's spies on alert: he warned his suspects and witnesses, Griebl included, that they would be called to testify before the grand jury in May. In April and May, at Turrou's request, the Southern District of New York Court filed complaints against a number of witnesses, requiring them to put up bail money. Thus, they retained their liberty and were free to leave the country.

Imprudent though his decision seemed in retrospect, Turrou remained for the time being Hoover's untouchable protégé. When Hoover released a diversionary blame salvo, he aimed it not at Turrou but at Lamar Hardy.

A native of Meridian, Hardy was the fifty-nine-year-old son of a Confederate soldier who later became a judge of the Superior Court of Mississippi. Lamar had captained the football and baseball teams at Vanderbilt University, and when appointed corporation counsel in New York City in 1915 with the mission of rooting out corruption, he had taken a firm stance. His first measure had been to fire his whole staff. Mayor Fiorello

LaGuardia of New York had accepted his recommendation that the city should have a commissioner of purchases to clean up the public contracting process. Hardy's record recommended him to both the mayor and to President Roosevelt, who had appointed him district attorney.[20]

Hardy's accomplishments failed to deter Hoover, who launched into full assault mode. On June 1 the FBI director issued the following statement via New York special agent in charge Vetterli: "The responsibility for the disappearance of Dr. Ignatz T. Griebl and the witness Werner G. Gudenberg is the responsibility of the United States Attorney and not of the Federal Bureau of Investigation." A little over four hours later came the riposte from Hardy: "I deny . . . that the disappearance of these witnesses was in any way the result of negligence in the slightest degree on the part of my office." The *New York Times* reported the exchange as part of its coverage of what it termed "the loss of two of the most important figures in the greatest attack on spies in peace time."[21]

All concerned recognized that the stakes were high. The blame game was in full swing.

12
BLAME GAMES

The escapes sparked a search for scapegoats. At the time, FBI director J. Edgar Hoover was left relatively unscathed. He managed to persuade the White House that he was doing a good counterintelligence job and gained the confidence of President Roosevelt just as the director would win the ear of every chief executive during his long tenure.

In more recent times, Athan Theoharis has questioned Hoover's reputation for competence. Theoharis worked for the US Senate's inquiry into the FBI, Central Intelligence Agency (CIA), and other agencies in the 1970s and established a reputation as the chief authority on the history of the FBI. Theoharis and, more recently, the historian Svetlana Lokhova have pointed to an area where Hoover's FBI failed to stop foreign espionage or even to find out that it existed.

They were talking about Soviet spies. The FBI director put up a convincing *show* of being an anti-communist and, as Theoharis and others have shown, persecuted the American Left. But when it came to the real threat against national security, he was less effective. In the 1940s, the world learned that Soviet spies had been active in the United States. In the 1990s, more information emerged when postcommunist Russia temporarily opened its security files and after the release of the "Venona" decrypts of secret Soviet messages that the US Army's Signals Intelligence Service intercepted during World War II and in the early Cold War. The combined information confirmed some of the Americans' worst fears about how Moscow's espionage damaged their nation.

We now know that in 1928 General Secretary of the Communist Party of the Soviet Union Joseph Stalin targeted US aviation technology. In 1931 the Soviet spy Col. Stanislav Shumovsky enrolled at the

Massachusetts Institute of Technology. Together with confederates, he successfully sought US military secrets over the next few years. Also, just as Lonkowski coordinated many of the Abwehr's US efforts, Aleksandr Ulanofsky, a military intelligence officer operating under the alias Nicholas Sherman, directed a number of the Soviets' US operations in the early 1930s.

Moscow's objectives were in some ways similar to those of Berlin. Its agents hunted for and obtained US State Department plans and details of military production. Preeminent among its agents was the research physicist Klaus Fuchs. Having fled Hitler's Germany, some years later he joined the Manhattan Project, which developed an atomic weapon. When the British finally arrested him for passing vital atomic secrets to the Soviets, J. Edgar Hoover fumed at London for monopolizing the case, but the truth is that Fuchs was a giant-size fish who evaded the security nets of both MI5 and the FBI until significant damage had been done.[1]

At least partly because Hoover opted for the easier task of persecuting radical minorities, the FBI remained blind to and even complacent about more serious threats. And the seriousness of those threats cannot be in doubt. Stalin's dictatorship would turn out to be as bloody as Hitler's. To quote a gruesome phrase, the Soviet leader presided over a "population deficit" of approximately 48 million people, of whom only 22 million were soldiers killed in action fighting Germany and its allies.[2]

Given what we now know, the FBI's performance against the Abwehr has to be assessed in a wider context of counterintelligence failure. In the 1930s, however, nobody knew enough about Soviet espionage to mount a serious challenge to the public narrative on the FBI's competence. The debate in the press and elsewhere was all about the bureau's competence against German espionage and about who should be held accountable for any deficiencies in that regard.

While the debates were vigorous and open in the United States, in Germany they were just as vigorous, but the government-controlled press kept the German public in the dark. Within the hidden world of officialdom, alarm grew over the Abwehr agents' exposure and its likely consequences. In Bremen Erich Pfeiffer had access to US newspapers through his couriers, and he anxiously followed the stories about the spy case debacle. He fretted that Ignatz Griebl was talking too much and erratically. Pfeiffer worried that the gynecologist-spy was building him up into some sort of superspy who could be blamed for the whole spying enterprise. When Pfeiffer heard that he was being accused of running the disastrous Jessie Jordan in Scotland, he breathed a sigh of relief, for he would be able to prove to his German superiors that she was instructed not from his base in Bremen but from Hamburg.

Schlueter was another problem for Pfeiffer, though he could also use him as an opportunity to divert the blame from himself. The Bremen chief portrayed his agent as a fanatical Nazi Party member and incompetent spy who had tried to show professional intelligence officers how things should be done. Schlueter had launched the inevitably exposed and very damaging McAlpin Hotel plot. Pfeiffer later recalled, "The colossal ambition of Schlueter, combined with bad crime literature [inspiring Schlueter's actions] was at the bottom of the madness."[3]

Such was the power of the National Socialist Party that Pfeiffer could not hope to have Schlueter disciplined, so he sent him on a cruise instead. Pfeiffer arranged for the discredited agent to join the crew of a vessel engaged in the Nazi-organized "Strength through Joy" tourist and propaganda program that sent over 10 million Germans on seaborne vacations in 1938. Pfeiffer saw to it that Schlueter's ship was "guaranteed not to call at American ports."

Pfeiffer's efforts at self-preservation might well have failed, for powerful factions were out to get him. North German Lloyd complained that the Americans' disclosures damaged its reputation and threatened its trade and profits. To aid and abet espionage was one thing, but it was quite another to be found out. The managing director, Pfeiffer recalled, "demanded a full explanation" from him.

Worried about the impact of the scandal on German-US relations, Berlin's Foreign Ministry also expected an explanation from the Bremen spymaster. At the Abwehr's Berlin headquarters, Hermann Menzel raged at Pfeiffer's alleged indiscretions and ordered his junior to curtail his operations and to concentrate on monitoring US press reports. Pfeiffer feared that too many forces were aligned against him. There was little support for him in Berlin. People were listening to hostile voices in the United States—not just the press but also the pier master Wilhelm Drechsel with his complaints about the spy scandal's impact on shipping line profits.

Matters came to a head when Wilhelm Canaris ordered Pfeiffer to present himself for a dressing down in Berlin. The naval intelligence officer duly arrived at the Tirpitzuferstrasse military building. He ascended to the Abwehr chief's suite, knowing that Canaris opposed the use of violence in intelligence operations and would be horrified by Schlueter's behavior. Pfeiffer had always found his boss to be a cold fish and feared he would be unable to dissuade the admiral from censure over the controversial American affair, for "in such cases [Canaris] used to go ahead regardless."

Pfeiffer entered the boss's office. Sitting as usual with his back to the windows overlooking the Landwehr Canal was the master of the master spies. Physically Pfeiffer towered over the five-foot-six chief, but psychologically he felt intimidated. He recalled, "The atmosphere was that of a deathbed scene."

Pfeiffer churned out his litany of excuses. It was Schlueter's fault; he was a rogue spy out of control and had been insubordinate in reporting to Hamburg instead of solely to Pfeiffer in Bremen. Furthermore, Schlueter had used Hamburg cover addresses contrary to Abwehr policy. The "stovepiping" principle—in the interest of security, each branch of intelligence looks after its own secrets independently of other branches—had been breached. Schlueter had ignored that requirement.

No doubt Canaris had worked all of this out for himself. He listened with forbearance. In spite of his intimidating summons, he had no intention of changing his view of the man he had handpicked as a promising spymaster. Pfeiffer may have missed a twinkle in the admiral's eye when he asked, "Well, Pfeiffer, have you got any complaint against me, too?" He now offered his junior a cigar, and at last Pfeiffer could relax, for "it represented the pipe of peace." Instead of punishing Pfeiffer, Canaris assigned him to other tasks.[4]

According to one of Turrou's newspaper articles some months later, Pfeiffer was actually promoted, the recognition being a reward for engineering the evacuation of Griebl from the United States.[5] Pfeiffer, as one might expect, was keen to defend his competence. He felt he had neither really failed in his US mission nor succumbed in his tussle with Turrou. To the extent that he had been brought down, he later told a British interrogator, it was because of collateral work by MI5 and not through good work by US counterintelligence.[6] Postwar British intelligence assessments tended to agree with Canaris's view that Pfeiffer showed more competence than his colleagues in Hamburg did, even if one such report noted that the quality of Abwehr intelligence made no difference anyway, for the leaders of Nazi Germany paid no heed to it.[7]

If a claim can be made for Pfeiffer's competence, does that reflect badly on the FBI? Must the bureau carry the responsibility for the Abwehr's damage to national security? Although the degree to which Germany's espionage had damaged US national security was never definitively ascertained, the FBI was worried. The loss of the Norden bombsight secrets, once discovered, would be treated as a significant setback, and great volumes of other military technology secrets were smuggled out of the United States. Pfeiffer claimed that the information his agents obtained conferred a military advantage. He gave as an example his spies' procurement of secret technology that improved the antiaircraft defenses of German pocket battleships.[8]

Ultimately the FBI took the view that Turrou's operation did not entirely wipe out Pfeiffer's spy ring. An FBI report sent to MI5 at the end of World War II noted, "Dr. Pfeiffer's activities in the United States were seriously disrupted in 1938 in the Rumrich case." However, the report continued somewhat apprehensively, "his representatives, if they actually existed, at Seattle, Washington, and Newport News, Virginia, have never been identified."[9]

Turrou was pulled both ways when discussing the strength of the German spy menace. In extolling his own achievements, he had to show that the Pfeiffer machine had been overcome. But as an anti-Nazi campaigner, he had to hype the monster. He recorded Pfeiffer's boast to Griebl at the high point of the Abwehr's operations: "In every strategic point in your United States we have an operative. In every armament factory in America we have a spy. In every shipyard we have an agent—in every key position. Your country cannot plan a warship, design a fighting 'plane, develop a new instrument or device, that we do not know about at once!"[10] Turrou said that "vital defense secrets were being smuggled out on virtually every Nazi ship which left our ports."[11] He knew that credible examples of German spying could be a way of defaming the Nazis, so he alerted Americans to the theft of blueprints for a new antiaircraft gun under construction in Fort Monmouth, New Jersey, and of plans to strengthen US battleships. He warned them that Germany had obtained "verbatim accounts of Cabinet conferences, secret military talks and Presidential telephone conversations." The Abwehr's successes were too tangible to be dismissed as just a story concocted to promote "European interventionist propaganda."[12] Aware of the need for tightened security, the FBI hierarchy parroted Turrou's findings without criticism.[13]

Turrou detailed a variety of security breaches. For example, he wrote up the case of W. Starling Burgess. A Harvard graduate who had served as a gunner's mate on the USS *Prairie* in the Spanish-American War, Burgess was further notable for having married five times and for having designed the *Enterprise, Rainbow*, and *Ranger* racing yachts that all won the America's Cup between 1930 and 1937. Burgess had successfully used aluminum in the construction of his boats and became a naval architect for both the Aluminum Company of America and the Bath Iron Works, which constructed destroyers for the US Navy in Maine.

Burgess believed that if an aluminum-steel alloy could be used in the hulls of destroyers, it would enable them to achieve speeds of up to fifty miles per hour and would help retard corrosion. In December 1937 Burgess had the first of two meetings with President Roosevelt to discuss the project. After the first meeting, a report of the discussion appeared in a Bath newspaper. It was a shocking breach of security. If a local journalist could obtain such information, what might the Abwehr be able to achieve? The FBI responded to the leak by demanding and obtaining lists of all those who had attended the meetings to discuss hull technology. It sent out a clear message about the need for security.[14]

The FBI's concern was not just about one isolated case. The FBI worried about Griebl's contention regarding Gibbs and Cox Company, a naval architecture and engineering firm. Griebl claimed that German authorities clandestinely received monthly reports on the firm's deliberations in their office at 1 Broadway, New York City, and thus knew all about US naval shipbuilding plans. Accordingly, on March 15, 1938, Special Agents F. I. McGarraghy and G. A. Callahan began a string of interviews with Capt. A. B. Court, a supervisor of construction for the US Navy who had advised President Roosevelt on naval procurement.[15]

Toward the end of the month, the bureau acquired some confirmation of how the Abwehr operated. Vetterli and Turrou, in company with two other agents, cross-examined Jacobus Mauritz. The subject of this new inquiry was yet another German-trained mechanic who fought in the war, migrated to the States, and ended up working on US defense contracts, in this case with the Newport News Shipbuilding and Drydock Company. The former artilleryman worked on the designs of the carriers *Ranger*, *Yorktown*, and *Enterprise* and of their aircraft arrester equipment, in which Pfeiffer and his superiors had expressed an interest.

In August 1937 Mauritz had sailed on the SS *Bremen* to visit his mother and other relatives in Germany. The ship's hierarchy had been ready for him. Though Mauritz was traveling tourist class, Werner Jarren, the *Bremen*'s commander, invited him to dine at the captain's table. Jarren declared that Hitler was wonderful and urged Mauritz to read the dictator's testament, *Mein Kampf*. Mauritz later said that at the privileged table he found himself in the company of three other pro-Hitler men. All three had doctorates, and one of them quizzed him expertly about his defense work. Under later FBI interrogation, Mauritz insisted that he had seen through the ruse, had refused to cooperate, and had never heard of Pfeiffer or Griebl. The FBI's examination of his personal finances—a standard procedure with the object of identifying irregular money flows—came up blank.[16]

The upshot was no arrests, but agents took more precautions. According to one of Turrou's reports, "Captain Court advised that he considered the general system of handling . . . confidential plans entirely too loose. He has taken several precautions; in fact he now has the waste paper destroyed."

The effectiveness of such precautions was open to question. A worker at the Bath Iron Works in Maine pointed out that all those who labored on implementing a design had to know about that design; thus, maintaining tight security was easier said than done. Mauritz offered a parallel critique. After being grilled at some length about who held which cabinet key and who could see what plans, he lost patience with his questioners. He snapped that the press usually found out about ship designs and that 90 percent of the details of America's new aircraft carriers could be found in the British annual reference book *Jane's Fighting Ships*. What Mauritz did not say, and what must have been evident to his questioners, was that a crucial 10 percent was not public, and that was the information the Abwehr sought.[17]

The spy case did not change everyone's view. A *New York Times* editorial made a similar point to Mauritz's. It conceded there were spies in the United States but asserted that "the spy problem is no real problem at all." The frenzied effort by the FBI and by US Army and Navy counterintelligence officers was "in itself symptomatic of the fear psychosis which has swept the world rather than of the alarming importance of the international spy." There were few real military secrets. How could there be, when Brazil was building destroyers using plans supplied by the United States? The *Times* exhorted its readers not to support any proposal for a new superspy agency, for spies such as Rumrich represented a low threat and could deliver only slim pickings as so much technical knowledge had already been internationally disseminated.[18]

If Americans lived in an open world community with no secrets, then espionage would indeed have been pointless, and there would have been no need for blame games. However, while the *Times'* vision was an attractive one, it was utopian. All the evidence points to the conclusion that the Abwehr obtained high-grade secret information (as well as a great deal of dross) about US military technology.

Yet if the Abwehr came away with booty, it was at a cost. In propaganda terms, it surrendered the last vestiges of American goodwill that remained in the German treasure chest. MI5's senior officer Guy Liddell saw this clearly. He emphasized not the damage done to US security but the instructive character of the spy story: "The most interesting feature of the case is the way in which the whole of the Nazi party machine . . . has been placed at the disposal of the German intelligence service for the purpose of espionage." Drawing on a "source," Liddell contended that the New York pier supervisor Drechsel, far from being an innocent party caught between a rock and a hard place, was the local representative of the National Socialist Party's Inspectorate, which had links with the Gestapo, and was "closely connected" with Heinrich Himmler's notorious Schutzstaffel (Protection Squadron, or SS). Like Turrou, Liddell saw the spies' activities as drawing Germany into serious disrepute. Once that perception gained traction, it was destined to undermine relations between Hitler's Germany and the Anglophone world, making Pfeiffer and his colleagues a liability to their country.[19]

Turrou was determined to win the psychological battle by exposing the perfidious Nazi character of his target spies. He pointed an accusing finger at the Abwehr's agents in the United States. He also wanted to complete his victory in the spy wars by securing the arraignment of those agents who were in custody. One day in June 1938, he achieved that objective.

Foley Square in Lower Manhattan was built on a swamp and named for a saloonkeeper with Tammany Hall connections. Times change and, by 1938, it had a newer, cleaner image. The imposing dimensions of the recently completed US Courthouse conveyed a stern message. In that edifice on June 22, 1938, Johanna Hofmann, Otto Voss, Erich Glaser, and Guenther Rumrich were arraigned on charges of spying. Rumrich, Glaser, and Hofmann were accused of stealing military codes, and Voss was charged with transmitting secret information about US Army aircraft designs. They all pleaded not guilty with the reservation that they might change their pleas later, and all remained in custody. The four were held in continuation of bail set at $25,000 each, an amount Hofmann's lawyer George C. Dix described as "outrageous." They could not raise the bail, and no funds were forthcoming from the German Consulate. Apparently, after all, the Berlin authorities had settled for the policy that pier manager Wilhelm Drechsel suggested earlier: a few should be sacrificed to protect the many.[20]

Assistant US Attorney Walter N. Thayer stated that fourteen of the indicted were abroad. Jessie Jordan was in prison in Scotland, and the thirteen others were in Germany, with three of them serving in that country's War Ministry. Thayer's superior, Lamar Hardy, persuaded the judge to issue bench warrants for the arrest of all fourteen. No extradition would be possible, but the warrants would assert a moral point, would establish the fugitive status of those named, and would render them liable to arrest if they returned to the United States. Bench warrants had lifetime validity.[21]

The court charges followed the handing down of indictments by the grand jury two days earlier. In a press statement, Hardy put a positive spin on the outcome. The FBI had been investigating since February, he said, and the grand jury had conducted a five-week investigation. The inquiries unveiled "a spy ring of extensive proportions." German government officials residing in their own country had directed the spies, all of whom were of German extraction. He acknowledged the work of his own assistants, Lester C. Dunigan and John W. Burke Jr., and singled out for special praise "Mr. Leon G. Turrou, a veteran agent who has worked unceasingly since the beginning of the investigation and has, in my opinion, done an extraordinary piece of investigative work."[22]

Turrou was the hero of the hour. In his tussle with Pfeiffer, he had emerged at least a part-winner, and his moral arguments were carrying the day. Unfortunately for his reputation, however, he was about to take an action that would place him at the center of the blame game.

13
DISMISSED WITH PREJUDICE

The grand jury issued its indictments on June 20, 1938. That very day, Leon Turrou quit the FBI. In his letter of resignation to J. Edgar Hoover, he said he had finished his work as leader of the spy investigation. He had worked so hard to achieve results that his health had suffered. His physician had ordered him to rest, and he owed it to his family to take the doctor's advice. As much as he loved the bureau, he had decided to turn to a literary career. In his writings, he would be sure to convey his admiration for the FBI and its fight against crime.[1]

It was a bold step. According to the *Washington Post*, Turrou was the "highest-paid of the G-men."[2] Barring a fatal shoot-out, if Turrou had stayed on as a special agent he could have looked forward to job security, paid vacations, and a pension. However, he was an ambitious person and wanted more. Being temperamentally unsuited to administrative duties, he could expect to rise no further in the FBI. As was immediately apparent, he had his eye on an alternative source of future income.

On June 22 the *New York Post* announced that the following day, it would start publishing Leon Turrou's account of the spy case. One of America's great campaigning newspapers ever since Alexander Hamilton launched it in 1801, the *Post* was pro–New Deal and vigorously anti-Nazi under its new owner, J. David Stern. But it lagged in the circulation wars. The paper needed a good story, and Turrou's revelations looked like a sure bet.

The broadsheet devoted two whole pages to promoting its scoop. The spread included a fulsome biography of Turrou and promised "the most astounding revelations ever published by any newspaper."[3] The rewards for Turrou seemed ample compensation for the loss of his $4,600 per annum FBI salary. Press reports claimed that Turrou signed a contract giving him a down payment of $25,000 and a total of $40,000 on completion of a series of thirty spy stories. A few days later, other reports cited an advance of $1,500 from the Warner Bros. film studio and a promised $25,000 annual salary. The amounts had been exaggerated for journalistic effect, but Turrou would indeed be well paid. He had always wanted to promote his anti-Nazi message, and now he would be amply rewarded for doing so.[4]

Such things take time to arrange, and Turrou had been planning his exit from the bureau for a while. In company with his New York boss Reed Vetterli, he had visited Stern in mid-May to scout the possibilities. In a later letter to Hoover's assistant Ed Tamm, he rejected the idea that in these proceedings he had been the "vile and woolly schemer and Vetterli . . . the gullible lamb." Turrou said Vetterli had heard of Hoover's own plan to publish a book on the spy case and sell the rights to Paramount Pictures for a reputed $25,000, and Vetterli had suggested to Turrou that they should make a preemptive move.[5]

Be that as it may, Vetterli then reported Turrou's negotiations to Hoover. The director did not like the *Post*'s attitude toward the FBI and was displeased with the news. He praised Vetterli for telling the tale, and on June 1, the New York special agent in charge tried to ingratiate himself further when he suggested Turrou might be removed from the spy case team. Hoover took no action, but nine days later Tamm complained that Turrou was "getting his picture in the paper too often" and was becoming a problem for the FBI. Though he blamed Lamar Hardy, not Turrou, for the escape of the spies, Hoover was now losing faith in his blue-eyed boy. Anticipating that there would otherwise be trouble, Stern had required that Turrou resign his position before the story went to press. Stern could not have anticipated just how bad that trouble would be.[6]

The *Post* was an afternoon paper, and Lamar Hardy did not have much time to react to the announcement of the Turrou series. He moved quickly. By 4:40 p.m., the district attorney had applied for an interim court injunction preventing publication of Turrou's stories. Two hours later, a signal came from Washington confirming that Attorney General

Homer Cummings had approved the move. The press seized on the story. Journalists reported Hardy's argument that publication would have prejudiced the spy case. Hardy said the grand jury still had matters to consider, including possible additional indictments aimed at the officers of the German shipping companies. He averred that Turrou's articles would divulge information that might unfairly sway the minds of jury members. Stern was unimpressed. He expressed anger at the injunction, which, he claimed, was "an unprecedented attempt to erase freedom of the press from the Constitution."[7]

The next day, June 23, Judge Murray Hulbert presided over a full hearing in room 506 of the US Courthouse in Foley Square to determine whether the injunction should be made permanent. FBI observers reported to Washington on the proceedings. They sent Hoover the good news that some papers were "taking cracks" at Turrou.

The newly retired FBI veteran was, however, far from defenseless. One of his lawyers was Robert F. Wagner Jr., who was destined to become the mayor of New York. He was just starting his law career and played a secondary role on the day. His presence on the team had psychological significance, for his father—a German American and the US senator for New York—was a pillar of the New Deal and had famously sponsored the 1935 National Labor Relations Act, guaranteeing the right of workers to join labor unions. And Senator Wagner was right there, attending the hearing. The pressure was truly on Turrou's opponents as well as on Turrou himself.[8]

Turrou's senior counsel was Simon H. Rifkind, a Lithuanian Jewish immigrant who had served a term as administrative assistant to Senator Wagner before returning to private practice in 1933. Rifkind argued that there was no precedent for prior restraint of a newspaper's reporting. It was, after all, a kind of advance censorship that was found in unfree countries. John W. Burke Jr., for the government, conceded the absence of precedent but insisted that publication would prejudice a fair trial.[9] Further advancing the government's case, Assistant US Attorney Burke said that Turrou had signed a confidentiality agreement. Rifkind said that he had not, and in any case he had resigned with immediate effect, giving up his right to vacation pay; therefore, he was no longer, by any definition, an FBI employee and thus not bound by confidentiality.

At this point Turrou displayed, for the first and almost the only time in his life, a willingness to attack the director of the FBI. He brought into court what was, in effect, a file on the bureau's boss. He gave his attorney a scrapbook on the FBI's major cases, and Rifkind showed it to Judge Hulbert, stating that "the most prolific source" of crime story leaks to the press "is Mr. J. Edgar Hoover himself for Mr. Hoover wants his picture in the paper." To reinforce the point, Rifkind handed the judge a pile of articles Hoover had written in the *American Magazine*.[10]

Judge Hulbert may have been impressed. However, he was primarily concerned about the First Amendment prior restraint issue and with the question of whether a former government employee could be bound to silence. He ordered the lawyers to reappear the next day armed with precedents.

The case might have become a constitutional confrontation, anticipating the landmark ruling in favor of the *New York Times* in the Pentagon Papers case of 1971 (403 U.S. 713). In the event, Stern agreed not to challenge the restraining injunction. Yet his agreement was with a mental reservation: his plan was for the *Post* to publish once the trial was over, whereas the government had not agreed to withdraw its injunction. Through his suspension, Stern had appeased President Roosevelt, and Hardy could keep Turrou as an effective witness, a desirable outcome in the absence of the absentee Ignatz Griebl. But the tension over the issue of free speech remained unresolved. That which is hidden is so often treasured, and the interest of the press and Hollywood in Turrou's suppressed story intensified.

While President Roosevelt found it politically convenient to blame Turrou, he also acknowledged some of the FBI veteran's arguments. Reacting to the *Post*'s threatened disclosures at a press conference on June 24, he said the government would make a greater investment in counterespionage and indicated that there would be more money not just for the FBI but also for army and navy intelligence. He implied a condemnation of Germany's behavior by saying that the United States would not embark on foreign espionage—a mode of behavior, he made clear, that was undesirable.

When a journalist asked him about the diplomatic repercussions of the spy case, the president sidestepped the issue, saying he had not recently heard from the Department of State. He resorted to distraction tactics, attacking an unnamed individual who was obviously Turrou. Revealing what the *New York Times* described as "disappointment and chagrin," he repeatedly emphasized that a former FBI agent had displayed question-able patriotism and ethics by selling his story to a newspaper.[11]

By fingering an American scapegoat instead of criticizing Germany, Roosevelt had avoided giving political ammunition to pro-neutrality crit-ics such as North Dakota's senator Nye. With midterm elections loom-ing, the president had no intention of moving quickly against Germany. It was his good fortune that the trial of the four alleged spies would not finish until the elections were over. The postponement of the *Post* series helped to sweep the issue of Nazi espionage under the carpet and provided the additional advantage that after the elections, the trial and Turrou's then-available account of events would cause the espionage issue to reemerge. This gave the president policy options, especially when the Democrats held on to their majorities in both House and Senate.

Hoover's dilemma was of a different order. He continued to rely on his former investigator's findings as set forth in his FBI reports. When the director of naval intelligence demanded a briefing some days after Roosevelt's pronouncements, Hoover sent him two of Turrou's reports, as they were (and would continue to be) the best available.[12] However, he could not forgive the apple of his eye for, as he saw it, turning rotten.

If Hoover had refrained from punishing Leon Turrou, it would have been inconsistent. A high-profile precedent had already been set. On July 21, 1934, an FBI team led by Chicago's SAC Melvin "Little Mel" Purvis had shot dead the mobster John Dillinger, who was known to have robbed ten banks and killed a policeman. There was intensive press interest, and Purvis, like Turrou, could be economical with the truth when narrating his own role. The diminutive agent made the error of publicizing himself as an ace G-man. He posed for a victory photograph at a Chicago railroad station with Attorney General Cummings, but the FBI director was nowhere in sight. Purvis even capitalized on his fame by marketing breakfast cereals.

Accordingly, Hoover took steps to reduce Purvis's image to that of a bit player, asserting that he had only a secondary role in the Dillinger incident. Purvis resigned from the FBI the following year. According to one of his sons, he felt betrayed by Hoover, yet he continued to love his boss, keeping a framed photo of the director in his office until the day in 1960 when he died of a self-inflicted gunshot wound.[13]

As his critics say, in Hoover's view there was only one vacancy for the position of FBI hero, and he was determined to be the sole applicant. At the same time, the director had three responsibilities that help explain his behavior toward Turrou. First, he had to rein in those special agents who were publicity mongers and who sought such fame that would lead to more lucrative opportunities outside the bureau. Had he failed to do so, the FBI would have hemorrhaged talent. Second, Hoover was responsible enough to know that mistimed publicity could wreck criminal trials. Hoover's final responsibility was for the integrity of the bureau's counterespionage work, which would be prejudiced if Abwehr officials could simply read all about the FBI's operations in the newspapers.

The danger in attacking Turrou was that Hoover would discredit the prosecution's main asset. He took the risk regardless. The director claimed that his fallen agent had always been a "problem child" who took advantage of a "gullible public." His claims did not convince the media. The *New York Times* recorded Turrou's view that Hoover was "jealous" of a "publicity rival" who had "scooped" him.[14] When the boss responded by publishing a searing indictment of the American press in *Collier's* magazine, one newspaper editor accused the FBI director of promoting "off the record" publicity one minute and abusing journalists the next.[15]

In the first spate of his rage against Turrou, Hoover recommended to the Justice Department that the former agent should not appear as a witness in the forthcoming spy trial. He said the success of the government's case would be "imperiled." He had it on the authority of the FBI's New York office that other agents could testify instead. In the relatively few cases where Turrou had interrogated people alone, the relevant witnesses could be reinterviewed by replacement personnel.

In a separate memorandum, Hoover asked the Justice Department's advice on how he might dismiss Turrou "with prejudice." One possible recourse was to the 1933 Act for the Protection of Government Records. This law had been passed in reaction to the controversial case of Herbert O. Yardley.[16]

A poker-playing American code breaker who could have given lessons to both Hoover and Turrou on how to cavalierly treat the dictates of modesty and discretion, Yardley had directed a cryptographic unit known as the American Black Chamber. In the 1920s the US government cut back foreign and domestic security expenditures, and in 1929 it closed down the chamber. Upset by this decision, Yardley published a memoir titled *The American Black Chamber.* The book shocked the Japanese, who learned from its pages that Yardley's staff had been spying on them during the Washington Naval Conference of 1921. Publication of the book had contributed to a downward spiral in Japanese-American relations, just as the Nazi spy case now threatened German-American relations. When Yardley wrote a sequel called "Japanese Diplomatic Secrets," the US government sought to limit the diplomatic damage and impounded the manuscript. Congress backed the executive branch by passing the Act for the Protection of Government Records, otherwise known as the Yardley Act.[17]

Commenting on Turrou's resignation, an editorial in the *New York Times* noted that the former special agent's plan to publish in the *Post* had created a mess and speculated the Yardley Act might be invoked. Two hundred miles south at the FBI's Pennsylvania Avenue headquarters, Special Agent Percy E. "Sam" Foxworth drew the editorial to the attention of his superiors, Ed Tamm and J. Edgar Hoover. Destined for high office in the FBI, Foxworth commanded the director's ear and was regarded as politically astute.[18]

Fearing that federal attorneys had been unable to advance watertight legal grounds in the injunction proceedings against the *Post*, Foxworth took legal advice on the applicability of the Yardley Act. His advisers variously told him that nobody remembered the act, that prosecutors were afraid of using it for fear of being accused of suppressing free speech, and that in any case Congress had not agreed to the legislation. The last assertion was incorrect, but Hoover and his advisers decided against invoking the Yardley law. It was just as well from their point of view, because the text of the law (of which FBI headquarters seemed to be ignorant) referred merely to an "official diplomatic code or any matter prepared in any such code." While the 1938 espionage indictments did refer to the theft of codes, the firing of Turrou had nothing to do with that; thus, the Yardley Act was inapplicable to it.[19]

The United States lacked any equivalent of the United Kingdom's Official Secrets Act, so the government faced a problem when it wanted to suppress information in the interest of a prosecution or of national security. Even allowing for that, the FBI was ill prepared for a contingency such as that created by the Turrou case. Had its lawyers been better versed, they might have considered referencing the 1875–76 Supreme Court case *Totten v. United States*. In 1790 Congress had voted President George Washington a contingency fund, authorizing unvouched expenditures on spying. The practice continued, and President Abraham Lincoln used spies in the Civil War. William A. Lloyd, one of his agents, accepted the mission of secretly penetrating the Confederacy in pursuit of military intelligence. His controller would authorize payment of a monthly salary of $200. But his supervisor never did so, because he was assassinated. For this reason, Lloyd received only his expenses. At the war's conclusion, he sued the government for back pay. However, the Supreme Court found against him, stating that he was in breach of his secrecy contract: "Both employer and agent must have understood that the lips of the other were to be forever sealed."[20]

Totten was a potentially useful precedent and has since been cited, for example, in the 2005 case *Tenet v. Doe*. However, there was no acknowledged criminal basis for the prosecution of those accused of betraying the secrets of the federal government. The contrast with the United Kingdom was stark. In 1932 the writer Compton Mackenzie published *Greek Memories*, a memoir of his time as a British intelligence officer. The authorities suppressed the book, and Mackenzie was prosecuted under the Official Secrets Act. Such options were not open to the FBI or to any other branch of the US government.

J. Edgar Hoover did have one card up his sleeve. He had cautioned Turrou at the outset of his career that he should observe the "no publicity" convention, but in 1935 the FBI director went one step further in the wake of the Purvis fracas. He made confidentiality a contractual requirement. Rifkind denied it, probably out of ignorance, but on November 13, 1935, in the presence of the notary public of Bronx County, New York, Turrou did sign the following sworn statement:

> The confidential character of the relationship of the employees of the Federal Bureau of Investigation with the public is fully understood by me, and the strictly confidential character of any and all information secured by me in connection directly or indirectly with my work as a Special Agent, or the work of other employees of which I may become cognizant, is fully understood by me, and neither during my tenure of service with the Federal Bureau of Investigation nor **at any other time** will I violate this confidence, nor will I divulge any information of any kind or character whatsoever that may become known to me to persons not officially entitled thereto.[21]

Notwithstanding the fact that he had resigned from the FBI before signing his contract with the *New York Post*, Turrou had breached his 1935 undertaking to reveal no FBI secrets "at any other time."

On this ground, Attorney General Cummings and FBI director Hoover wrote to tell Turrou he was being released, with notices of the dismissal going to special agents in charge right across the nation. The envelope containing the original of Cummings's letter was dated June 25, but the letter within was backdated to June 20, making the point that the government did not accept Turrou's resignation and that he was being fired. In February, Turrou had signed another contract stipulating that the resignation of a special agent should take place with immediate effect. At the time, he had welcomed the change, and even later he may have thought it would release him to start publishing right away. Immediate severance meant he lost his holiday pay entitlement, and Hoover stipulated that he would also lose his pension. In light of Turrou's writing contracts, this loss was less punitive that it would otherwise have been.[22]

There was, however, a sting in the tail. In his dismissal letter, Hoover used the phrase "with prejudice," meaning that Turrou was officially in disgrace. The director explained what he intended this to mean in practice: "Turrou can never get back into any Government Department as long as he lives." As punishment for breaking the code of omertà, Hoover's onetime favorite had incurred a vendetta.[23]

As Hoover intended, dismissal with prejudice was a real shock for Turrou, whose very identity was wrapped up with a patriotic attachment to his adopted country and with a loyalty to the FBI and its leader. He tried to defend himself and continued to be, for a limited period, critical of the FBI director. He said the four accused spies had already signed confessions, so his published utterances could not affect the forthcoming trial. Succumbing to apparent amnesia about the oath he signed in 1935, he at first claimed, "There exists no pledge, no rule, no statute and no regulation which forbids publishing any of the facts acquired by me."[24]

Turrou then claimed that the 1935 oath was a supplementary order that Hoover rushed through in the wake of the Purvis affair: "After Purvis resigned and wrote stuff, [Hoover] became jealous."[25] Next he asserted that he had signed the oath "casually," scribbling his signature in haste on a whole bunch of official documents that had been presented to him for his authentication. His suggestion was that there had been an effort to trick him into silence.[26]

Turrou observed that Hoover had published stories with a view to educating the public, just as he intended to do, and that the director had been well paid for his contributions. What impressed the media was his charge of hypocrisy against his former boss. The *Washington Post* ran his defense under the headline "Hoover Writes, Why Can't I?"[27] American newspapers were wedded to the principle of free speech, and from Hoover's perspective, the distinct danger was that Turrou would remain a hero. Turrou's fame might have got him into trouble with the director, but it was also his shield. Hoover's publicity staff accumulated clippings with such headlines as "Turrou, Ace of FBI, Cracked Hard Cases."[28]

It was not a foregone conclusion that Turrou's trial testimony would prevail. For one thing, his amnesia defense over the omertà oath threatened to become a liability. On July 1, the *New York Post* published yet another Turrou statement on the sworn promise to remain silent: "I have no recollection of having signed this statement. Nor can I recall the circumstances." Quoting this statement, Johanna Hofmann's lawyer, George Dix, focused on the detective's professed memory lapse. In an affidavit filed in relation to the spy case, he stated, "Since Mr. Turrou admits he has a poor memory, and his recollection may be equally inaccurate in my client's case, I insist that it is all the more important that I obtain the testimony of witnesses having knowledge of the facts." He claimed that Turrou had a financial interest in Griebl's departure for Germany, as the absence of the key witness licensed the detective to publish without fear of contradiction. Dix requested that a commission be set up to interview Griebl and Karl Schlueter, another key witness; and he demanded more time to gather this and other evidence in the defense of his client.

The FBI had already dishonored Turrou. Dix was determined to complete the job.[29]

Wilhelm Lonkowski. An agent code-named Sex, Lonkowski
played a key role in setting up the Nazi spy ring before
making his dramatic escape to Germany in 1935. (Federal
Bureau of Investigation)

The steamship *Bremen*. Holder of the Blue Riband for the fastest transatlantic crossing and the pride of the German merchant marine, the vessel and its sibling ships fell under Hitler's control and were vehicles for the Nazi spy ring. (Deutsches Schiffahrtmuseum [German Maritime Museum], Bremerhaven, Germany)

The Bendlerblock, Berlin. This military office building housed the headquarters of the Abwehr, Germany's secret service. Wilhelm Canaris, its director from 1935 until February 1944, worked from a desk with his back to the balcony on the facade overlooking the Landwehr Canal. (Stefani Werle)

Jessie Jordan. The Scottish spy whose activities alerted first Britain's counterintelligence agency, MI5, and then the FBI. Was she a conniving pro-German adventurer or a sad and rejected woman in search of adventure? (The National Archives, Kew, Surrey)

Talgarth postbox. Here in Powys, Wales, Jordan the spy posted items intercepted by MI5. They included reports on military dispositions in Aldershot and a forged letter from her aunt offering to finance Jordan's deep-cover hairdressing business in Dundee. (Author's collection)

Guenther Gustave Maria Rumrich. From a distinguished family in the old Austro-Hungarian Empire, he was an undistinguished spy. His service as an FBI informant resulted in a reduced prison sentence in the espionage trial of 1938. (Federal Bureau of Investigation)

USS *Yorktown*. This 1939 image is of a state-of-the-art aircraft carrier commissioned in the US Navy. Germany's spies were desperate to get their hands on its high-tech secrets, such as the design of its flight deck arrester equipment. (Library of Congress)

Heinrich Lorenz. A ship captain who helped the Nazi spies, Lorenz hoped to retire in the United States. The Nazis detained his wife, Alice, suspecting her of spying for America. His daughter Marita had a relationship with Fidel Castro and spied for the CIA. (Deutsches Schiffahrtmuseum, Bremerhaven, Germany)

Wilhelm Drechsel. An influential Nazi fellow traveler, Drechsel supervised German shipping in the port of New York. He gave every assistance to spies and the Nazis, yet he also cooperated with Turrou, who refrained from arresting him. (Deutsches Schiffahrtmuseum, Bremerhaven, Germany)

Erich Pfeiffer and Hilde Gersdorf. Seen here with his secretary and mistress, Pfeiffer was the German spymaster in charge of purloining US military secrets. (The National Archives, Kew, Surrey)

Mata Hari. Executed by the French in 1917 after being convicted of spying for Germany, in the 1930s the Dutch-born dancer and courtesan became an obsession of the media—and of Nazi spies. (Fries Museum [Freisian Museum], Leeuwarden, the Netherlands)

Dr. Ignatz Theodor Griebl. The leading anti-Semite was a womanizer who promoted the idea of a "Mata Hari"–style honey trap "salon" in Washington, DC. He confessed and helped Leon Turrou crack the German spy ring. (Federal Bureau of Investigation)

Kate Moog, pictured on the Upper West Side of New York in December 1938 or January 1939. Her lover Ignatz Griebl told German intelligence chief Canaris that she could run his envisaged Washington, DC–based "salon," a vehicle for blackmail that would yield the secrets of US national security.

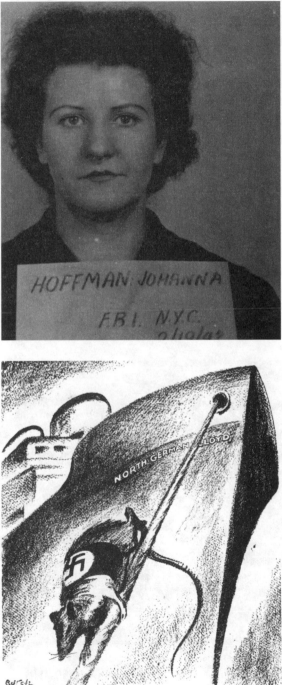

Johanna Hofmann (not Hoffman). Her Gestapo-linked lover, Karl Schlueter, abandoned her to the FBI. The American press labeled her a "minor Mata Hari." Her imprisonment for espionage took away what remained of her youth. (Federal Bureau of Investigation)

Jacob Burck cartoon, "The Brown Pest." The Polish-born, Jewish American artist and Pulitzer Prize winner here gives an impression of the sinking reputation of the once-prestigious SS *Bremen* and its sibling ships. (The image appeared in the *Daily Worker* in 1935. Burck, *Hunger and Revolt* [New York: Daily Worker, 1935])

Leon Turrou. Acclaimed in his day as the FBI's best detective, Turrou finally exposed the Nazi spy ring. (Bob Turrou)

In even more dramatic pose, World War I veteran Turrou effortlessly conformed to the compulsory manhood norms of the FBI in the 1930s. His contributions to national security were, however, deductive and educational. (Bob Turrou)

J. Edgar Hoover (*left*) "arrests" Louis "Lepke" Buchalter (*center*). This photo opportunity of Hoover's apprehending a criminal who had surrendered in advance and without firing a shot typified the FBI director's determination to stay center stage. That determination spelled the doom of the high-profile Leon Turrou. (Library of Congress)

Farewell, German-American friendship. Germany's ambassador Hans Dieckhoff had worried about the impact of the 1938 spy revelations on US public opinion. Here, on November 22, 1938, he bids goodbye to American journalists he had befriended prior to his abrupt recall to Berlin. (Library of Congress)

14

SEEKING THE EVIDENCE

Anti-fascists looked for a well-publicized trial and conviction of the four incarcerated spy suspects. Turrou's removal from the FBI had been a blow for the prosecution. In another setback, George C. Dix secured a delay to the start of proceedings. To compound still further the difficulties of the prosecution and its supporters, the FBI's New York office was in disarray.

In the wake of Turrou's severance, Reed Vetterli also quit the FBI. Tom Tracy, a former special agent now running a private detective business, was recruiting former colleagues. Turrou had refused to join him in September 1937, but Vetterli now accepted Tracy's offer of $12 a day. The former SAC also wrote for newspapers and irritated Turrou by asking for an introduction to Hollywood.

J. Edgar Hoover charged Tracy with organizing a conspiracy against the bureau. Just after Vetterli's resignation on August 22, the FBI director confided to his senior colleague Clyde Tolson, "We have been having considerable trouble in our New York Division relative to mal-contents and griping." Turmoil in the FBI's New York office did nothing to expedite a successful spy case prosecution.[1]

The delay that Dix had achieved meant all four of the accused languished in prison in a state of limbo. For Rumrich, the ultimate prospects seemed not too bad, as he hoped to be rewarded for testifying against the other three. His confederate Erich Glaser could look forward to no such special treatment. Otto Voss, very evidently the most effective spy of the four in custody, was in serious trouble. Charles W. Philipbar, his attorney, in mid-July demanded full details of the charges against his client, no doubt with the object of picking holes in them. Without the provision of bail, though, Voss, like the other accused, had to stay in jail.[2]

Jenni Hofmann stared at the walls of her cell with one consolation. In George Dix, she had a fighting lawyer. Dix perceived from the outset that Turrou would be the main and indispensable witness for the prosecution. With the former special agent already under a cloud, Dix sought an opportunity to complete the destruction of his credibility.

Turrou saw Dix as a person who hated him with an irrational intensity, and he reciprocated the animosity. In truth, the former detective and the lawyer shared certain characteristics. They both had a propensity to exaggerate, and each of them fought hard for his chosen cause. In the course of World War II, Dix would take more than three hundred civil liberty cases and, at a time of intense patriotic fervor, courageously defend citizens who had been detained as enemy aliens. All this lay ahead, however. In 1938, still a lawyer on the make, Dix defended Jenni Hofmann with formidable energy.[3]

When Dix appeared in court on June 29, he supplied a taste of his future tactics. The attorney charged that Turrou had been corrupted by the "arrogance of office" and had habitually lied. He leveled a charge that muddied the waters and delayed proceedings: Turrou, he claimed, had deliberately allowed Griebl to escape. When Judge Vincent Leibell asked him what proof he had, he said, "None, but I'll try to get it." Questioned again by the judge, he confessed to his "personal animus" toward the detective. Turrou was in court at the time, shaking his head in denial of the charges. The judge reprimanded Dix for impugning the reputation of a government official of many years' standing but allowed him time to find his proof.[4]

There ensued a battle by affidavit. Each side presented its arguments by this means to the court. Dix fired his next salvo on July 2. He toned down his invective slightly, saying that he did "not impute the receiving of a bribe," insisting instead that Turrou had been "naïve." He still argued that the former detective was "glad that Griebl escaped," as "Griebl, fugitive, necessarily would arouse more interest in such articles [as Turrou planned to publish] than Griebl as a witness who could or would not tell anything of importance."

Dix took aim also at Lamar Hardy and Lester Dunigan. Neither the district attorney nor his assistant had interviewed Griebl or Schlueter. How could they assume that the evidence of these individuals, if given, would not have affected the outcome of the case? Dix claimed that Griebl could have been forced to testify. He could have been extradited from Germany on a charge of larceny, but Dix did not specify whether he was referring to the Jewish land deal or to Griebl's sleight of hand over his automobile accidents and the damages claimed. Because of negligence at the very least, he argued, the attorneys and Turrou had let slip an opportunity.[5]

Dix appealed for more sympathetic treatment by claiming that the odds were stacked against him. He painted a picture of Texans who were conspiring to defeat him. Hardy hailed from the Lone Star State. More important, Dix complained that Assistant US Attorney Dunigan had told government witness Senta de Wanger, "I have a Texas judge here who will do anything I ask him to." The target of his barb was Judge T. Whitfield Davidson, who was in Manhattan on a temporary assignment. Davidson sprang to the defense of Dixie: "We may be regarded as old fashioned down in Texas, but we still believe in a God, we still believe in law and justice as expounded by John Marshall, and we are proud of a civilization that has given to the Union such men as George Washington, Robert E. Lee, Andrew Jackson, Sam Houston, John Garner." The judge held Dix in contempt of court.[6]

In a supplemental affidavit sworn on August 22, Dix indicated that he was "familiar with the German language." He had been in touch with Maria Griebl, who on August 4 had shown him a letter from her husband that had been mailed in Germany on June 26. Dix quoted extracts from the letter in his own translation. In his letter Ignatz Griebl indicated what was perfectly true: he had never signed a confession for the G-men. He told his wife he was not a fugitive from justice and had never been in contempt of a subpoena to appear before the grand jury. This was technically true but only because the date for the grand jury meeting had been postponed from the original day of May 5, and Vetterli had then phoned him to say his summons to appear had expired.

On May 10 Turrou told Griebl and Kate Moog that a new date would be set for their appearance. The following day Griebl took action to ensure he would not be served with a writ compelling him to appear in court: he disappeared, abruptly leaving his wife and his mistress to stow away on the *Bremen* with its obliging crew. In his conjugal letter he recalled that Turrou and Hardy were "furious" at him, because by leaving the country he had taken out of their hands "all possible legal control."

Warming to his theme, Griebl claimed Turrou could not be a believable witness "because he himself is the investigator." There was no possibility of an objective trial, for that was not the FBI's intention. The real aim was "to serve the American Public for breakfast a sensational 'Spy case' with highly interesting Anecdotes. What these G-Men, including Mr. Turrou, assert sounds like an interesting spy romance, which exists only in his brain, but never occurred. These little fellows are making themselves ridiculous. . . . [Turrou's] action is against the Ethics of a G-Man, and therefore, not permissible."[7] Griebl's letter encouraged Dix to believe that its author could be deployed to destroy Turrou's credibility as a witness.

Dix's plan was for a commission to visit Germany to reinterview Griebl, using the authority and facilities of US consuls in Bremen, Bremerhaven, or Berlin. To support his request, he had Johanna Hofmann file an affidavit suggesting that Turrou had never regarded her as a prime actor in the spy ring; he had seen her merely as an accessory. To his formal application, Dix attached three appendixes. The first minuted a conversation he had had with Griebl on April 30, saying that Griebl refused to talk for fear of incriminating himself and had denied all knowledge of Jenni Hofmann. The second told of Dix's encounter with Turrou on June 21, the day when Jenni Hofmann appeared before the grand jury. The lawyer alleged that on this occasion Turrou implied Hofmann was innocent, and then he assaulted Dix and threatened him with arrest. The third appendix was an affidavit on the subject of an interview he had conducted with

Maria Griebl on June 24. In the interview, Maria claimed that her husband was convinced that Turrou wanted him to disappear.[8]

On July 28 Judge Leibell ruled against the commission proposal and ordered Dix's supporting narrative struck from the records of the court on the grounds that it was "scandalous."[9] However, once he had dropped the provocative elements in his plea, the persistent Dix got his way before a more sympathetic judge. Early in September, a commission did travel to Germany. Lamar Hardy remarked that it was the first time that a federal court in the Southern District had sent such a commission abroad. Like the spies, the commission traveled in luxury, sailing on the SS *Champlain*. A French Line ship constructed in Saint-Nazaire, the fast and elegantly designed *Champlain* was one of the new breed of "cabin" ocean liners. The commission members who sailed on this well-appointed ship were George C. Dix; Hardy's assistants, Lester C. Dunigan and John W. Burke Jr.; and FBI special agent John T. McLaughlin.[10]

On September 19, 20, and 21, 1938, the commission interviewed Dr. Griebl at the US Consulate in Berlin. The fugitive said he was prepared to return to the United States to testify on certain conditions: immunity from prosecution, freedom to publish his own account of events, and all expenses paid, with transatlantic fares and legal fees included.[11] The attorneys refused to agree to those conditions. Thereupon, Griebl offered to make a statement at the consulate, provided his wife, then under detention in New York as a material witness, was released. The attorneys agreed to this condition.[12]

Griebl insisted that Jenni Hofmann was a spy. Agent McLaughlin reported that the former New York doctor was trying to persuade the German Foreign Ministry to tell all four accused to plead guilty; if true, he was adhering to the Drechsel damage limitation plan. Griebl stated that Turrou had no credibility, as he was a Jew and a radical. Undoubtedly Griebl had picked up on some of the spurious anti-Semitic stories about the ex-G-man being a communist. As ever, however, the trickster was enigmatic. Off the record, he confided to McLaughlin, "You can understand what would happen to me here if I did not say that and did not contradict the things I told the FBI. . . . Personally, self-preservation has always been my god."[13] Griebl rambled on in a manner that the attorneys felt was "silly" and "half crazy," and finally he supplied a written statement that ran to seventeen thousand words.[14]

Back at FBI headquarters, officials impatiently awaited reports from McLaughlin. The envoy later explained to Ed Tamm that the six messages he had sent via diplomatic pouch were the only communications he had been able to get out of Germany. The German authorities restricted what he could send by coded telegrams, and he did not have enough money to make phone calls. Finally, McLaughlin arrived in New York with two copies of Griebl's statement on the morning of October 6. Turrou was at the pier when the ship arrived and, according to the FBI's Dwight Brantley, in a "frantic" mood. The plan was to restrict dissemination of the statement until the trial opened; as Turrou was no longer with the FBI, McLaughlin would not tell him what Griebl had said. McLaughlin also refused to speak to the members of the press who were there in force. Dix was another interested party at the pier. Griebl's confirmation of Hofmann's guilt must have been a blow to him, but he still fought for his client. He exchanged "venomous glances" with Turrou before regaling the newspaper reporters with his conspiracy theory about Turrou's helping Griebl escape. Another FBI agent who observed that harangue reported that the press was just not interested in Dix's version of events.[15]

Just as George Dix sought to defend his client by seeking evidence in Germany, so Lamar Hardy sought foreign evidence that would bolster the government's case. His idea was to put Jessie Jordan on the witness stand. She had already confessed and had been convicted in Scotland, so her words would carry some authority in court. True, Jessie's knowledge about German espionage was limited, but she could testify about the Crown affair and about the Abwehr's poste restante system. That testimony would add credibility to the prosecution's narrative.

American-British contacts over the spy case and its Jessie Jordan dimension are a chapter in the history of the special relationship that developed between the two countries' intelligence communities. Because of the news leaks at the time of Rumrich's arrest, US authorities had been unable to honor their promise to keep the Jessie Jordan angle under wraps, yet the intelligence relationship continued to be important to both sides.

MI5's Guy Liddell kept a close eye on developments in the United States. In March he visited the States and spoke to officials in the State Department, the FBI, and the military intelligence services. He noted a "slight contretemps" between Hoover and the State Department over the handling of the spy case. More interested in arrests than in diplomacy, the FBI did not put the smoothing of US-German relations at the heart of its agenda. The State Department's James Dunn had a different approach. He said he was anxious to exchange information about the Nazi threat *provided* it was kept secret to avoid the possibility of awkward questions being asked in Congress that would prejudice relations with Germany.

Over the next two months, Liddell exchanged information with US Army intelligence and the FBI over the case and kept the anti-appeasement civil servant Sir Robert Vansittart abreast of events. He agreed that the Crown letters could be used in the US prosecution and advised that a qualified witness could be sent from the United Kingdom to testify at the trial, though he did not specify Jessie Jordan.

Lieutenant Colonel Lee, America's military attaché in London, was convinced of the need for US-UK cooperation to meet the German espionage threat. In October he would ask MI5 for advice on how a new US counterespionage service might be constructed. MI5 responded by outlining how things were done in the United Kingdom. The FBI would take advantage of such thinking, and J. Edgar Hoover was destined over the next two years to play a key role in boosting counterintelligence and in US-UK intelligence collaboration. Meanwhile, in the summer of 1938, Special Agent Sam Foxworth strove to promote cooperation over the approaching spy trial. In seeking British cooperation over the deployment of Jessie Jordan, Lamar Hardy had grounds to be optimistic.[16]

Through the summer, the American press reported on the progress of anticipated British cooperation. In mid-May Lamar Hardy had spent two hours questioning Leon Turrou before the grand jury, and although he refused to answer questions after the session, evidently he was looking across the Atlantic for support. The *New York Times* sanguinely reported,

"British Evidence Made Available to U.S. for Colleagues' Trial."[17] In June Britain's *Daily Herald* echoed the *New York Times*' assumption that prosecution witnesses who had been lined up for the Jessie Jordan trial would cross the Atlantic and testify in New York.[18]

On June 29, with the British press poised for a sensation, Lamar Hardy crossed the Atlantic. He sailed on the SS *Normandie*, the world's biggest ocean liner and an even more luxurious ship than the *Champlain*. He took with him his daughter, Micheline, whom he had long promised a trip to Paris to see her mother's relatives. On the eve of his departure, he told the ever-attendant American press nothing about his objectives, other than saying he might look into "angles" of the case in "France and England." A *Daily Mail* sleuth tracked him down on board the *Normandie* and conducted what he tried to pass off as an interview. He quoted the canny Texan as saying, "I've got important clues." The journalist injected an air of mystery into his revelation that Hardy was alighting in France as well as in England (hardly news, as this was the *Normandie*'s usual route) and predicted that he would travel to Scotland. With the district attorney's having told him nothing, the journalist finished his story with speculative remarks about the dangers Hardy faced in traveling without a G-man bodyguard.[19]

The *Daily Express* considered Hardy to be America's "spy-catcher No. 1."[20] But if Hardy expected Jessie Jordan and possibly other witnesses to testify in New York, he did not understand MI5's mission to shield sensitive matters from prying eyes. In the event, that problem did not arise, for Hardy discovered to his cost that he had reckoned without Scottish legal scruples. Whatever MI5's views about Anglo-American intelligence cooperation, it could not deliver a result in the Scottish courts.

On July 22 and 23, MI5 director Vernon Kell orally conveyed to P. J. Rose, assistant secretary of state for Scotland, Hardy's request to interview Jessie in prison "in the expectation of ascertaining from her that she is only a post box." The word "only" jumps off the page for its irrationality, as Jessie's postbox function was potentially much more dangerous to all concerned than her amateur forays into direct espionage. But Hardy's seemingly illogical deployment of the word was calculated. It conveyed the message that the Americans would not come down too heavily on Jessie and that Scottish cooperation would not infringe on her legal rights. Hardy was interested in documenting the links to the mastermind behind the Nazi spy ring. He diverted Jessie from that frightening thought by using the minimalist word "only."

Unfortunately for Hardy's plan, Rose had already spoken with and explained to Kell that allowing a foreign inquisitor to interrogate a prisoner would be contrary to Scottish legal practice. In the spirit of cooperation, Kell now tried to broker a compromise. If the Americans were to drop charges against Jordan, could they then interview her for informational purposes? Rose said yes, if she gave her consent, if her solicitor were present, and (in a special Scottish touch) if the Americans paid all attendant expenses. He tartly added that the Lord Advocate had already told the "American Authorities" that Jessie Jordan "was just a post box." The Scottish legal grandee and the New York lawyer were talking at cross purposes, for the Crown-Jordan correspondence was what interested Hardy most of all.

Rose concluded with a further note of caution, pointing out that Jessie was likely to be deported to Germany on the completion of her prison sentence. Her position there "will be very difficult if she has given evidence [to Hardy or in New York] against her American associates." In the event, Jordan played no direct part in the New York prosecution. As a setback for British-American cooperation, her nonappearance could be discounted as a blip and blamed on the Scottish lawyers. As a setback for the trial prosecution in the United States, it was potentially more serious. It dictated a fallback to plan A—that is, relying on the testimony of Leon Turrou.[21]

Both Hardy's trip to Scotland to gain evidence from Jessie Jordan and his deputies' trip to Berlin to interview Griebl were official ventures that were sanctioned by federal officials in Foley Square and reimbursed by the US taxpayers. In addition to these trips, according to Erich Pfeiffer, two private American forays in search of evidence occurred.

Toward the end of the summer, a person whom Pfeiffer identified as "Lorenz of the *Bremen*" contacted him with a warning. When later under interrogation, Pfeiffer claimed that he knew little about Heinrich Lorenz and was even unaware of his first name. He then did concede Lorenz had worked for him from 1935. As the spymaster put it, Lorenz, as a captain with the North German Lloyd Line, "gave permission for stewards on his ship who were working for us, to land." If Pfeiffer suspected that Lorenz, the husband of an American woman, was acting as a double agent, he did not mention it.[22]

Lorenz's warning concerned Leon Turrou. Earlier in the year, the FBI detective had been in hostile pursuit of German military personnel who were facilitating the spy ring. Now, though, he wanted to interview Pfeiffer "on a friendly basis" to obtain copy for his intended book about the case. The following paraphrase of Pfeiffer's account indicates how the German intelligence officer took precautions: "The naïveté of the suggestion amused [him], but he removed his nameplate from the door of the house in Misslerstrasse and warned his wife to stall off any callers."

Pfeiffer continued by saying that Turrou's attempt at a visit was the first of two abortive approaches. The Misslerstrasse measures had been "a wise precaution, for shortly afterward another American, apparently Jenni Hofmann's lawyer, called at the house, to be told that Pfeiffer didn't live there any more. The lawyer promptly had recourse to the Gestapo HQ, whence Haupt. Schultz phoned the news to Pfeiffer, who got him to sidetrack this very simple American."[23] It was an unusual spectacle. The spymaster who normally lived a tranquil and sheltered life while he dispatched his agents to work at their peril suddenly had to behave like a fugitive in his home city, hiding from Turrou and then from the terrier-like George Dix. Pfeiffer's precautions were yet another signal that from the German perspective, the United States, with its tradition of free investigation, would be a difficult country to deal with.

Of the two unwanted visitors, the former G-man would turn out to be the greater threat to the Abwehr. While Dix was nearing the end of the line, the forthcoming trial would show that Leon Turrou had been anything but naive.

15

THE NAZI SPY TRIAL

On October 14, 1938, a jury of ten men and two women filed into a federal courtroom in Foley Square. The accused, the witnesses, and the other parties having also assembled, the spy trial was set to begin at last. John C. Knox, presiding, had been the prosecution counsel in spy cases in World War I, and in 1918 President Woodrow Wilson had appointed him as one of the youngest-ever federal judges. By 1938 he was thus an experienced member of the judiciary. He met with Leon Turrou's approval.[1]

Judge Knox opened proceedings in a trial that would have a political impact at home and abroad. At home, the view from the White House was distinctly unsettling. Midterm elections loomed on November 8. American internationalists might well exploit the case. Champions of US neutrality such as Senator Nye would then cause real trouble.

The significance of the event was apparent to commentators abroad. Describing the trial as the "biggest show in town in twenty years," London's *Daily Express* reported that war ministries all over Europe and Asia were watching the case. In the Soviet Union, both *Pravda* and *Izvestia* devoted their front pages to coverage of the courtroom drama, which, they held, proved Stalin had been right to drive through the Moscow purges and spy trials of 1936–38. Only in Germany did the authorities discourage public interest in the Rumrich-Voss-Glaser-Hofmann case. *Völkischer Beobachter*, the Nazis' official organ, ignored it, as did other German newspapers.[2]

While the German press may have been silent, the diplomatic reaction was one of alarm. The German Embassy in Washington saw a looming public relations disaster. Ambassador Hans Dieckhoff, a non-Nazi who had held the number 2 post in the German Foreign Ministry until the Hitler regime exiled him to the US mission, regarded the tussle unfolding on Foley Square with dismay. Following Wilhelm Drechsel's recommendation, he had been agitating for guilty pleas to shorten the trial and minimize German-American friction, but the American defense lawyers were having none of it. Now the eyes of his country's enemies would feast at length on the spectacle of Nazi malfeasance.[3]

These were jumpy times. Just before the trial began, Hitler's troops invaded Czechoslovakia. The dictator's action ended the illusions of those who still hoped that the carnage of 1914–18 had been the "war to end war" and that the peace settlement of 1919 would hold.

Other nerve-jangling events occurred at the time of the trial. At 8:00 p.m. EST on October 30, the eve of Halloween, twenty-three-year-old Orson Welles's radio spoof broadcast *The War of the Worlds* persuaded some Americans that a Martian invasion was taking place (a few even thought Germany was invading). After the trial ended, Kristallnacht occurred in Germany on November 9–10. The smashing of Jewish business premises signaled Berlin's anti-Semitic course and gave force to the message that Turrou and other anti-neutrality campaigners were trying to broadcast.

Because of recent events in the United States as well, "spy" had become a dirty word at just the wrong moment from the Germans' point of view. From 1936 to 1939, Sen. Robert M. La Follette Jr. (R-WI) chaired the Civil Liberties Committee hearings and showed how corporation executives were systematically spying on American workers. People have always looked down on spies, but the La Follette hearings commanded a national audience and for a period made espionage especially repugnant. It was "a veritable insecticide upon the Great-Man treatment of history," in the words of the contemporary writer Richard Wilmer Rowan.[4]

Plenty in the spy trial's proceedings stimulated public interest. Notably, Mata Hari rose from the dead. According to the *Los Angeles Times*, Jenni Hofmann was a "minor" Mata Hari. She was minor, that is, compared with the star of the show Kate Moog. When Kate testified about her rendezvous with Canaris on the banks of the Landwehr Canal, the

New York Times ran its account under the headline "Spy Witness Bares 'Mata Hari' Offer."

While there was general agreement on the perfidiousness of Otto Hermann Voss, some expressed sympathy for Erich Glaser on the grounds that he had been led astray by Rumrich and had ambiguous feelings about the United States, having endured US bombings in the last war. The press took a wary interest in the FBI's use of wiretaps and noted the repeated (but unproven) charges that Germany was passing US military secrets to Japan.[5]

While there was interest in such matters, one of the main features of the trial was the absence of fourteen fugitives who would not testify and who would not be held accountable for their actions. Nobody had seriously expected senior Abwehr officers such as Udo von Bonin, Hermann Menzel, and Erich Pfeiffer to appear. The absence of Jessie Jordan, however, was more frustrating. She was, of course, in prison in Scotland and, in mid-trial, was under armed guard in the Edinburgh Royal Infirmary having a fibroid operation. MI5 had supplied information about her activities, and the FBI and prosecution lawyers had a duplicate set of the Crown correspondence. Assistant US Attorney Lester Dunigan in court was able to read aloud depositions on Jordan's correspondence and the circumstances of its interception, but he did not mention MI5. He claimed his evidence had been prepared by the Dundee Post Office.[6] All this damning evidence still lacked the dramatic impact of a personal appearance by the Scottish spy.

Ignatz Griebl was the other notable absentee. In his absence, his wife, Maria, might have testified. Turrou at one point suggested she could have things to say. During her mission to Germany between September 12, 1937, and April 21, 1938, to leverage the expropriation of the Jewish Berliner family's property, she had frequently telephoned and corresponded with Erich Pfeiffer. After her husband absconded to Germany in May 1938, Maria had planned to join him but was taken into custody as a material witness. In prison, she loyally protested her husband's innocence and was not cowed by Hardy. She had already confronted his predecessor, George Medalie, a few years earlier, when Ignatz faced charges of Nazi subversion. On that occasion, she had dismissed Medalie as a biased Jew. On June 6, 1938, she was placed on bail set at $5,000, and it was too much for her to pay. Her husband had transferred property to her to avoid liability for car accident damages, but he had assumed power of attorney and was now missing. Seward B. Collins came to the rescue and paid the $5,000. The influential editor of the *American Review* was a stranger to Maria Griebl, but he had developed fascist sympathies. He also accused the government of holding his new protégée "hostage."

Maria Griebl testified to the grand jury on July 28 and on several other occasions. However, she sought to avoid a court appearance in the subsequent full trial, saying she needed an operation in Germany (her physician said she had "a fibroid tumor of the uterus approximately as large as an orange"). She also claimed she could not be a competent witness if required to testify against her husband.

In response, Lamar Hardy argued that her plea of ill health was opportunistic, that she would not be testifying against her husband as he was absent, and that in any case her argument was outdated. He cited a recent Supreme Court case in support of his contention that "recognition by the common law of a wife's privilege not to testify in a criminal case against her husband has become questionable as the cause for recognition of equal rights for women has triumphantly progressed." The court denied Mrs. Griebl's petition on September 16.

However, the court released her from her bail conditions soon afterward, as Assistant District Attorneys Dunigan and Burke, when interrogating Ignatz Griebl in Berlin, had agreed to release her in return for his provision of a statement. In November Maria traveled to Vienna to join her husband. Theirs was a reunion of partners in crime rather than a rekindling of conjugal bliss. They would separate the following year. Ignatz had taken up with yet another woman.[7]

While Maria Griebl would have contributed some—though not much—detail at the fall trial, Ignatz Griebl would have been a compelling material witness. If he had testified in person, he might have influenced the course of the trial. As things stood, the court had at its disposition Griebl's mutually contradictory evidential transcripts. First, there were the unsigned depositions and "confessions" he had supplied to Turrou when under interrogation in New York. The FBI's Ed Tamm feared that their authenticity might be challenged, as the stenographer had destroyed her original notes. Tamm disbelieved Turrou and Vetterli when they claimed they had instructed the stenographer to preserve them, and he saw the confessions as weak evidence.[8]

Second, the court had the self-exculpatory transcript Griebl supplied to Dunigan and his colleague when questioned in the US Consulate in Berlin. The exculpatory statement was potentially a damp squib, as Griebl had confessed to Dunigan privately that he had made it under duress from the German authorities. The statement was nevertheless read into the court record on November 9.

Dix exploited it. He said it proved Turrou had "coached" Griebl to make his earlier statements and that Hofmann was the victim of a "frame-up." But according to Turrou, the reading of Griebl's Berlin deposition provoked laughter among members of the jury. It lacked the credibility to be useful to Dix in conducting his client's defense. From the FBI's perspective, it had the effect of creating a double negative; Griebl's earlier narratives supplied to Turrou were, by implication, not incorrect. It was good news for the prosecution, even if Griebl's accounts were always questionable.[9]

Guenther Rumrich took the stand as a state's witness and testified between October 17 and 24 against the other three accused, all of whom, regardless of any previous confessions, had pleaded not guilty. With an eye on a lenient sentence, he tried to ingratiate himself with the court. Pretending to hold anti-Nazi views, he ventilated the rumor that Germany's winter relief funds had been diverted to pay for the program of espionage against the United States. He had joined the US Army because it gave him three meals a day at a time when he was starving. Then he had deserted the army because his drinking had got the better of him and because his fellow soldiers had mocked his German accent. He had spied for Germany and accepted payment for it, but his real motive was to find out all about Germany's spies so that he could reveal their identities to the American authorities. In that way, he told his incredulous listeners, he had planned to earn redemption for the sin of deserting the army.[10]

In between his flights of fancy, Rumrich told what he knew about the workings of the Nazi spy ring. His words carried little weight. Defense attorneys dubbed him a "beermug romancer." The *Washington Post* poured scorn on his "inexhaustible supply of spy-plot tales."[11]

Jenni Hofmann, like the other two who pleaded not guilty, faced up to twenty years in prison. Her tactical predicament is summed up in the words of a later FBI report:

```
JOHANNA HOFMANN's cooperation with the Government
ceased after she had furnished original statement
and at the time of trial of this case, she recanted
her former testimony not only to representatives
of the Bureau, but also her testimony to the Grand
Jury. During the course of the trial of this case she
obviously perjured herself in attempting to avoid
conviction.[12]
```

When she appeared in court on October 20, the jury heard that in her confession to Turrou she had said she spied because "I believed I was doing my duty to my fatherland." At least she was unambiguous in her loyalty, and that made her a more sympathetic figure than Rumrich. Being a twenty-six-year-old redhead did her no harm as well. Some members of the jury may have been swayed by the tears she shed in court, though with repeat performances, the charm may have worn thin over the course of the trial. Whether Dix's shouted protests at the reading out loud of her confession helped her case in court is open to question.[13]

Dix was nevertheless doing the best he could for Jenni. For example, on her behalf he prepared a petition to the court, saying that when the FBI seized her locked case on Lorenz's vessel the *Europa*, it had violated her right to privacy under the Fourth Amendment. The incriminating letters found in the case therefore should not be used in court.[14] That attempt failed, as did the effort to obtain her exoneration via Ignatz Griebl.

Jenni Hofmann was an unlucky young woman. Her betraying lover, Karl Schlueter, had sent her to her fate in the first place, and now Griebl wanted her to be convicted.

The Drechsel plan was being implemented. Having just a small number of spies convicted would be a reasonable outcome for Germany under the circumstances and would help to resolve an embarrassing affair. Hofmann was to be sold down the river.

The German authorities had underestimated Dix, who would just not play ball. On October 17, as the spy trial court got down to serious business and heard the opening statements by the prosecution and defense, the lawyers representing Glaser and Voss took a conservative approach, but Dix rose to deliver a fiery indictment of Leon Turrou. He told the jury the special agent was interested solely in publicity and money. Turrou had told Griebl that he had an offer of $40,000 for his story and had attempted to groom the doctor in a series of out-of-office meetings. He wanted Griebl to flee the United States, because he feared that Dix would interview the alleged spy and obtain the truth from him.

To infuse his claim with credibility, Dix averred that Turrou had also tried to frame an unnamed government inspector at the Sperry Gyroscope Company by getting Griebl to approach him and recruit him as a German spy.[15] The inspector had complained via military channels about his rough treatment at the hands of the FBI. As noted in chapter 10, Turrou did interrogate an inspector named Johannes Karl Steuer about the Sperry bombsight, and perhaps Steuer was left with bruised feelings. However, Dix had taken a misguided tack, for the inspector had already signed the following statement: "Nobody ever contacted me representing any foreign power and I have no information that any of my men were contacted."[16]

Lacking reliable witnesses for the defense, Dix redoubled his attack on Turrou's credibility. He called J. David Stern to the stand. Under the compulsion of a subpoena, the *New York Post*'s editor produced the contract he had with Turrou. Contrary to earlier press speculation, it was dated July 19, some time after Turrou's resignation from the FBI. Under cross-examination, though, Stern failed to remove the impression that he and the special agent had an understanding prior to that resignation and that perhaps earlier agreements had been torn up for convenience's sake. Dix thus succeeded in showing Turrou was interested in publicity and money.[17]

He was less successful in his effort to portray Turrou as a "crooked agent who embarrassed his government."[18] Dix suffered one particularly embarrassing setback in his attempt to dishonor his opponent. Aware of Turrou's tendency to embroider the truth in discussing his past, Dix decided to take a chance. He called to the witness box Turrou's boss at the time of the 1921–23 US-led effort to relieve famine in Russia. William N. Haskell was by now a major general and a commander of the New York National Guard. Dix had picked up from junior members of the American Relief Administration rumors about Turrou's unpopularity and unreliability. Griebl had assured him that Turrou was a communist Jew, and Dix had high hopes of undermining the prosecution's case when he questioned the general:

DIX: Didn't you receive reports from members of your staff that Turrou was suspected of being disloyal?

HASKELL: Oh, I heard some gossip, but I paid no attention to it.

DIX: Didn't you tell me last July that you used an interpreter named Lears whenever you could instead of Turrou?

HASKELL: Yes, but I also told you why. I said Lears didn't have as much brains as Turrou, and anybody who has used interpreters a lot knows that the less brains they have the better they are apt to be, so long as they know the language.

Dix appears not to have picked up the point that Turrou hated the communists and for an excellent reason: he thought at the time they had wiped out his wife and children. That hatred must have contributed to his overaggressive translation. *The Sun* of New York summed up the impact of Haskell's testimony in one word, "boomerang."[19]

The poor relationship between J. Edgar Hoover and his former agent might have played into Dix's hands, had he known how to play the card. It was a clash of megalomaniacs. One of Ed Tamm's reports gave an indication of the scale and nature of the problem as well as of Turrou's sense of mission:

> I was advised that Assistant Dunigan, who is handling the trial . . . has agreed to use Turrou just as little as possible and Vetterli as well. [Special Agent in Charge Dwight] Brantley further stated that Turrou told McLaughlin, among other things, that he was working for a corporation receiving a salary of $10,000 a year; that he would be in a position soon to give other agents in the service jobs . . . ; that Turrou made statements to the effect that the President and Attorney General of the United States are behind him, Turrou, one hundred percent; that the only Government official who now is his enemy is the Director; . . . that if it had not been for his, Turrou's work in uncovering spy activities in this country, the President would not have come out with his statement concerning his intention to coordinate the activities of the agencies investigating espionage; and that his, Turrou's work had made the public conscious of the spy conditions.[20]

Turrou had basked for so long in the rays of Hoover's approval that he had lost the ability to predict the director's behavior. This came to light when he asked Assistant US Attorney John Burke to subpoena the FBI director to appear in court so he could confirm that the former agent had served the bureau faithfully and that he did not employ third-degree methods. Burke dismissed the request as a joke but duly informed Hoover. The director wrote "that if Burke mentions matter again he should be told my testimony would thoroughly discredit Turrou & that in turn might react unfavorably upon case of the government & wouldn't want to harm the case but I would have to tell the truth." It was fortunate for the prosecution that Dix did not put Hoover on the witness stand.[21]

Turrou felt that the bureau was withholding information that might have eased the prosecution's case, but Hoover made the distinction between evidence that was strictly relevant to the court proceedings and "general intelligence" that had "no pertinency to the prosecutive action . . . but which may be of vital interest to the intelligence services." If mistakes had been made, they were the fault of the New York office of the FBI, and any embarrassment arising was attributable to "the dishonest viewpoint of former Special Agent in Charge Vetterli and former Special Agent Turrou."[22]

Ed Tamm saved the day. He was able to counterbalance Hoover's wrath because of his special standing within the bureau. The organization had undergone a number of name changes since its founding in 1908, and it was Tamm who in 1935 pressed for the adoption of its final label, the "FBI." He lobbied also for the adoption of the bureau's new motto, "Fidelity, Bravery, and Integrity."[23] He was preeminent among those who had shaped an identity for the FBI. The FBI's number 3 man could see that the outcome of the trial was vital to the FBI, as well as to national security, and that Turrou was vital to the trial's success.

Tamm turned to Special Agent Sam Foxworth for assistance in managing the event. With the help of New York assistant SAC Dalton, Foxworth kept a close eye on the trial, and the two men guarded Turrou's credibility. Foxworth reminded Tamm that the bureau had investigated Turrou's alleged maltreatment of Steuer and had exonerated him; the relevant documents should be given to the US attorney.[24] Two weeks later—in a memorandum "for the files" and not "for the director"—Tamm noted with evident satisfaction Dalton's report "that Turrou has been standing up under the cross-examination very well and has been making general denials of the accusations which Dix is insinuating in his questioning."[25]

In an inspired move toward the end of the trial, Dix demanded to see Turrou's FBI file. He had already requested it at the time of the Berlin trip, and McLaughlin had on that occasion told him to proceed through official channels. Dix's request, if granted, had the potential for explosive impact because the FBI's personnel file for Turrou was being transformed into a file *on* Turrou, with derogatory information supplied especially by those agents who were sycophantic toward Hoover. With the file in hand, Dix might have delivered a killer blow in court, showing how unreliable Turrou was as an autobiographer and how much Hoover reviled him. But—and the director's minders may have played their part here—when Dix made his official request for the file, Hoover was "out of the city." Without an authorization for the file's release, Jenni Hofmann's counsel never received the smoking gun.[26]

When the trial drew to a close on December 2, Turrou signed his contract with Warner Bros., and David Stern planned to start the multipart Turrou series three days later. But the US attorney's office announced that the restraining injunction was still in effect, and Stern would be liable to contempt charges. The attorney's action was based on the rather fanciful logic that the case was not yet closed, as fourteen defendants were still under indictment and might be tried one day. Stern shot down to Washington, where he volubly demanded respect for the principle of a free press. Whether because of his visit or not, word reached the US attorney's office to "lay off."[27]

Next it was Lamar Hardy's turn to travel to Washington to meet "the Great White Chief." He was due to deliver to President Roosevelt a file on the US Army's incompetence in dealing with the Lonkowski spy case. Hardy's plan was to take advantage of his brief meeting and to protest against the dropping of contempt proceedings. By this time, though, wiser counsels had taken hold. Unlike President Richard Nixon at the time of the Pentagon Papers case, President Roosevelt did not risk incurring political fallout by challenging the First Amendment. Turrou escaped prosecution and was able to publish.[28]

The combined, if fractious, efforts of Tamm and Hardy were successful in the end. The jury believed Turrou. On November 29 its members returned guilty verdicts in the cases of Otto Voss and Johanna Hofmann. The next day they convicted Erich Glaser. Together with Guenther Gustave Rumrich, who had pleaded guilty, all four now awaited sentencing.

During the hiatus, the prosecution and the defense gave their reactions. Lamar Hardy showed himself to be on the side of Turrou and his growing support when he pointed to the urgent need for stronger US counterintelligence efforts. George C. Dix said he would appeal "if Hitler would send us the money."[29]

At 2 p.m. on Friday, December 2, Judge John C. Knox began to sentence the four prisoners. Jenni Hofmann produced a handkerchief and sobbed into it. In her case, the judge showed leniency: "She was thrilled to think that she served her government; but she has been abandoned." Jenni's sentence was four years' imprisonment, and a photographer caught her weeping again as she left in a police vehicle for the Federal Prison Camp for Women at Alderson, West Virginia. Glaser and Rumrich each received two years. On Voss, Judge Knox imposed a six-year sentence, observing that he was "inspired by a dream of *Deutschland über Alles*."

Judge Knox backed up his sentences with a moral verdict: "Had these defendants been apprehended within the confines of Germany, their fate would have been much more fearful. . . . We have no sawdust sprinkled on our prison yards."[30]

16

OF PROPAGANDA
AND REVENGE

The conclusion of the spy trial released Leon Turrou to tell his story and to launch a propaganda campaign against the Nazis. He pursued no less a goal than to shift the United States from its position of neutrality. Ranged against Turrou and his allies were formidable figures who had hitherto commanded a majority of US public opinion. In Congress critics of a powerful pro-neutrality bloc stigmatized its members as "isolationist" and backward looking, but those members included progressives whose support was vital to the administration's New Deal legislative program. Senators such as Gerald Nye and Hiram Johnson (R-CA) held aloft the anti-interventionist banner and had President Roosevelt over a foreign policy barrel. Turrou also found himself politically opposed to Charles Lindbergh, whose son's killer he had helped convict. With Nye, Lindbergh in 1940 founded the totemic anti-interventionist movement America First. The Nazis' atrocities abroad were not enough to shift opinion against this charismatically led pro-neutrality bloc.

On December 5, 1938, the *New York Times* carried an advertisement in heavy bold that marked the start of Turrou's propaganda barrage. It appeared in every other metropolitan newspaper as well: "Today It Can Be Told—Here are the articles, withheld until now by the New York Post at the request of the United States Government—Inside Story of the Spy Conspiracy in America—Revealed by Leon G. Turrou, former Ace G-Man, as told to David G. Wittels."

Wittels was a journalist who had covered the spy case for the *Post*. In the course of the next year, he helped Turrou write *The Nazi Spy Conspiracy in America* (published in the United States as *Nazi Spies in*

177

America), a write-up of the *Post* articles. Turrou also gave his name to another collaborative work, *How to Be a G-Man*, which was aimed at a juvenile audience.

Turrou's writing activities did not stop there. Having contracted to write the *Post* articles for a set fee of $10,000, he also promised twelve contributions to *Cosmopolitan Magazine* at $150 a piece, with each giving the story of one of his earlier cases. These pieces would be an advance serialization of the book *Where My Shadow Falls*, which appeared in 1949. The money was clearly important to the former detective, but so was the message about anti-fascism and the need for better US security.

Reed Vetterli also got in on the act. He accepted an offer from a newspaper syndicate of $100 per article for a series on the recent spy case. This annoyed both Turrou and Hoover, but the efforts of others in reality lent force to Turrou's campaign. Those efforts were becoming a contagion. The FBI's Ed Tamm wailed, "The newspapers will all start running spy articles of one sort or another in an effort to compete with the articles in the New York Post."[1]

Turrou's literary imitators multiplied. In a review for *The Nation*, Ludwig Lore deemed *Nazi Spies in America* to be different only in being "less sensational" than two other spy books that had appeared by July 1939. One was by the veteran spy history writer Richard Rowan and the other by the communist John L. Spivak, who claimed (in Lore's paraphrase) that "Americans without a drop of German blood in their veins are functioning as agents of the Nazi regime." Spivak was especially critical of Henry Ford, postulating a link between the automobile manufacturer's extensive espionage against his firm's workers and the Nazis' infiltration of the United States. Lore, a Jewish immigrant from Silesia who edited the daily *New Yorker Volkszeitung* (People's Daily) and wrote a foreign affairs column for the *New York Post,* predicted that the three books' exposés about German spying in the States would be "a shocking revelation to those who think there is safety in isolation."[2]

Nazi Spies in America remained the most important of all the posttrial publications in the United States. In Germany it was a different matter. When the book appeared early in 1939, Kate Moog mailed a copy to Erich Pfeiffer. He gave the book his closest attention. Outside the Abwehr, however, *Nazi Spies* had no impact in Germany. Media censorship was now absolute, and there were no reviews or mentions in the press. Ordinary citizens in Germany had no means of knowing how the reputation of their country was crashing in the United States.[3]

Americans felt the impact of Turrou's message not just through the printed word but in other ways too. For a man who cited exhaustion as his reason for resigning from the FBI, Turrou showed remarkable energy as a public speaker. As late as February 1940, he was scheduled to give an additional fifty-three lectures, each for a fee of $500, giving him a projected total of $26,000. The proceeds had allowed him to buy a house in Long Island, and he was putting two sons through college.[4]

In his speeches, Turrou did not claim to have put an end to the spy menace in the United States. In April 1939 he spoke to the Baltimore and Washington Kiwanis Clubs. He warned them that the Nazis were acting on the assumption that all German Americans were ready to betray the United States. A "huge network" was "systematically working from coast to coast, rifling American files of military secrets," and his work in New York the previous year had "only scratched the surface."[5] A few days later, he gave a near-identical speech at a federated clubs' luncheon in the world's second-largest hotel, the William Penn in Pittsburgh. A local newspaper reported his view that public indifference explained why the United States was "swarming with Nazi spies." In Pittsburgh, as in his addresses all over the nation, Turrou appealed for heightened public vigilance, stricter espionage laws, and a boost to FBI finances and personnel.[6]

Toward the end of the year, Turrou told a gathering at the Chilton Club in Boston that Americans were at last becoming "spy conscious," though there was still a need to increase the resources of the FBI, especially its counterespionage branch. He praised J. Edgar Hoover for his determination in tackling the spy problem. Hoover meanwhile was engaged in more than the bureau's administrative expansion. In 1938 he had escalated the efforts of the FBI's recently formed Crime Records Division, whose purpose, in spite of its name, was public relations.

Here, it should be noted that although Turrou and Hoover in one way sang the same tune, there were discordant notes. Hoover might well have preferred to continue with anti-communist programs as his dominant FBI-boosting tactic. There was a ready-made audience for anti-communist rhetoric, and the newly formed House Un-American Activities Committee was strongly anti-communist, even if it also opposed the fascist version of totalitarianism. Turrou's campaign obliged Hoover to devote both resources and rhetoric to the anti-fascist cause, and Hoover hated being coerced. He wanted to be the sole owner and shaper of the FBI's image. When he received a press clipping about Turrou's praise for him in the Chilton Club address, he wrote in the margin, "This is like a kiss of death."[7]

Attempting to convert myth into reality through frequent repetition, Turrou continued to praise Hoover, and he recited an improved version of how their sweet relationship had originated. At a meeting in Indianapolis on February 3, 1940, he omitted all references to the times when the FBI had turned him down; instead, he said he had come to the rescue of the bureau. He reminisced that it had amounted to little in 1928. But he went to Washington to meet Hoover: "I then told him of my experiences, my knowledge of languages, and he was somewhat impressed and gave me an application to fill out, and stated he would let me know later on. A week or so thereafter I received a wire to the effect I was appointed a special agent, to proceed immediately to Washington to take the oath of office."[8] Turrou modified his message according to his audience. For example, in early April 1939, he was returning to New York from Hollywood, when a local journalist caught up with him. At the time, the train was approaching Kansas City, Missouri. Turrou had written about his work on the Kansas City Massacre case, but he now reassured the reporter that "Kansas City is not to blame" and did not deserve the "crime center of America" label that out-of-state newspapermen once attached to it.[9]

To please his audiences, Turrou varied his biography. In some places, he told his tales about his Polish birth and struggles as a boy and young man. In others, he became French. He gave one midwestern journalist to understand that he "was a native of France who came to America at the age of 16," thus explaining his "broken accent." Broadcaster Mac Parker introduced him on a Philadelphia radio station with the words "quiet looking, unassuming, a bit of the ancestral French accent." There was never a hint of Turrou's Jewish identity.[10]

Turrou's literary and public speaking activities gave him a voice in what was a crucial US debate. In 1923 Italian Americans had formed the world's first anti-fascist organization, the Anti-Fascist Alliance of North America. Mistrust of fascism increased sharply in the Hitler years. There were worries that the Nazi "brownshirt" movement was taking root in the United States, and fears that acts of espionage and sabotage would be perpetrated on US soil escalated.

Nazi atrocities in Europe may have seemed like far-away events, but they were brought home to the American public. World-famous anti-fascist exiles arriving from Germany—for example, Thomas Mann, Albert Einstein, and, later, Hannah Arendt—contributed to the clamor. The novelist Ernest Hemingway was just one of a number of leading Americans who took up the anti-fascist cause in the 1930s. Hemingway had witnessed and helped to resist the fascist insurrection in Spain and, with fellow novelist John Dos Passos, scripted the propaganda movie *The Spanish Earth*. Narrated by Orson Welles, it was screened in the White House in July 1937 after Hemingway had dined privately with Franklin and Eleanor Roosevelt.

Hemingway also linked foreign events to domestic worries. His play *The Fifth Column* highlighted the danger posed by fascist "fifth columnists," traitors and spies who plotted to advance totalitarian objectives within free societies. It was published on October 14, 1938, the first day of the spy trial. Images created by writers such as Hemingway gelled with Turrou's depictions of Ignatz Griebl and his brownshirt connections and with fears of an *American* fifth column. William J. Donovan, who had sponsored Turrou for his FBI post in the 1920s, would write a booklet on the issue.[11]

The movie *Confessions of a Nazi Spy*, based on Turrou's book, ensured that his anti-neutrality campaign would have mass appeal. The impact of the movies had been huge ever since the silent era, when they had reached out to all of America, regardless of literacy or a grasp of the English language. America's 16,500 film theaters showed films that could touch ordinary people's feelings in ways that the written word could not.

Turrou had had early dealings with Warner Bros. The studio had dispatched screenwriter Milton Krims to be an observer at the spy trial, and he came away impressed with the dramatic potential of the underlying story. But it was not a foregone conclusion that Hollywood would be ready for heavy investment in a highly political, anti-Nazi movie.

Until very recently, the omens for such investment had been poor on both sides of the Atlantic. In 1930 Goebbels had led a riot at the Mozart Hall in Berlin to protest a showing of *All Quiet on the Western Front*, a Universal Pictures movie based on Erich M. Remarque's antiwar novel of that title. After Hitler took power, there was blanket censorship and information control. The German government made it clear it would take offense at any film anywhere showing the Nazis in a bad light. When Universal Pictures in 1937 produced *The Road Back*, based on Remarque's sequel novel, German officials complained, and the critics panned it. The same fate awaited Universal Pictures' *The Spy Ring*, a 1938 film starring Jane Wyman about agents with heavy German accents stealing a device to improve artillery accuracy.

Moving images that depicted the realities of life under the Nazis simply did not make it out of Germany. Prior to running the main feature film, American theaters in those days showed newsreels, or footage of events that had occurred two weeks earlier in Europe; however, US news cameramen were barred from filming in Germany. The adverse impact of one newsreel was inadvertent. Shot by Hitler regime loyalists, it showed the book-burning event of 1933 that signaled the end of free speech in Germany, giving Americans a glimpse of Nazism in the 1930s.[12]

Against this background of political interference and earlier marketing flops, it would take courageous commitment to invest major funds in an anti-Nazi movie. Turrou's campaign was perhaps aided by the fact that many studio moguls of the era were Jewish. William Fox, for example, was a Hungarian Jew. However, these people were not necessarily radical. The author of a critical study of Hollywood's Jews once remarked that they aped the Eastern Establishment, voted Republican, and adhered to the maxim that "Jews were to be seen and not heard."[13] Leaders of the Jewish community faced a conundrum with which Turrou was all too familiar: if as a Jew one spoke out against the Nazis, one's argument might not be taken seriously, as it would appear to have come from a biased source.

The Hollywood moguls were nevertheless acutely aware of the threat Hitler's Germany posed not just to Europe but to the United States as well. Secretly, they funded and encouraged propaganda and even espionage against the Bund and other fascist groups on the West Coast. Neil Ness, for example, was a gentile anti-Nazi who penetrated the German American Bund on behalf of the Los Angeles Jewish Community Committee and exposed the role German shipping played in transporting to the United States German anti-Semitic pamphlets that were written in English and falsely claimed to have originated in the States.[14] Hollywood's studio bosses may have been social climbers, but they were ready to take on the Nazis when the time and opportunity arrived. *Confessions of a Nazi Spy* would be, in the words of one historian, "Hollywood's first marquee posting of a four-letter word that had blackened newspaper headlines since 1933."[15]

Like Turrou, the Warner brothers were of Polish Jewish heritage. Their 1936 movie *Black Legion* starring Humphrey Bogart had already pointed to the danger of American fascism. Jack Warner nevertheless remained wary right up to 1939 of making an explicitly political film: "If I want to send a message, I'll use Western Union."[16]

Now the studio decided the time had come to back a major anti-Nazi movie. On January 30, 1939, Warner Bros. announced the start of production for *Confessions*. The film shoot would last fifty-five days, and there were seventy-eight speaking roles including a Mata Hari part for Berlin-born actress Lya Lys. Eighty-three different sets would portray "scenes in Germany, Scotland, Washington, DC, New York, aircraft factories and shipyards which figured in the international spy system."

The movie's story was based on the revelations by Turrou, who appeared in a cameo role as an assistant to his celluloid self, special agent

Ed Renard—*renard* being French for "fox." The initial budget ran to $1 million, and there was a 50 percent overrun. In a perverse stroke of good fortune, a set of stage lights fell in unexplained circumstances on the actor who played Renard, Edward G. Robinson. His injuries did not render him unable to perform, but it was a golden opportunity for the studio to release stories about death threats sent to members of the cast. Adding to the air of mystery and intrigue, the film had to be shot in conditions of secrecy.[17]

Robinson's appearance in the leading role was in one way remarkable. He had become a Hollywood star by acting in gangster roles. He was an everyman's underdog fighting the powers that be, including the forces of law and order. Now the man who had shot to fame in *Little Caesar*, about a small-time mobster, was all of a sudden playing an FBI agent. According to one journalist, Robinson physically resembled Turrou. In another similarity, Robinson was a cosmopolitan who spoke seven languages. His fans had not previously appreciated that Robinson had been born Emanuel Goldenberg in Bucharest and had painful memories of anti-Semitism there. His attitude toward Hitler was unambiguous. At the end of the 1938 spy trial, he had called for a boycott of German-made goods. Writing a piece called "Little Caesar Joins G-Men," a Hollywood journalist concluded, "Mr. Robinson and Mr. Turrou have one thing in common: They just don't like Adolf." A great film actor is always a story in himself, and from Turrou's propagandist point of view, Robinson could not have been better cast.[18]

With the film in mid-production, Jack Warner and his wife Ann paid a visit to President Roosevelt in the White House. It cannot be confirmed, but the presidential diary indicates they were there long enough for the president to see some rough cuts of *Confessions*. Certainly there must have been some discussion of the latest Warner movie.[19] The cause for which Turrou battled, if not the man himself, had come into its own.

Confessions opened at the Strand, New York, in late April 1939, with armed police theatrically posted on the roof of the great movie palace, which was now part of the Warner Bros.' property empire. The film was a direct piece of propaganda, with scenes straight out of Turrou's book and the Foley Square courtroom. It used a "Voice of God" voiceover and other state-of-the-art techniques. Its scenes depicted Jessie Jordan's treasonable actions, spies who desperately pleaded not to be sent back to Germany, brownshirt summer camps in the United States, and "Trojan horse" references to the fifth column threat. The characters' names were fictionalized, yet the film had a documentary character. The preliminaries dispensed with two conventions: there was no legal disclaimer, such as "all characters are fictional," and no initial credits. Instead, the cast list appeared at the end of the movie, flagging the theme that the stars were not the message even if Robinson was a box office draw.

Turrou now switched from promoting the book to promoting the movie of the book. Across the continental United States, he followed a schedule so frantic that he once found himself stranded in Harrisburg, Pennsylvania, having lost his New York–Chicago railroad ticket.[20] In June he turned up in Glasgow for the British launch of *Confessions*. He told a UK *Daily Worker* journalist that virtually the entire film was "absolutely true" and expressed his regret at having too little time to visit Dundee to meet the famous postie who had triggered the great tip-off. The English novelist and film critic Graham Greene welcomed *Confessions* as a movie that applied "documentary technique . . . excitingly to fiction." In an unusual move, the British censors allowed younger viewers to see the film despite its violent scenes.[21]

The $45,000 box office takings for *Confessions'* first American night were the highest so far recorded for 1939. There was a critical reception to match. *The Nation* praised the excellence of the cast and the movie's verisimilitude, though it did hint that propaganda could not really be art. The *Los Angeles Examiner's* Louella Parsons thought that Lya Lys was "efficient" in her role, but the true message was the courageous statement by the Warner siblings. New Deal documentary filmmaker Pare Lorentz announced, "The Warner brothers have declared war on Germany with this one. . . . Everybody duck."[22]

There were limits to the impact of *Confessions*, especially in Hitler-controlled areas of Europe. The movie did make its way to the German military's high command bunkers at Zossen, twenty miles south of

Berlin. According to Eric Pfeiffer, he and his colleagues enjoyed "frequent showings" at that location.[23] But the film was banned from general distribution; thus, as in the case of Turrou's book, it had no impact on German public opinion.

Regarding its impact in the United States, one should keep in mind that *Confessions* appeared in what was a bumper year in Hollywood's Golden Age. Other movies that opened in 1939 were *The Wizard of Oz*, *Mr. Smith Goes to Washington*, *Stagecoach*, and *Gone with the Wind*, with a record budget of $3.85 million. People still sought escape from the problems of a depressed decade and delighted in Scarlett O'Hara's waistline instead of worrying about Hitler. *Confessions* did not create spy neurosis overnight. Greta Garbo, star of the 1931 movie *Mata Hari*, later in the year appeared in *Ninotchka*, a Metro-Goldwyn-Mayer film about Soviet spies. In one way the film was a reminder of the problem of espionage, but it was mainly a romantic comedy.

Yet *Confessions* did break the mold. It marked the moment when millions of moviegoers began to realize the full enormity of what was happening in Europe and what that might mean for the United States. In the spring of 1940, another spy case broke that kept the issue of espionage in the forefront of the public's consciousness. Tyler Kent, a code clerk in the US Embassy in London, illegally secreted copies of confidential messages exchanged between President Roosevelt and the British prime minister in waiting, Winston Churchill. Kent was an anti-Semite and anti-interventionist, and his aim was to leak the messages to political opponents of the American president. On May 20, MI5 secured his arrest in time to prevent a leak that might have affected the 1940 presidential election. Details of the Churchill-Roosevelt exchanges were kept under wraps. Anti-neutrality partisans such as Bill Donovan stated that Kent had colluded with Germany; the FBI in later years suspected that Kent had Soviet connections. Whether an "isolationist" or a totalitarian secret agent, Kent contributed to contemporary jitters about espionage.[24]

Meanwhile, Turrou's propaganda campaign irritated J. Edgar Hoover. The FBI director did not object to what Turrou advocated. How could he, when his former favorite constantly boosted the FBI? But Hoover could not reconcile himself to the fact that Turrou had jilted him. Nor could he forgive him for a single instant for having become famous.

The boss set out to besmirch Turrou's record. In June 1938 Reed Vetterli had turned over to the FBI boss the spy hunter's personnel file.[25] Hoover instigated a faultfinding investigation of Turrou's past. FBI special agents gathered new evidence. For example, one morning in August, Louis Loebl interviewed Joseph Davidowsky, the long-term acquaintance of Turrou's who had by now fallen on hard times and ran the Izba, a Russian-themed bar in Brooklyn. By 10 a.m. when Loebl turned up at the Izba, which he described as a "dive" of ill repute, the fifty-five-year-old had been drinking heavily. But in spite of downing "numerous" further cocktails of indeterminate composition in the course of the five-hour interview, he spoke lucidly. He had turned against Turrou and obliged Loebl with a character assassination, branding his sister's former lover as a liar, a cheat, and a womanizer. All this went into Turrou's file. The interview became part of Hoover's long-running campaign to defame his former agent, one of the FBI's greatest detectives, and eventually to drive him into exile and obscurity.[26]

Turrou continued to campaign publicly against the Nazis right up to the moment the Japanese attacked Pearl Harbor and brought the United States into World War II. He even endorsed in July 1941 the kidnapping of Adolf Hitler.[27] By this time, however, he was thinking of returning to public service, and Hoover did his utmost to prevent that from happening.

When Turrou asked Mayor LaGuardia if New York City might have a job for him, Hoover sent a letter stating that the applicant was a disgraceful character. For a while, Turrou worked instead for a private philanthropic organization dedicated to the anti-fascist cause. Finally in 1943, saying he was younger than he really was, he enlisted in the US Army and went through basic training. Hoover lobbied against his promotion to officer rank: "Everything should be done to prevent this. It is an outrage." When Bill Donovan established the Office of the Coordinator of Information—the precursor to the Office of Strategic Services (OSS)—Hoover told him not to touch the man whose career he and Donovan had conspired to promote a decade earlier. When Turrou spun an improbable line, saying he saw signs of reconciliation with his former boss, Hoover scrawled another comment: "The damned liar!"[28]

Mel Purvis, that other former FBI agent consigned to purgatory by the vengeful FBI director, sympathized with Turrou's predicament and helped him get a commission in the military police.[29] This launched Turrou on a significant new commitment, for when Gen. Dwight D. Eisenhower learned of his talents, he assigned him to work with Brig. Gen. Walter Bedell Smith in the US Army's Criminal Investigation Division. To the dismay of Hoover's office, Purvis and Turrou began to recruit Americans for work in counterespionage. Turrou worked closely with Bill Donovan, who was now head of the OSS (established in June 1942) and in the Washington power games a rival to J. Edgar Hoover. With new patronage and boasting first-rate credentials, Turrou became the director of the Central Registry of War Criminals and Security Suspects (CROWCASS) headquartered in Paris. This well-funded organization hunted down Nazi war criminals, extraditing them to countries where harsh penalties awaited them. In some controversial cases, if they were potential "assets," CROWCASS recruited them to work for US intelligence.[30]

According to a 1949 article in Der Spiegel, Turrou's successful application of IBM computers in the work of CROWCASS brought him "worldwide fame." The German magazine credited his work against the Abwehr, but Turrou's previous success against Pfeiffer's spies did not really register in Germany and was everywhere fading from the public's consciousness.[31]

From Turrou's personal perspective, these later achievements were overshadowed by family tragedy. First of all, his wife died. On May 1, 1942, Teresa was committed to earth in the Holy Rood Cemetery right across the railroad tracks from the family home at 401 Union Avenue in Westbury, New York (just four miles from the Lonkowskis' old haunts in Hempsted). Immediately afterward when notifying Hoover of Turrou's application to become an army officer, Ed Tamm mentioned that Leon was "extremely upset" about Teresa's demise, and it was on this letter that the FBI director expressed his handwritten "outrage" at the thought of Turrou's army promotion.[32] Then on August 16, 1943, Leon's son Victor was killed in action when his bomber was shot down over Italy. Although both the United States and the city of Paris decorated Leon Turrou for his war work, for the recipient, the plaudits must have had a hollow ring.

Turrou's decision to spend the rest of his life abroad contributed to the erasure of his reputation in the United States. Two weeks after the Allies' victory against Germany, he remarried, and his new wife, Anna B. Mc-Lester from Atlanta, Georgia, was a frequent European traveler. In 1949 they settled in Paris, where he became billionaire J. Paul Getty's security man. He lived in France not because of Hoover's persecution but because he loved the country: "France is all the contrasts that one could wish for in life." His profile has suggested to one historian that he continued to work for US intelligence through the period when his wartime boss Bedell Smith was the director of the CIA (1950–53). After Turrou died in 1986 at the age of ninety-one he was interred at the Neuilly-sur-Seine New Communal Cemetery outside Paris, where his name is inscribed at the American Legion Memorial Mausoleum.[33]

In April 1965 Turrou had written to Hoover, saying as he was almost seventy, the removal of the "dismissal with prejudice" stain would be wonderful for his grandchildren and great grandchildren, and that the exoneration could no longer be regarded as a move that might gain him federal employment. It was the latest of his many such appeals, and others had been lobbying on his behalf. One of Hoover's acolytes recommended that this appeal, like the previous ones, be ignored, but this time the boss appended an initialed instruction: "Remove 'with prejudice.'"

On June 21, 1965, Hoover signed a Notification of Personnel Action form giving effect to his decision. Turrou had received a coldly worded advance notification from the director. Still cleaving to his supplicant stance, he had replied, "Permit me once more to express to you my deep thanks and appreciation for your kindness and thoughtfulness in expunging the disgraceful blot from my service record which has tormented and haunted me since I left the Bureau."[34]

Fifteen years earlier, the New York federal court had issued a nolle prosequi order, dropping the charges against the spies Turrou had so effectively exposed as well as against Jessie Jordan. The spies had been reprieved, while the detective who exposed their felonies had remained under a cloud. The reprieved, though, had not shown any repentance.

17

SPY SEQUELS

Leon Turrou blew his own trumpet but did not blow it too hard. He did not want to give the impression that he had ended the German spy threat in the United States. That would have run contrary to his insistent campaign for more resources to be devoted to counterintelligence.

The FBI took the same line and ensured that its leaders across the nation remained alert to the spy ring's personnel and their possible successors. A few days after the spy trial's conclusion, New York's latest special agent in charge, Dwight Brantley, sent a briefing to his corresponding SAC in Seattle with notes on all those who had been indicted. There were clearly loose ends. Brantley had "little information" on the German War Ministry's Udo von Bonin other than what Ignatz Griebl supplied. The same could be said of Hermann Menzel of the same ministry. The bureau had "no information" about Erich Pfeiffer, though he was "apparently" the head of the spy ring that had operated in the United States. Brantley speculated that Sanders might be Pfeiffer.[1]

Thus, a great deal remained unknown, and there was no ground for believing the named officials or their successors would refrain from waging future intelligence operations against the United States. The FBI knew it had a duty to be alert, but it lacked the resources to be fully effective, especially when it came to foreign counterintelligence. Once the United States was in the war, the FBI could dispatch personnel to foreign countries, especially in South and Central America. But in the 1930s, information about foreign intelligence agencies came only from indirect sources: US military attachés serving overseas, information from decoded international communications, and liaison arrangements with friendly countries.

The latter arrangements were helpful in the case of Jessie Jordan. In that particular case, the FBI could be confident that there was no cause for concern. Although Jordan was technically a fugitive from American justice, she was safely incarcerated in the United Kingdom. In fact, she remained under lock and key until the end of the war and suffered from a number of problems that neutralized any espionage ambitions she may have continued to nurture.

Jordan's daughter, Marga, had in the meantime met a Glaswegian named Thomas J. Reid, and they went through a marriage ceremony at Gretna Green, the Scottish border community famous for its accommodation of runaway brides. The suspicion was that she acted to obtain British residency rights; like her mother, she was a German citizen.

Marga, and possibly Tom as well, had neglected to divorce her previous spouse. When Marga visited her mother in prison, Jessie comforted her daughter with her view that she would not be prosecuted for bigamy in Germany, as the offense had been committed under Scots law.[2] The polygamous arrangement did not work out financially. Reid was not paid at a sufficient level to satisfy his partner, and he lost his job with little immediate prospect in those hard times of finding another. Marga appeared not to return his affections, and she sailed for Germany on October 25, 1938. Photographers who pursued her onto the Hamburg-bound ferry at the port of Leith snapped a mischievous wee Jessie making faces at them around the corner of a cabin door. The photographers did not notice that Marga by this time was pregnant with another child.[3]

Meanwhile, the grandmother's health had declined. She began to complain of constant constipation, saying she was used to a fresh fruit diet, which was not available in Saughton Prison. In late August, she was admitted to Edinburgh's Royal Infirmary under twenty-four-hour guard because MI5 wanted to shield her from the press "in her own interest." The gynecologist W. F. T. Haultain performed what his junior described as "a sub-total hysterectomy and bilateral salpingo-oophorectomy for a large fibroid."[4]

Back in prison, the convalescent Jordan remained under twenty-four-hour surveillance. MI5's Hinchley Cooke felt sorry for her and relaxed the invigilation, but then Jordan suffered another blow. Late on the eve-ning of January 20, 1939, Marga died at the Finkenau Women's Clinic in Hamburg. The death certificate stated, "The deceased was not married, divorced." Her unborn baby also died. Marga's death certificate appears to support Reid's contention that the catastrophe was the result of an "illegal operation."[5] Reid declared his intention to adopt his stepchild, Jessie, but Grandmother Jessie did not trust him. The paperwork formal-ities for such a procedure in Germany were formidable. Reid said it was beyond his capabilities, and the following year he married a third wife.[6]

When World War II started, Jessie Jordan was evacuated to Aber-deen Prison. There, she suffered from further illnesses and complained about damp and cold conditions. The prison governor described her as "insolent to all officials" and said she stirred up discontent among the women prisoners. She had complained to him that laundry was hung to dry in the women's quarters—"the whole place has never been without wet clothes"—whereas the men did not have to put up with such damp conditions. "Why we women?" she asked, and it was not an isolated ex-pression of feminism. Rumrich had criticized her for calling herself Mrs. Jessie Jordan and not, as was the custom in 1930s Scotland, using her first husband's full name, as in Mrs. Frederick Jordan. It was poor tradecraft, he thought, as she was drawing attention to herself. But the reason for it may well have been Jessie's desire for independence.[7]

Like Mata Hari, who had complained about prison conditions for women as she awaited her execution, Jessie Jordan had a penchant for resistance.[8] To male officials, Jordan seemed difficult. P. J. Rose, assistant secretary of state at the Scottish Office, referred to her as "a woman of tortuous mentality and of a designing nature."[9] In a contrasting vein, Jordan's conduct reports categorized her as a model prisoner who worked hard and broke no rules; her recommendation for release on license summed up her conduct as "excellent." She is reputed to have converted to Christian Science when in prison.[10]

Jessie Jordan's good behavior qualified her for early release on January 14, 1941. It was to no avail. The moment she set foot outside Aberdeen Prison she was rearrested as an enemy alien and interned for the duration of the war. At the war's end, the British authorities deported her to Germany. Her granddaughter, Jessie Wobrock, who had spent the war in an orphanage, was able to join her. Jessie Jordan became a missionary for the Christian Scientists. She fell ill in 1954, and in accordance with the precepts of her adopted religion, she refused medical treatment. She died in Hanover without having given the FBI a moment's serious concern since her arrest in 1938.[11]

A little more disturbing, the FBI lacked information on Dr. Ignatz Griebl. He appears to have enjoyed the fruits of his misdemeanors, owning property in Germany and Austria, and practicing gynecology in Vienna. He and the long-suffering Maria divorced, but he apparently made no attempt to take up with Kate Moog. At the end of the war, he applied to the Allied Military Government for a travel permit. The military authorities were forewarned and arrested him in Salzburg. They did not, however, remove him to the United States for trial. He remained a fugitive from US justice until the nolle prosequi order of 1951 and as much a mystery to the FBI as he ever had been.[12]

The FBI had been unable to touch Udo von Bonin. As noted previously, when the British interrogated the senior Abwehr official in Denmark at the end of the war, he claimed he only became involved in American spy work because he spoke English and the responsible official was away from his desk when Griebl and Moog presented themselves in 1937.[13] Bonin's interest in the United States, however, was not transient. For example, in 1942 he sent a Dutch-born agent to the country. A terrified Alfred Meiler was trying to keep his Jewish identity secret. He was an easy recruit for Bonin, who promised to protect his brothers from persecution in the German-occupied Netherlands. Issued a forged US passport in the name of Arthur Koehler, Meiler was initially tasked with finding out about the US nuclear weapons program. Right up to the end of the war, "Uncle" (as the Hamburg office now called itself) gave him a whole variety of other missions. The evidence indicates that the FBI had Meiler under surveillance and used him to send disinformation to Uncle. He may well have been complicit in this procedure, making him a double agent. Still the FBI did not have a rounded knowledge of Bonin until the

British interrogated him and passed what they knew to J. A. Cimperman, the FBI's representative in the US Embassy in London.[14]

Turrou and his colleagues had glimpsed the fish, but Bonin swam nowhere near the FBI's net. The same could be said of Hermann Menzel. According to Bonin, in the mid-1930s Menzel was his immediate superior at the Berlin headquarters of the Abwehr. These senior intelligence bosses were well outside the FBI's control.

Nikolaus Ritter, who pulled off the Norden bombsight coup, eluded the FBI's grasp. He managed to remain an unknown entity until he became a focus of FBI interest in 1941. His former wife, Mary Aurora, helped the FBI with its inquiries once she had shaken the bureau's suspicion that she was herself a German agent. Not until September 1945 did the FBI finally get to interview him and find out about his childhood, his training to be a textile engineer, his unemployment in the 1920s, his services as a spy in the years 1918–33, and his subsequent operations against both the United Kingdom and the United States.[15]

Ritter became a spy of note in World War II because of his dealings with Arthur Owens, code-named Snow. Owens was a double-double agent, working for both the Abwehr and MI5, and betrayed both sides. For example, he promised the Abwehr he could deliver a Plaid Cymru (Welsh Nationalist) saboteur. Such persons could be found—the cultural nationalist Saunders Lewis is an example—but Snow was in no position to deliver. MI5 was on to him, and from Wandsworth Prison while under the tutelage of British intelligence, he transmitted carefully crafted misinformation to Uncle. It was the beginning of the famed double-cross system.[16]

Many years later, when Ritter learned from the American journalist Ladislas Farago that some wartime intelligence documents had survived and would be released, he wrote a memoir and was to a certain degree forthcoming. In 1945 he had told his British interrogators he had never joined the National Socialist Party, and in his book he reiterated his claim to have been an apolitical patriot. "I was a soldier and served my fatherland under the Emperor in the First World War and under Adolf Hitler in the second, and would, God forbid, serve under the leader of my fatherland should there be a third." He also revealed how much he admired tall, blond, and blue-eyed people like himself; how he scorned American women with their "regal" expectations; how he shamelessly abused his American wife; and how he worked with Wilhelm Canaris and with Hilmar Dierks, the inventor of Sanders. Such personal details would have been of great interest to Turrou and his collaborators, but until the 1940s Ritter's page was largely blank in the FBI's inventory of spies.[17]

How much did all this ignorance matter? While every piece in a jigsaw is significant, what really concerned the FBI was its performance against spies who tried to operate in the United States. Here, the bureau built on what Turrou had started, and its agents operated with determination and effectiveness. The New York trial marked the end of one FBI operation, but it spurred an expansion of counterespionage surveillance. Special agents pursued all kinds of leads, responded to tip-offs from members of the public, and kept an eye on the four convicted spies.

Guenther Rumrich attracted continuing attention. On July 10, 1940, he was released on probation from the federal prison in Milan, Michigan. The FBI placed him under surveillance. It emerged that the former agent was interested solely in the exploitation of women and in petty crime.

Rumrich returned to New York City, working for short spells as a doorman. He took up with a new mistress, Lottie Einsele, who dumped him when she discovered he had been a spy. After a short visit to see his children in Montana, he got a job in the Portland, Oregon, shipyards.[18] Production was already booming because of wartime demand, and Rumrich worked first as a timekeeper, then as an apprentice welder. In the meantime, he engaged in criminal behavior to an almost compulsive degree. He deceptively signed on to the crew of a merchant ship under the assumed name of Joseph de Bors, using his mother's maiden name. He fraudulently tried to join the US Coast Guard in Seattle, giving a false name and address and denying his criminal record. He cashed three bogus checks in Seattle and temporarily gave his FBI watchers the slip.[19]

By now, his wife had divorced him and remarried. An FBI report filed in October 1943 told a sad story. The released prisoner had issued four more dud checks in the name of Joseph Rumridge. He preyed on the kindness of others and had defrauded an old lady. Rumrich used the

Ramapo Hotel in Portland as a place of sexual convenience. The report listed eight women he had dated there. He did not make a good impression on them. One of his lovers was Mrs. Juanita Carol Raney, a "full blooded Indian" who was prepared to turn him in.

His sons, now ages six and seven, visited him, and perhaps they inspired their father to try to reform. Rumrich explored ways to find a path out of his fix but did not follow through with them. An FBI search of his travel trunk uncovered, interleaved with love letters from yet another woman in the Bronx, the drafts of several short stories. The serial US Army deserter also tried to reenlist in the military, and that would have been a potential cause for concern had he succeeded. Finally he had ceased to be a threat to US national security, and that was what mattered most to the FBI.[20]

The FBI watched the spy case witnesses as well as those who had been indicted. Kate Moog had escaped prosecution but was of interest because of her former association with Ignatz Griebl. She promised to keep the bureau informed of her whereabouts, and in January 1939 she told the New York office she had moved into a new apartment in the city and was moving to Florida for a number of weeks. She promised to contact the New York office immediately if she received any communication from Griebl.[21]

The bureau focused mainly, however, on those who had received prison sentences. It maintained a watch on their posttrial legal moves. The Rumrich conviction had been cut and dried, but the cases of his three codefendants had judicial developments. The FBI followed the proceedings on December 16, 1938, when counsel representing Erich Glaser called for the verdict in his case to be set aside on the grounds that juror number 4 should have been barred from serving because he had concealed his Jewish identity. Judge Knox slapped this down and refused to pass the request to the Circuit Court of Appeals. "So far as this Court is concerned, the record made at the trial will stand."[22]

The Circuit Court of Appeals did hear a plea from Glaser to be allowed to appeal in forma pauperis, meaning that he had no money and wanted his court expenses waived. The Court of Appeals dismissed the motion. In a "comprehensive" FBI review of the spy convicts in 1943, the FBI intimated that Glaser, having completed his term in prison, was working as a caretaker on a farm in Vermont and recommended that he should be stripped of his US citizenship.[23]

An FBI parole report on Johanna Hofmann two weeks into her prison sentence took an unsympathetic line. She had initially admitted both to her work as a spy courier under the instruction of Karl Schlueter and to her trip to Czechoslovakia to recruit Gustav Rumrich. But after her trial, she ceased to cooperate with the government. She recanted her testimony and "obviously perjured herself in attempting to avoid conviction." Hofmann remained in the Federal Prison Camp for Women at Alderson until her conditional release on December 30, 1941. By this time, the United States was at war. Attitudes toward spies and traitors harden under such circumstances, and like Glaser, she could expect little leniency. Immigration and Naturalization Service officials immediately rearrested her upon her release and removed her to Ellis Island, where she awaited deportation. There, she was arrested yet again, this time as a dangerous enemy alien.

The Alien Enemy Hearing Board for the Southern District of New York examined Hofmann in March 1942 and recommended to the US attorney general that she should be interned. Confronted with this probability, Hofmann chose to be repatriated, under the terms of the original deportation order, before the attorney general handed down his decision. On May 7, having plucked her eyebrows for the last time on US soil, the beautician departed on the SS *Drottningholm*. The Swedish American Line's ship had once transported Greta Garbo to America and ultimate stardom in the movie *Mata Hari*. By arrangement with the Axis powers, the US State Department had recently chartered the passenger liner to repatriate civilian internees and diplomats from both sides. The deportation option would prove to be a short-lived arrangement, but Hofmann had availed herself of the opportunity. When the vessel arrived in the neutral port of Lisbon, she disembarked a lucky woman.[24]

The FBI's parole report on Otto Hermann Voss was never going to be exculpatory. It observed that Voss had perjured himself to avoid conviction. It opined that "the information furnished by Voss to agents in Germany was by far the most damaging," as he had divulged the latest design details of the US Army's pursuit planes. The parole report also noted that "during the trial of this case Voss was asked whether he believed in the principles of the National Socialistic Party in Germany and he stated he could not answer the question." Voss appealed his sentence but pragmatically "elected to serve the sentence imposed upon him during the pendency of his appeal." Still under observation by the FBI, he served his term in the high-security US Penitentiary in Lewisburg, Pennsylvania.[25]

In the aftermath of the 1938 spy case, the FBI received increased support from the Roosevelt administration. Over the next year or two, however, there was little sign that this backing would boost the bureau's *foreign* counterintelligence aptitude. Even if its skills had increased to the degree that it could have produced persuasive evidence, Germany would have refused to extradite senior officials such as von Bonin, Menzel, and Pfeiffer, and in all probability it would have protected lower-ranking intelligence officers as well.

The FBI's protection of the continental United States, however, was another matter. The bureau watched the captured spies of 1938 very closely, and events would show that the FBI remained vigilant when it came to future German spy ventures on US soil.

18

THE CASE NAMED FOR DUQUESNE

In June 1941 the Americans discovered that Germany was once again spying on their nation and on a considerable scale.

The Duquesne spy ring, the cause of the new alarm, was named for a man with a lurid image. Fritz Duquesne was a South African of Dutch and Huguenot heritage. Fond of embroidering his life story, Fritz told the tale that as a preteenager, he had fought the "Kaffirs," a derogatory term for the Zulus, whose lands the Dutch settlers aimed to appropriate as if by divine right.

In the Second Boer War, Fritz Duquesne fought against the British. When the might of the empire prevailed, they took him prisoner and exiled him, somewhat benevolently, to the island of Bermuda. He escaped that paradise to enter the United States illegally. Some years later, he boasted of having achieved his revenge by killing the British general who had crushed the Boers. The official version of Lord Kitchener's death holds that he died when the armored cruiser that was taking him on a diplomatic mission to Russia struck a mine off the coast of Orkney on June 5, 1916. Duquesne, however, asserted not only that he was with Kitchener aboard the HMS *Hampshire* as it left Scapa Flow for Archangel but also that he signaled a German submarine. The U-boat torpedoed the warship, and Kitchener perished along with 736 others. The signaler escaped by swimming to the submarine through the cold North Atlantic waters.

Subsequently, Duquesne said that he was glad to spy for Germany because he hated the British. The Nazis' racism in any case appealed to him. Their money was a further attraction for a man who bore the twin burdens of a low income and a taste for expensive women.[1]

Duquesne first met Nikolaus Ritter in 1931. Billing himself as "the man who killed Kitchener," he had by this time made up a whole inventory of heroic exploits and had promoted himself to the rank of colonel. He told Ritter that as a boy he had watched his mother die in a British concentration camp. His tales impressed the German agent, and the two men became drinking friends, meeting in a private New York university club where they were able to quench their thirst in the dry decade. Ritter then left for Germany. By the time he returned, Prohibition had ended, but old habits die hard. One day in November 1937, as he was waiting to hear that the Norden bombsight plans from Hermann Lang had been safely smuggled out of the country, Ritter visited Duquesne at his apartment on West Fifty-Seventh Street. They once again drank whisky.

The time had come to recruit Duquesne. The sixty-year-old "colonel" had the qualification of speaking several languages. Ritter also recalled that while his host "never had money," he had "excellent social connections." He gave Duquesne the code name Oskar, the code number A.3518, and a check for $100. The South African celebrated what was to be his new income stream by moving to more upscale accommodations with his wife, Evelyn, a Southern belle who was twenty-six years his junior and a fashionable sculptress.

Ritter saw Duquesne as "a daredevil with nerves of steel and whatever he aspired to, he succeeded in." He claimed that when Duquesne brazenly asked for secret information from official sources, "he was rarely rejected and all his information was immediately transferred to Germany." The reality is that compared with Lang's espionage, Duquesne's activities were trivial. Fritz gave his Abwehr controllers information about the design of a new US gas mask, but the source of his data could not have been more open; it was the *New York Times*. He did have credentials as an investigating journalist and obtained other information simply by writing to people and requesting it, but it is doubtful that the intelligence was at all important. As in the earlier instance of Rumrich, Duquesne was not entrusted with any of the Abwehr's inner secrets. FBI files on the 1938 and 1941 spy rings were named for Rumrich and Duquesne, respectively, but that was deceptive. Like Rumrich, Duquesne gave his name to a spy ring but was not a productive member of it.[2]

By virtue of his seniority, Ritter was in a position to achieve more. The architect of the Lang coup became the principal spymaster operating against the United States. He operated from Hamburg, which had always been a larger Abwehr station than Bremen. Pfeiffer left Bremen following the 1938 debacle, and Hamburg from then on directed espionage against the United States. In 1946 London's Counter Intelligence War Room produced a "liquidation report" on the activities of the Hamburg station and noted that its headquarters from 1937 were at 14 Knochenhauerstrasse. "Very few records were left undestroyed" after the war, but clearly its operations against the United Kingdom and the United States were "practically unrestricted." The report noted a sharp increase in Hamburg's activity in 1938, with some thirty agents dispatched to the United States and more to Latin America. As Pfeiffer relinquished his US responsibilities that year, Canaris was thought to have given Hamburg the kind of pep talk that could not be ignored.

The writers of the liquidation report observed that Ritter showed poor judgment and tradecraft, and he tended to "cross swords with his superior officers over policy." They belittled the performance of his American agents: "None . . . can be considered successful." In 1940 Ritter's unit in Hamburg redoubled its efforts, instigating extensive technical training for its agents, but the commanding officers lacked the skills to orchestrate major results. "It was probably for this reason that the successes they achieved were very few." The liquidation report's conclusion that Hamburg's overall performance was poor was not entirely objective. Reflecting a British victory hubris and an ignorance of the Abwehr's successes elsewhere, the writers claimed the German intelligence organization failed everywhere. They added that it made no difference that Germany's democracy was in a straightjacket, for its fascist leaders both ignored intelligence that might have suggested a different course and would not have listened even if their spies had delivered accurate findings.[3]

The tone of the liquidation report contrasted with the FBI's caution in its earlier, 1941 assessment. This FBI review of the Duquesne case saw ominous signs. Looked at together, the Rumrich and Duquesne files indicated "that the conspiracy of the German Government to engage in espionage activities in the United States existed continuously from 1935 to date." In harmony with its exiled prodigy, Leon Turrou, by the date of this review the FBI firmly believed in the continuous existence of the German spy menace.

The FBI's review dwelled on links between the Lonkowski, Pfeiffer, and Ritter phases in German espionage. It had evidence on the courier connection. The FBI had a note from Sex (Lonkowski), apparently addressed to Pfeiffer, saying he proposed to use the courier Eitel. Lonkowski had used another courier, Schlueter, who was connected with Hofmann and thus with Griebl and Moog. In another connection, Duquesne had been active in the now-defunct German Aviation Club, which was located near Roosevelt Field, Long Island. The club had National Socialist leanings, and one of its members, Ulrich Hausmann, had helped Lonkowski flee the country in 1935.[4]

The FBI's 1941 report did not fully credit the damage Turrou's detective work caused the Abwehr operation in 1938. In the authors' anxiety to point to a national security threat, they undervalued their own organization's efficacy. Unlike the authors of the 1946 British report, they did not have the comfort of having just won a war.

If the Abwehr's threat to US security was low, it was to no small measure the result of the FBI's improving skills. Like a hitherto overlooked younger sibling, the bureau was catching up with its peers. British counterintelligence had a longer tradition than its US counterpart, and Great Britain's entry into World War II accelerated MI5's expertise at a time when the United States was still neutral and unengaged. But US intelligence would pull abreast and then ahead in some domains. Military code breaking was a notable example. The FBI, too, improved its performance. It even began to impress MI5 with its expertise in particular areas.

One of those areas of expertise was the Hamburg spy station and its director of US espionage, Niki Ritter. In its assessments of Hamburg, the

FBI was edging ahead of MI5. An MI5–MI6 exchange in March 1942 revealed that the British knew two of Ritter's code names, Rantzau and Renken, but not all of them; and the security services had no reliable photograph of the Abwehr spy. The FBI had both a list of his code names and photographs. Noting that "the FBI has quite a quantity of information about the Hamburg Stelle [office] which is new to us," an MI5 official wondered whether the bureau might agree to send a report, "as we still have several cases on our hands which originated from Hamburg."[5]

The FBI had also developed more than its regional expertise. Hoover had always been keen on the FBI's keeping up with technological change, and such change was constant in the spy profession. Gone, for example, was the reliance on rolled umbrellas as the means of transporting secret documents on the ocean liners plying between New York and German ports. In 1928 a professor at Dresden Technical University had developed microphotography, and a decade later Germany's spies began to take notice. Big documents were out, and the microdot was in. Nor would Germany be so reliant on transatlantic telegraph cables as it had been, to its cost, on the eve of World War I. The coded telegram was giving way to the coded radio transmission.

The FBI kept up with these changes and exploited them with the assistance of what every successful intelligence operation needs—a stroke of luck. That stroke of luck came in the shape of a walk-in spy.

The spy who walked in was Wilhelm Gottlieb Sebold. Born in 1899 in the city of Mülheim in Germany's industrial Ruhr area and, like so many German children of the era, named after the reigning monarch, Wilhelm trained as a mechanic. In World War I, he joined the Imperial German Army as a machine gunner. He spent months in the Somme area of the western front and inhaled mustard gas, an experience that affected his health for the rest of his life. His wartime experience left him in a troubled state. In a hotheaded moment in the postwar days, he struck a police officer and served a short prison sentence.

Life was grim in his part of Germany after the war, and in 1922 he migrated to the United States. Wilhelm became William and then just

Bill. He moved around, served as a merchant sailor, and worked in South America, where he developed his knowledge of diesel technology. In 1931 he married Helen Büchner, an American of Bavarian stock. They settled in San Diego, where he worked at the Consolidated Aircraft Corporation.

They did not stay long. Moving east for medical reasons, Sebold settled into greater New York City's Yorktown suburbia (not to be confused with Manhattan's Yorkville neighborhood) and applied himself to working at any jobs he could find in the Depression-torn 1930s. In 1936 he became a US citizen. He encountered pro-Hitler militants in Yorktown's German American community, but unlike some of his fellow veterans who were embittered by the World War I experience, he took away from the Somme campaign the lesson that peace should be cherished. After the rise of Hitler, Sebold was convinced that American democratic values were superior to those of Nazi Germany.[6]

In the winter of 1937, surgeons at Bellevue Hospital removed half of Sebold's stomach after diagnosing an ulcer problem. His recuperation was slow, and at the same time he experienced marital problems, resulting in a temporary separation from Helen in 1938. He decided to return to his mother's house in Mülheim, where he arrived early in 1939. He recovered sufficiently to work for a local manufacturing company.

One day the Gestapo arrived on his doorstep. They had heard about his employment in the airplane manufacturing industry and considered him a potential asset. They said they knew he was part Jewish and reminded him of his brush with the law in 1918. Had the American authorities known about his criminal record, he would not have obtained his US citizenship. The Gestapo took away Sebold's American passport and threatened to inform American officials of his past misdemeanor if he applied for a replacement without first agreeing to cooperate. In a finishing touch, they referred to the funeral clothes that lay in wait for him if he did not comply.

Sebold traveled to Hamburg to meet a Dr. Renken, who was really Nikolaus Ritter. As in the case of Jessie Jordan's recruitment, the Abwehr took up where the Gestapo had left off. Sebold underwent training as a spy, learning about microphotography, encryption, and radio technology. He expressed enthusiasm for his role and presented himself to the credulous Ritter as a German nationalist.[7]

In January 1940 the Germans issued Sebold a new American passport in the name of Harry Sawyer and gave him $1,000 in cash, half of which he was to deliver to Everett Roeder, an Abwehr agent who had worked at the Sperry Gyroscope Company. They gave Sebold five microphotographs of documents containing espionage instructions; each was the size of a postage stamp. Two carried encryption and password information for his own use and were for his retention. All five fitted into a pocket watch that the Abwehr also supplied. Ritter told him his task was to establish a shortwave radio transmission facility and use it to relay communications between Hamburg and its agents in the United States. He also was to make contact with Hermann Lang and deliver the three remaining micro documents to Roeder, Lilly Stein (a model whose chief role in the spy ring was that of femme fatale), and Col. Frederick Duquesne.

Having made these arrangements, Ritter accompanied "Sawyer" to Genoa, Italy, for his embarkation on the crack US liner the SS *Washington*. With war having broken out four months earlier, the voyage across the Atlantic was potentially hazardous, even if the United States was not yet a belligerent. The line had to protect the *Washington* from accidental attacks by belligerent warships, so on each side of the hull were painted two large Stars and Stripes, one on each side of the words "United States Line." On February 8, 1940, the vessel arrived safely in New York. Special agents of the FBI discreetly greeted Sebold/Sawyer there. Sam Foxworth, veteran of the 1938 spy trial and now the special agent in charge of New York, had arranged the reception committee and already had over fifty agents working on the case. Prior to his departure from Germany, Sebold had given the Gestapo the slip long enough to confide his story to US consular officials in Cologne. One of them, it is unclear who, advised him secretly to play along with the Abwehr's designs. The FBI duly received notification. If Sawyer was to be trusted, he could become a double agent.[8]

The FBI allocated Special Agent James C. Ellsworth to work with Sebold. First, he established the double agent's bona fides; then he helped him achieve his goals. To oversee the case, Hoover parachuted in one of his trusted colleagues—Earl Connelley, Turrou's former boss in Chicago, who now carried the rank of inspector. Connelley moved to New York from Washington, and Foxworth returned to his original duties of running the FBI's New York office.

The bureau refrained from making immediate arrests. Instead, it put Sebold on a monthly retainer and let the spies run so that they could be followed, watched, and identified. It supervised and assisted Sebold in his work of tracking down spies and finding evidence that could be used to prosecute them. Agents secretly took over the Abwehr's banking arrangements.

The bureau also turned to the businessman and philanthropist W. Vincent Astor for help. In private life, Astor was a neighbor of Franklin Roosevelt's in Hyde Park, New York. They had been close friends since the 1920s when the future president had comforted his polio-afflicted legs in the Astors' heated swimming pool. Astor had conducted informal intelligence tasks for the president and, as managing director of the Western Union Telegraph Company, had a feel for technology. He helped the bureau set up an office on the sixth floor of the Newsweek building at 152 West Forty-Second Street. This FBI facility masqueraded as an Abwehr office that, in turn, was masquerading as a research center, and the bureau's technicians had bugged it. At this special facility, hidden film cameras and microphones recorded eighty-one spy meetings in all.

The FBI helped Sebold set up the shortwave broadcasting facility the Abwehr had requested. As information came in from spies, it was encoded and transmitted in messages to Hamburg. Following standard practice, encryption followed key words selected from a literary work, in this case Rachel Field's novel *All This, and Heaven Too*. A breathless best seller, it featured such lines as "'Paris—Paris—Paris,' her pulse beat over and over."[9]

As an additional security measure, the Abwehr had familiarized itself with Sebold's "fisting" signature. Like every code operator, Sebold had individual idiosyncrasies in tapping out messages. The FBI realized this and had its own man, Morris H. Price, learn how to mimic Sebold's fisting style. Thus, the bureau was able to send out disinformation. By April 1941 Friedrich Busch (not to be confused with Canaris's alias) was in charge of the Abwehr's American espionage in Berlin, where he received spy reports forwarded from Hamburg. He was convinced that Sebold was "controlled," noticing, for example, that Sebold had sent a report on US aircraft engine production based on 1939 figures, when its output was one-twentieth of what it had achieved by 1941. Busch claimed nobody listened to him, and both the case officers and the Luftwaffe hierarchy insisted on taking the US disinformation at face value. Though the United States was still at peace, the FBI was successfully using deception techniques that mirrored those being used by the warring British and Germans.[10]

By the end of June 1941, the FBI feared that members of the spy ring would resort to sabotage. For example, Fritz Duquesne proposed to Sebold the bombing of St. James Episcopal Church, President Roosevelt's place of worship in Hyde Park. While the policy of watch and deceive had much to commend it, acts of terrorism could not be tolerated. The FBI prepared to pounce. Its agents arrested thirty-three spies, and this time there would be no escapes. All the spies were kept in custody until the trial.

Compared with the 1938 case, the result at first sight looked good. This was partly because the FBI adopted a more prudent indictment policy. It did not charge untouchable members of the German spy hierarchy, nor did it indict lesser agents who lived abroad and could not be arrested. According to one tabulation, in addition to the thirty-three arrestees, there were a further thirty-seven "unindicted Duquesne ring coconspirators," making seventy spies in all. The extra thirty-seven ranged from Nikolaus Ritter to minor field agents across the globe. Had all thirty-seven of these extras been indicted, the FBI's arrest rate would have been a more modest thirty-three detained out of a total of seventy.

Disregarding such niceties, Hoover announced that the FBI had achieved the "greatest round-up of its kind in the nation's history," adding that "this is one of the most active, extensive, and vicious groups we have ever had to deal with." Officials made an effort to paint Duquesne as a dangerous spymaster. The media dutifully made various references to the betrayal of US military secrets to Germany. The greatest news story was, however, the delayed revelation about Lang's theft of the Norden bomb-sight. This event had occurred four years earlier, before the engagement of Duquesne and prior to the 1938 fiasco that had prompted a renewal of the Abwehr's efforts in the States.[11]

The Pearl Harbor attack of December 7, 1941, was significant for the Duquesne case in two ways. First, as it occurred before sentencing, it may have affected the punishments meted out. Lilly Stein—a minor figure and little more than a "Viennese prostitute," according to Hoover—received a sentence of ten years, a much harsher punishment than that handed to Johanna Hofmann in the 1938 trial.[12] Everett Roeder's sentence was six-teen years. Lang received eighteen years, and so did Duquesne. Nations at war do not treat espionage lightly.

Second, Pearl Harbor and the US entry to the war stripped the case of its potential significance as an opinion shaper. The spy ring of 1938 had helped galvanize Americans' opinions on Nazi Germany. The spy ring of 1941 did not. Because Pearl Harbor, and Hitler's declaration of war on the United States in its wake, had a definitive impact on opinion, no spy case could make Americans angrier than they already were.

Thus, the political impact of the so-called Duquesne case was one of history's what-might-have-beens. But it did raise another question: What made a few dozen German Americans betray the United States? In a way, that is the wrong question. For in spite of the high profile of the German spies, of the German Bund activities, and of the alleged German fifth col-umn in the United States, the great majority of German Americans were loyal US citizens. *Confessions of a Nazi Spy* had made this point. In one of the movie's opening scenes, Dr. Karl Kassel (a fictionalized Dr. Ignatz Griebl) harangues an American Nazi meeting. He is in military uniform, most of the other men are wearing Nazi headgear, and swastikas adorn the room. Kassel rants against racial equality, demanding that the coun-try must be "our America." A member of the audience rises to interrupt the proceedings. It is one of the movie's powerful moments. Hatless and dressed in his ordinary best clothes, the man protests, "But we German Americans are not like that."

This became evident once America entered the war. A short list of US military leaders of German heritage—Eisenhower, Carl Spaatz, and Chester Nimitz—makes the point in one way. To offer another perspective, during World War II thirty-three thousand men who fought in the US Army were born in Germany, and fourteen thousand of them were not yet American citizens. German exiles also fought in the US armed forces and served in the OSS.[13]

In Germany itself, opposition was extremely risky, yet Allen Dulles of the OSS, who had the job of cultivating the opposition, estimated that around 10 percent of the Abwehr was hostile to Hitler.[14] The Bendlerblock, the building complex on Berlin's Landwehr Canal that housed the German military command, supplied a mini illustration of how resistance and repression occurred. The July 20, 1944, plot to assassinate Hitler was hatched in the building, and its perpetrators were executed in one of its courtyards. Admiral Canaris, whose office remained in the Bendlerblock's Abwehr suite until bomb damage prompted a move to the Zossen bunkers, was later executed for shielding the plotters. Today, the Bendlerblock (controversially) houses a section of the Ministry of Defense. But it also accommodates the German Resistance Memorial Center dedicated to showing that even under repressive Nazi rule some brave Germans resisted Hitler. On the other side of the Atlantic, that resistance was the norm.

Looking at why certain individuals spied, it is true that German Americans often felt uncomfortable in their adopted land. In both the 1938 and the 1941 episodes, the spies were predominantly first-generation immigrants to the United States; in the latter case, twenty-eight of the thirty-three arrestees were US citizens, but only one of them was not born in Germany. A decade later, Oscar Handlin (a historian of Russian Jewish heritage) wrote of the alienation that first-generation immigrants suffered. With their different ways and manner of speaking, they met with hostility. While some American racist theorists postulated the superiority of Teutonic nations, which included Germany, others narrowed their preference to the English-speaking nations, making outsiders of German immigrants.[15]

The vast majority of German Americans overcame these difficulties. The tiny minority of German Americans who did succumb to their feelings of alienation and spied tended to be bitter about the 1919 peace settlement, with its imposition of humiliating terms on Germany. Typically they had fought in the 1914–18 war, felt robbed of both victory and justice, and found inspiration in the rhetoric of Hitler, who promised to restore German pride.

A good number of them had experienced identity confusion not just while in the United States but also before they left Germany. Secret agents, of whatever nationality, tend to act out a process of splitting. They can live double lives, just like a person who is unfaithful to a spouse (as many of the spies were).[16] Several of the spies discussed in the foregoing pages came from borderlands such as East Prussia and Alsace, where identity confusion and split loyalties were endemic.

It is notable, too, that the Abwehr's agents who operated in the United States came from lower-middle-class backgrounds. The prize catch for the Abwehr was a machinist who understood military technology. As for the couriers, they were hairdressers or ship stewards. All this was evident not only in 1938 but also in 1941: six of the later arrestees were mechanical engineers, and eleven of them worked on ships. While the role of social status has been a matter for debate, the weight of historical evidence supports the popular view that Hitler typically drew his followers from the lower middle classes. The typical Hitlerites belonged to a place in society that made them resent both the working class, with its socialist tendency, and the traditional ruling elite. The agents who served in the United States had a social status that made them just such Hitler supporters—unlike the officers who controlled them and unlike the better-educated German émigrés who hated the führer.[17]

Loyal to the United States though the great majority of German immigrants were, the presence among them of potential traitors offered a special opportunity to the Abwehr. Against this background, it was a credit to the FBI that its special agents succeeded in neutralizing both the 1938 and the 1941 spy rings. The occasional potent microdot must have gotten through, but the FBI appears to have effectively snuffed out the Abwehr's operations against the United States after 1938.

The bureau continued to reap the reward of fame—for example, through a new movie. *The House on 92nd Street* (1945) was to the 1941 spying episode as *Confessions of a Nazi Spy* had been to its 1938 precursor. The former's plot was about the 1941 unraveling of the Ritter-Lang story of 1937. It was recognizably about the theft of the Norden bombsight's plans but updated to appeal to end-of-war concerns about spies potentially stealing US atomic bomb secrets. The substitution of the bomb for the bombsight reflected the realities of 1945. As noted in chapter 17, Udo von Bonin did dispatch Alfred Meiler to Manhattan with hopes of obtaining information on US nuclear physics.[18]

The 1941 arrests may not have been significant politically, but Berlin still reacted angrily to them. The German authorities dismissed the architect of the ring, Major Ritter, and dissolved his section of the Hamburg branch of the Abwehr.[19] Ritter subsequently served in ground-to-air flak artillery units in Sicily and Italy, and in April 1945 he surrendered to Allied troops in the Harz Mountains in northern Germany. His days in intelligence were a fading memory.[20]

19

PFEIFFER'S STORY

It was April 21, 1945, a spring day in the Aegean. An eleven-thousand-tonne steamship eased its way out of the Dardanelles and headed for the wider reaches of the Mediterranean. Capt. John Nordlander did not want the ship mistaken for a combatant. Its name, *Drottningholm*, appeared in very large letters on its white-painted hull, along with the words "Sveridge" (Sweden) and "Diplomat."

It does not take too much imagination to picture a cluster of individuals who gazed at the receding Turkish coastline while engaged in desultory talk. A casual observer might have noted among them a hulking figure of military bearing. We know that Erich Pfeiffer stood more than six feet tall and weighed 210 pounds. His head was large, even for one who was so strongly built. He had a crop of fair, graying hair, a small mouth, and a jutting chin. A scar ran down his left cheek to the nostril of his long, straight nose. He had the disconcerting habit of standing on one foot while talking, then swinging away, and gazing into space when someone tried to reply.[1]

Down below, Pfeiffer's copious luggage pointed to a person of substance and to a man who was unusually well prepared for travel. It consisted of three suitcases, a kit bag, and a brief case. Pearl cuff links, gray kid gloves, silk shorts, and a bottle of scent hinted at the voyager's extracurricular interests. There was a white metal star with a swastika in the middle. And money. Pfeiffer had US dollars, Swiss francs, Swedish kroner, Turkish lira, and smaller amounts of currency from the Netherlands, Denmark, Portugal, France, Greece, and Yugoslavia.[2]

The voyager's luggage had not traveled for a while. Pfeiffer had spent the last few months confined to the German Consulate's compound in

Istanbul. His cover job had been the deputy naval attaché until August 1944, when Turkey broke off diplomatic relations with Germany and interned that nation's diplomatic staff. Unable to leave the compound, he whiled away the time learning to play bridge and, being an ambitious man, waited for word from Berlin about the promotion he felt was his due. By this stage in the war, Berlin had other matters to consider, and Pfeiffer waited in vain.

Having left Turkey, he hoped the quiet hum of the *Drottningholm*'s steam turbine engines would serenade his return home. On May 1 the steamer berthed at Lisbon, where Pfeiffer made two trips ashore. Portugal was a conservative dictatorship; though it had been neutral in the war, he remembered the days when Germany had intelligence assets on the banks of the Tagus. His agent Karl Eitel, formerly of the US run, had operated there during the war until he was recalled to Bremen in May 1944. Perhaps Pfeiffer did not realize that early in 1944 Eitel's Lisbon landlord had informed on him to the OSS, which recruited him as a "diver," or a double agent. Thereafter, Eitel fed British and American "chicken feed" and disinformation to his Abwehr spy bosses.

Lisbon was no longer a reliable outpost of German intelligence. Nevertheless, our voyager requested orders from Berlin. None was forthcoming. Hitler had just killed himself, and his capital city was about to fall. Resigned to his fate and suspecting, as he put it, that "the British would pick [him] up," Pfeiffer continued his voyage on the *Drottningholm*. A few days later, the ship docked at Merseyside for military inspection, or "control."[3]

As he must have foreseen, Pfeiffer was at this juncture "rerouted." He traveled from Liverpool to an establishment called Camp 020. Situated in Latchmere House, a barbwire-surrounded Victorian mansion near Richmond on the outskirts of London, the camp was a secret interrogation center run by the British Security Service. It came to be celebrated for MI5's recruitment of double agents, perhaps most famously Eddie Chapman, who was known to the Abwehr as Fritzchen and to his British controllers as Zigzag. A monocled half-German colonel, Robin "Tin Eye" Stephens, presided over an outfit that had quizzed 480 spies and other prisoners in the course of the war. Stephens later survived a court-martial, having been charged for the brutality of his interrogation techniques. He banned the use of violence, but his interrogators did use psychological techniques such as silence, head bagging, bright lights, and sleep deprivation.

Tin Eye also had at his disposal another way of concentrating prisoners' minds that was a consequence of wartime legislation. Early in the conflict, Parliament had passed the Treachery Act. The law on treason had hitherto applied to British citizens and was medieval; its 1351 enactment prescribed death for whoever warred or plotted against the king. Revised in 1534, it targeted religious dissenters. One of its victims was the Catholic Guy Fawkes, who was condemned to hang in 1606 for plotting to blow up the House of Lords. The act's 1940 revision, a reaction to the Tyler Kent affair, had stimulated a debate in the House of Commons, with members questioning the efficacy of the death penalty and expressing doubt about enemy military personnel being "handed over and shot" whether they were in uniform or not.[4] The bill that received royal assent on May 23, 1940, enabled trials for treason—which could result in execution—of non-British as well as British "traitors." In the course of the war, the British authorities executed sixteen persons convicted under the new Treachery Act. For example, Charles Albert van den Kieboom, a Dutchman who spied for Germany, was hanged in Pentonville Prison on December 17, 1940, after he resisted efforts to force him to become a double agent.

Camp 020 produced fourteen of the unfortunates known as "the unlucky sixteen" who were executed for infringement of the Treason Act. Three of them were Germans, men who were still deemed "treasonous" despite the fact that their country was at war with Britain. There was uncertainty about who was to be executed and why. The uncertainty must have been terrifying for Camp 020's inmates, who can only have thought of themselves as subject to the whims of Tin Eye and his fellow MI5 officers.[5]

By the time Pfeiffer arrived in Camp 020, the war in Europe was over, but British and American interrogators were still at work. They were turning their minds to the prosecution of Nazis for war crimes. They had other reasons, too, for continuing. Though currently allied to the United States and Britain, the Soviet Union with its newfound military might was emerging as a potent threat to democracy. So Germans with knowledge about the Soviet military could be helpful. Indeed, the Americans recruited and made an ally of Reinhard Gehlen, who had been the Reich's senior intelligence official on the eastern front. From 1956 to 1968 Gehlen would head the Bundesnachrichtendienst (Federal Intelligence Service, or BND), the Abwehr's peacetime successor. Camp 020 interrogators anticipated Germany would revive its intelligence activity after the war. They wanted to know more about the Abwehr not just out of curiosity about a former foe but also because it would be good to know about one's future friends.

How did Pfeiffer come to be an inmate of Camp 020? Its accounts of how this happened vary. One version holds that Pfeiffer was loyal to his country to the last. The officer who wrote up a conclusion after Pfeiffer's interrogation saw him as a "good and loyal German," while Pfeiffer's own account suggests he waited passively in captivity until the arrival of the *Drottningholm*.[6] Quite another version appears in 020 correspondence. It indicates that the exterminator sent to deal with the "rats leaving sinking ship" joined them.[7] As soon as Turkey broke off diplomatic relations with Germany, Pfeiffer had approached an OSS intermediary with a view to going over to the Americans.[8]

The British objected to the proposal that Pfeiffer should become an OSS asset. They felt Turkey fell within their sphere of influence. They furthermore charged that the Americans were less well equipped to interrogate Pfeiffer. Some Americans did feel that they could learn from the interrogation techniques used in Camp 020. General Bedell Smith of US Army intelligence, the former employer of Leon Turrou who would serve as a future director of the CIA, had visited the camp and arranged for US personnel to study its methods. This fed into a British superiority complex: when people show a willingness to learn from you, it is all too tempting to believe that they know less than you do.[9]

Pressing the British case, an MI5 representative wrote to MI6's Aubrey Jones and insisted that Pfeiffer's fount of knowledge could "be more suitably tapped by interrogation at 020." Stressing the urgency of a proper resolution, he added, "If they wish him sent to the United States, he should be routed via the United Kingdom." Jones accordingly got in touch with Robert D. Murphy, a career diplomat who had worked closely with the late president Franklin D. Roosevelt and for General Eisenhower. At this time, US forces were swamped with offers of surrender by Germans who wanted at all costs to avoid falling into the hands of vengeful Russians, Czechs, and others. From the US viewpoint, handing over some cases to the British must have seemed an attractive proposition. Murphy acceded to the British request for jurisdiction in Pfeiffer's case and lobbied OSS director Bill Donovan. So Camp 020 got its man.[10]

That did not spell the end of the Americans' interest. Back in 1942, the British had agreed with the OSS's Whitney Shepardson to share the benefits of interrogation.[11] In 1945 they responded to each other just as they had in the preceding three years: the FBI sent 020 its own report on Pfeiffer and a list of questions he should be asked; 020's interim report on Pfeiffer went to the US Embassy; and a copy of the report found its way back to 020 bearing notations in US diction (for example, "fall" as opposed to "autumn"), indicating that an American official had taken the trouble to read it carefully.

Appendix III to 020's Pfeiffer report was of special interest to the FBI. It contained the German spymaster's detailed, page-by-page commentary titled "Observations by PHEIFFER on 'THE NAZI SPY CONSPIRACY IN AMERICA' by Leon G. Turrou, London Edition (George G. Harrop & Co., 1939)." In his commentary, Pfeiffer gave his interpretation of how his spy ring had operated in the United States. He rejected the account rendered in the book by the FBI's crack detective. First, he objected to Turrou's use of the term "Nazi" to describe the German spy "conspiracy" of the 1930s. Next, he accused Ignatz Griebl of issuing "wild fabrications" and Turrou of being "absolutely rotten" in testifying to the veracity of Griebl's comments on "high-placed German personalities."

He then denied helping the Griebls sequester Jewish property. Pfeiffer's commentary found its way into the FBI's counterintelligence files.[12]

MI5 may have had to share its secrets, but Pfeiffer was still a prize catch, as he knew the Abwehr inside out. Yet what about his character and reliability? His reputation had preceded him in a dubious manner, for Karl Eitel had expressed his opinions on his former boss. In September 1944 with the Allied invasion in full swing, the Free French had detained Eitel just outside Nancy and handed him over to the US Army's Counter Intelligence Corps for questioning. Interrogator Oliver Burglund noted that Eitel had been born in the Alsatian community of Mulhouse (in German, Mülhausen). Mulhouse had witnessed heroic scenes of French resistance, and its inhabitants insisted that they spoke an *autonomous* version of the German language.[13] But it was also an area of disputed loyalties, which were replicated in the personal life of Karl Eitel. His mother was French, his father German. His mistress in Brest, Marie Cann, had been French, but his wife, Magda, was German. Burgland concluded Eitel's story, about being a French patriot who had worked against Germany at every opportunity, had "several outstanding weaknesses." He determined Eitel should be sent to London for further investigation, and if his "story is not proved, he should be executed."[14]

Skeptical and taking heed of his claim to have worked with the OSS in Portugal, MI5 decided to treat Eitel "with a velvet glove." Facing death, the double agent decided to distance himself from his espionage escapades for Pfeiffer, whom he described as a "complete egotist, ambitious, unscrupulous."[15] Transferred to 020's custody, he continued in that vein, but he also made some remarks that were indirectly helpful to Pfeiffer. For example, Eitel inadvertently assisted what would be Pfeiffer's defense—that is, he had not been in control of what Hamburg was doing—when he said that Pfeiffer had been furious with him for dealing with Lonkowski, insisting that Lonkowski was being run from Hamburg. Further, according to Eitel, Pfeiffer insisted that Lonkowski should deal only with his own agents; it was a cardinal principle of good intelligence. Another of his remarks potentially helped Pfeiffer at a time when captured German officers were desperately trying to establish that they never had been Nazis: contrasting his former employer with Griebl, who was "a fanatical Nazi," Eitel said that Pfeiffer was "too much of an egotist to be interested in politics."[16]

When Pfeiffer arrived from Istanbul five months later, 020's interrogators at last had the opportunity of assessing the master spy who had been Leon Turrou's principal opponent. They were in awe of him. They reported that he had the "doubtful distinction of world-wide notoriety as a spy master" and realized that Pfeiffer indeed had a deep fund of knowledge about secret intelligence. 020 further noted that Pfeiffer was a "superior" type and a "snob." These personality traits helped explain his deep resentment of the disdain with which the German hierarchy had treated the Abwehr over the past decade. 020 concluded Pfeiffer was "never a nazi."[17]

When Colonel Stephens wrote a final report on his unit's activities, his prejudices were evident. He admired Pfeiffer and despised his manservant in equal measure. The manservant Pfeiffer had been allowed in captivity was none other than Karl Eitel. He may have chosen him on the grounds of familiarity or, very possibly, to save him from the gallows, as a prosecutor might have taken the line that Eitel was a Frenchman who had spied for Germany. Stephens had an ominously low estimation of a person who was short, fat, and of indifferent social standing. In a potentially lethal opinion, he judged Eitel as "a bad spy, a bad German, and a bad man" who had enjoyed "a long run for his unearned Abwehr money." Tin Eye fondly recalled the occasion when Eitel ventured an opinion, and Pfeiffer told him to stick to the things he was good at, "cooking and scrounging." To Tin Eye's evident delight, Eitel "winced and wept and whimpered a sycophantic 'Ja mein Kapitän.'" The class-conscious Stephens made no attempt to disguise his perception of superior qualities in a prize captive: "PHEIFFER could never be wrong."[18]

Pfeiffer took a line and got away with it. He denied that he was a Nazi and that those who spied on the United States under his aegis were part of a Nazi spy ring. Also he rejected Turrou's idea that he was a master spy who pulled all the strings regarding the espionage effort against the United States. Yes, he had administered Lonkowski, but Lonkowski was "an agent of Berlin."[19] He did not originate the Kate Moog–Mata Hari plan, nor did he connive in the expropriation of Jewish property. His close associate Eitel, he maintained, never had any Gestapo connections. He disclaimed responsibility for the Crown correspondence and thus for both the McAlpin kidnapping-murder plot and the passport application forms scam. Instead, he tied these escapades to rogue fanatics who were out to please the party hierarchy and who answered not to Bremen but to Hamburg or to Berlin directly.

According to Pfeiffer, the villain of the piece was Karl Schlueter. Though admittedly one of Pfeiffer's agents, Schlueter was a maverick with Gestapo connections. In plotting extreme endeavors to ingratiate himself with the party and Abwehr hierarchies, he had committed a breach of security in using one of Pfeiffer's own code names, Spielman. The mysterious Spielman who had briefed Rumrich and Hofmann was then Schlueter and not Pfeiffer, as Turrou had supposed. Schlueter as a Bremen agent had poached Rumrich from the Hamburg Abwehr station, whose asset, so Pfeiffer claimed, he was supposed to be. By contravening the Abwehr's security procedures in these ways, Schlueter had contributed to the 1938 debacle and had given Pfeiffer's spy program a bad name that it did not deserve.[20]

Clearly at least some of his interlocutors saw that Pfeiffer, despite his self-exculpations, was an opportunist and a fellow traveler with the Nazis, but the interrogators were dazzled by the information he chose to divulge. So well informed was he, that, in the words of his interrogators, the "exhaustion of PHEIFFER's encyclopedic knowledge of the Abwehr and its personalities defies the very attempt." He passed on his knowledge in large, if not exhaustive, quantities. For example, he supplied mini biographies of 438 German spies with whom he had been in contact. His interrogators did realize that Pfeiffer held some things back, sometimes "by design," but they concluded that he talked well, perhaps because his country was no longer at war.[21]

020 interrogators were able to piece together, for the first time, the story of Pfeiffer's life and espionage activities. The narrative illustrated that, by and large, Pfeiffer succeeded in his spying efforts. His successes

elsewhere threw his failures in the States into relief and underlined the impressiveness of Leon Turrou's achievement in combating his German rival. Some of the German's successes predated the disaster of 1938, and others occurred through World War II. Pfeiffer claimed that his methods improved because of his tussle with the FBI. "It was his principle that neither agents nor officers should know more of each others activities and interests than was necessary for the execution of their assignments; the American lesson had not been lost on him."[22]

Pfeiffer's European operations were successful. In 1936 he took on Marc Aubert, a French naval officer who had offered his services to the German attaché in Paris. At their first meeting, Aubert was indiscreet. He turned up with a woman he introduced as his wife, but "she was the type of wife to whom the French refer between quotes." Pfeiffer was in no position to preach on such matters, and when Aubert delivered a package of secret documents that weighed fully ninety-five pounds, he became an enthusiast in spite of his contemptuous view that Aubert was a "born traitor" and in it for the money.

The traitor continued to be a "gold mine" until 1938. In that "calamitous" year for Pfeiffer, the French and British services tracked spy correspondence that was going through a poste restante address in Dublin. They identified Aubert and played him back as a double agent. Pfeiffer saw through the play-back, realized that the French authorities had identified Aubert as a traitor, and knew it was just a matter of time before they arrested his agent. He told his interrogators he was so upset about Aubert's likely fate that he told his wife, Lotte, to cancel the family's New Year party planned for January 1, 1939. He was also fearful of Berlin's reaction to Aubert's demise. In the event, Canaris received the news with his usual aplomb, saying that two undetected years was a good run for a spy in Aubert's risky position. For all his professions of grief, Pfeiffer basked in the rays of Canaris's approval. The venal Aubert was less fortunate. In March 1939 he met his death in front of a Toulon firing squad.[23]

After the war began, Canaris entrusted Pfeiffer with intelligence and counterintelligence responsibilities in France. The former Bremen station chief found himself in charge of the Abwehr station in Brest, the seaport in the Celtic province of Brittany, with the mission of gathering intelligence on Britain and France. A few of his Bremen staff had traveled with him, including his mistress-secretary and another familiar culprit, Karl Eitel.

Eitel did not contribute to Pfeiffer's success story. In the summer of 1940, Pfeiffer learned that Breton fishermen were sailing beyond the limit prescribed for them by the German authorities and communicating with the British. He turned for help to Eitel, who spoke French and, as a former wine steward on a German ship, claimed he knew how to handle sailors. Pfeiffer requisitioned the forty-five-tonne *Breiza Isel Arvor* and gave the boat and a scratch crew to Eitel to patrol the Atlantic approaches. This and similar missions met with indifferent success. The Celtic name of their boat suggests that Eitel's crew may well have spoken their own language, and the Breton workers had no time for the Alsatian-accented Karl Eitel.[24] They stole maritime equipment, engaged in "go-slow" laboring, and concealed Allied agents.

In 1940 Pfeiffer played a more constructive role when he took part in preliminary planning for the invasion of Britain dubbed Operation Sealion. Ever since his days in Wilhemshaven, he had been an authority on maritime logistics. Now he concluded the invasion scheme was impractical. He believed the Germans simply did not have enough ships and troop barges to do the job. His findings were among those that percolated upward, and on June 20 the navy chief, Adm. Erich Raeder, informed Hitler that Germany lacked the maritime capacity to transport an army across the English Channel. The Luftwaffe nevertheless attempted to prepare the way by asserting its air supremacy in what came to be known as the Battle of Britain (July–August 1940) but lost. The survival of the Royal Air Force's strike capacity meant that even with an adequate fleet, an invasion would have been hazardous. In a minor way, by pointing to the armada's inadequacy, Pfeiffer contributed to the wise German decision to cancel Operation Sealion.[25]

In March 1942 Pfeiffer moved to Paris and undertook work against the French Resistance. This time only one survivor of his Bremen staff accompanied him—Hilde Gersdorf. They lived together at Rue St. James in Neuilly, using the surname Kross. 020 staff noted that when an Allied bomb hit his home in Bremen, causing Lotte to lose one eye, Pfeiffer managed only a five-day visit to comfort her and his children, and to move the family to a safer location in Siegen, Westphalia. His interests lay elsewhere. Paperwork consumed more and more of his time, and, he told 020, he had pined for command of a fighting ship.

Pfeiffer at that time worried about the penetration of the Abwehr by Heydrich's Sicherheitsdienst (Security Service, or SD), an outfit with a terrifying reputation. Perhaps with his own safety in mind, he told his 020 interrogators that he had scruples about interrogation methods. His role model, Max Ronge, had interrogated prisoners of war without "invasive methods," arguing that the offer of a cigarette or a glass of wine at the right psychological moment could produce miracles, especially when combined with *rumors* of torture. Ronge's disciple told his Camp 020 questioners that he had resisted political pressure to employ "special methods to make a man talk . . . drugs, rays or hypnotists."[26]

Not long after taking over in Paris, Pfeiffer said, he "was summoned to Berlin to meet 'The Knights of the Green Table'—the supreme chiefs at HQ."[27] The reference calls to mind the ideal of medieval chivalry as conveyed, for example, in the anonymous poem *Sir Gawain and the Green Knight* (circa 1400). More recently, Kurt Jooss had developed in 1932 a macabre theme in his ballet *The Green Table: A Dance of Death in Eight Scenes.* The Essen-based choreographer opened and closed the piece by depicting the futility of peace negotiations with diplomats seated around regulation-green baize tables. He pointed to the inevitability of militarism and death without endorsing the philosophy of Nazism.

Whatever one makes of the image, the skies were closing in on those who struggled to keep the Abwehr professional and military in purpose. The Nazi political squeeze continued until, in February 1944, Himmler persuaded Hitler to abolish the agency and give its functions over to the Ausland-SD, the party's foreign intelligence wing. Canaris was arrested for having plotted against the führer that July. A few weeks before the war's end, he went on trial in Flossenbürg concentration camp, was stripped naked, and, within earshot of approaching Allied artillery, hanged.

Pfeiffer had operated out of Berlin since mid-May 1943. His desk diary reveals that over the next twelve months he traveled all over Europe performing his new supervisory duties. In May 1944, four months after the axing of the Abwehr, the same source indicates that he awaited the urgent delivery of a Turkish entry visa. Berlin had ordered Pfeiffer to restore German intelligence in Turkey, where three agents had defected to the Allies. At this point, Pfeiffer welcomed the prospect of a break. His health was deteriorating, his mentor was under suspicion, what remained of his cherished Abwehr had been rehoused in a section of the Reich's politicized bureaucracy, and the war was going badly. He told his mistress to pack her bags, for the ever-obliging Fraulein Gersdorf would accompany him. She could not have foreseen that within a year, her lover would desert her for the bachelor confinements of Camp 020.[28]

On October 9, 1945, after he had spent four months in Camp 020, the British authorities allowed Pfeiffer to leave. Under escort and in company with eight other recent inmates of 020, he went to Croydon Airport.[29] Their airplane took off for Germany. As it soared to cruising altitude, Pfeiffer no doubt turned his mind to a coming reunification with his family or what remained of it. At least he had remembered to repack his bottle of scent.[30]

Perhaps as he stared into space, as was his wont, or gazed down at the receding mists of London and then at the infernal English Channel, which had not since the sixth century yielded to German invaders, his recollections flickered for a moment over the time when he was in charge of great ventures in Abwehr Bremen. Yes, he had seen setbacks in the course of his work there. But according to what he told the British, his failures had sprung from political interference by zealots on his own side. He held firmly to his delusions that Leon Turrou was a naïf and that the Americans had never outwitted him.[31]

20
DIPLOMATIC FALLOUT

Foreign attempts to infiltrate or manipulate the United States have always run the risk of counterproductive consequences. It was thus in the 1790s, when Citizen Genêt plotted to entangle the United States in revolutionary France's war with England. Edmond Genêt succeeded only in provoking a distinct antipathy toward the French, an antipathy that later governed the actions of President John Adams's Federalist administration. It was thus in the 1940s, when Soviet espionage produced a hostile reaction. (So did the spying efforts of Wen Ho Lee on behalf of China in the 1990s.) These cases helped turn American opinion and American policy against the perpetrators. Similarly, the 1938 revelation that Germany was stealing US military secrets helped recast viewpoints in the United States and helped reshape the nation's foreign relations.

The shift in opinion affected not just US policy but also the attitude of Germany's diplomats. If the 1938 spy revelations caught America's champions of neutrality off guard, Berlin's emissaries were just as dismayed. It was not like the corresponding period of US neutrality in World War I, when the embassy in Washington had run Germany's spies. No, the agents of the Hitler regime had reported directly to their homeland controllers and, until trouble brewed, the denizens of the embassy on Massachusetts Avenue remained blissfully ignorant.

The spy revelations were a shock because a misleading impression had gained ground in the embassy and beyond. The notion had taken root that Germany, America's enemy in 1917–18, had since that war won a measure of sympathy and even affection. With Wall Street in bad odor following the 1929 crash and in the ensuing Great Depression, opinion turned against financiers and arms manufacturers, whom "isolationists" now accused of having dragged the United States into World War I. Historians and others further argued that Germany had been badly treated in the postwar settlement; its punitive terms imposed the payment of reparations that had effectively stimulated hyperinflation in the new German republic, causing a loss of faith in democracy and the rise of Hitler. A concomitant feeling was that the whole issue of Germany's war guilt should be revisited. All this looked good for German-American relations. Then came the spy ring scandal, which threatened to reverse the trend.[1]

The perceived impact of the revelations on domestic opinion rocked the complacency of Germany's diplomats. In January 1938, when new in his post, Ambassador Dieckhoff had warned that the Bund's activities were causing a decline in Americans' regard for Germany.[2] Just after that, the first spy arrests occurred. By that fall, the ambassador's monthslong efforts to limit the fallout from the arrests seemed doomed to failure. Undersecretary of State Sumner Welles remarked, in the wake of a conversation, that the envoy was "in a distinctly emotional and nervous condition."[3]

The meeting between Dieckhoff and Welles was tense. The ambassador tried for a whole hour to justify Germany's policies of expansion, and he complained about criticisms of his country in the American press. Welles replied that the American press was critical because Germany's treatment of Jews was intolerable. He added that the German press was just as hostile to the United States, with the difference being that it was ordered to take this line, whereas the American press was free.

"Finally," Welles recorded, "I said the trial of alleged German spies now going on in New York . . . had deeply incensed public opinion in the United States and would continue to arouse the deepest indignation." This worried Dieckhoff. He knew that Welles was a confidant of the president's. He felt personally vulnerable, as the press had linked his name to Theodore Schuetz, the spy who had escaped via Havana. Dieckhoff told Welles he had nothing to do with the spy ring and that the German War Department, Foreign Office, and intelligence service "had all been completely ignorant of any activities of this kind." He admitted the spies were likely to be found guilty but asserted they had received their orders "from persons of lesser authority in Germany who were acting on their own initiative without orders from the top."[4]

Dieckhoff's remarks could be regarded as a common diplomatic response to a situation where spies from one's country have been exposed. To explain away one's secret agents as rogue elements is a standard cover-up. In this particular case, though, there is a hint of tragedy. It seems likely that Germany's envoys had not been briefed but were aware that covert operations were under way. While uncomfortable, the best they could do was to speak in a coded language. Dieckhoff's "persons of lesser authority" might be a reference to Nazi Party functionaries. As has so often been the case, the prudent course of action is to blame a ruler's advisers—in this case, Hitler's party officials—and not the ruler himself.

Soon after his meeting with Welles, Dieckhoff was summoned to Germany. The abrupt termination of his mission was only indirectly connected with the spy case. It was Berlin's response to President Roosevelt's recall of Hugh R. Wilson, the US ambassador to Germany, for "consultation." Wilson had made the mistake of expressing admiration for Hitler at an unfortunate moment. At the time, the Kristallnacht and other anti-Semitic atrocities were occurring in Germany, and the spy scandal was in full spate in the States. Dieckhoff's recall, then, was for a number of reasons. That he was never replaced by a person with ambassadorial rank, however, reflected a chill that emanated at least in part from the spy scandal and its continuing reverberations.

A month after his return to Germany, Dieckhoff warned his government that Wilson's recall might well herald a complete break of diplomatic relations. He said that would be a disaster, as it would give President Roosevelt a reason for spending "billions" on the US military under the pretext that a German attack was imminent. Given what he described as the subjective approach of American judges, the "political trials" taking place in New York were going to result in convictions. The American press had already taken an anti-German stance, and the US government would seize the opportunity for further propaganda in the wake of the inevitable guilty verdicts.[5]

With Dieckhoff detained in Europe, the embassy's counselor, Hans Thomsen, took over as Germany's representative but with the lower rank of chargé d'affaires. One of his first actions was to arrange for securer delivery of confidential letters, telegraphs, and "secret political files"; the US Postal Service was no longer to be trusted. It was a response to fears that the United States would tighten its counterintelligence measures.[6]

In May 1940 Thomsen found a new reason to complain to the Foreign Office in Berlin. He asserted that Germany's secret agents were still at large and a real problem. They were using methods that might be justified in times of war but could not be defended in peacetime, and while Europe was by this time at war, the United States was not. He said the source of his information about German undercover activities was a one-legged agent called Bergmann, who reported that a Major Osten was directing him to conduct sabotage operations in the United States. The agent had obeyed orders and had already caused an explosion in a munitions factory and had sunk a ship at a Baltimore pier. In spite of his complicity therein, Bergmann believed these operations to be counterproductive. Thomsen wrote, "It was his opinion that when his activities were discovered, America's entry into the war would be inevitable."[7]

Foreign Affairs State Secretary Ernst von Weizsäcker later confirmed that an agent with the alias Bergmann existed. He claimed the agent worked only in counterintelligence but, as a precaution, ordered his repatriation. However, Thomsen and his military attachés agreed with Bergmann's view. In a memorandum on which Germany's foreign minister Joachim von Ribbentrop scrawled "For the Führer," Thomsen declared that his main task was to keep the United States out of the war, but the reckless deeds of secret agents "are the surest way of bringing America into action on the side of our enemies and of destroying the last vestiges of sympathy for Germany."[8]

Thomsen was not entirely out of step with Berlin, for although Hitler regarded the United States as a potentially inconvenient obstacle, he was biding his time. He knew he would have to force western Europe into submission before turning his attention elsewhere. This meant keeping the United States out of the war until such time as he was ready, with

Europe prostrate at his feet and perhaps with Japan ready to strike the country from the rear. His diplomats continued their efforts to maintain friendly relations, and no doubt some of them harbored genuinely good feelings toward the United States.

The diplomatic assessment and stance toward risky espionage enterprises persisted into 1941. When Ribbentrop heard of the Duquesne ring arrests, he told Admiral Canaris he would hold him personally responsible if the latest spy scandal caused the United States to declare war on Germany.[9]

In spite of the ready availability of such evidence, historians have paid scant attention to the impact of the Nazi spy ring case on the US relationship with Germany in the run-up to the former's entry into the war.[10] Diplomatic historians have credited the influence of other spy cases.[11] Yet, in part because of Hoover's obliteration of Turrou from the historical record, the 1938 spy case has not yet featured in discourse on foreign relations.

The omission is all the more striking because there is a growing recognition of the case's impact in other spheres. Indeed, that diversity of impact needs to be acknowledged. First of all, historians have shown how the affair spurred the growth of US counterespionage efforts.[12] Notably that growth had its own, distinctive impact on foreign relations. Boosting intelligence and counterintelligence resources was a way of preparing for future conflicts, and especially when done in collaboration with the British, it was a departure from neutrality.

The spy scandal's likely impact on security policy received contemporary recognition. MI5's Guy Liddell noted in a report dated March–April 1938 that Turrou's "enquiries have been very much of an eye-opener to the State Department, War Department and FBI." He foresaw that the last two in particular would exploit the situation politically by bidding for more power and resources.[13]

Percy Hoskins, the crime correspondent for Britain's *Daily Express*, thought the scandal would accelerate what was an international trend. "War ministries all over Europe and Asia," he claimed, "are watching New York's spy trial, where espionage is having the biggest show-down in twenty years." France was saturated with spies, and in 1938 Britain was spending £550,000 on espionage and counterespionage compared with just £180,000 four years earlier.[14] American journalists agreed that spying was an international threat that called for action, and they plucked figures out of the air to prove their point. The *New York Times* reported in June 1938 that the "European nations alone are now estimated to be spending between $50,000,000 and $80,000,000 annually on spying." The *Los Angeles Times* claimed a year later that ten thousand Nazi spies were at large in Europe and the United States, and it cited a *Paris-soir* report that Germany had ten training schools for spies.[15]

In May 1938 as the Nazi spy case gained momentum, the FBI had announced that because of budgetary pressures it would reduce its force of special agents. In response, President Roosevelt asked Congress to appropriate $108,000 as an emergency measure. Consequently, the number of special agents did not decrease in 1937–38; instead, it rose from 623 to 658. The bureau had 896 agents by 1940.[16]

At the time of the grand jury's indictment of eighteen spies in the summer of 1938, Roosevelt backed an increase in army, navy, and FBI intelligence. US expenditure on military intelligence had declined since the end of World War I, reaching a low in 1937. The numbers of US military attachés in foreign capitals dwindled, and F. H. Lincoln, a G-2 general staff officer, estimated in that year the US government spent only $1.5 million on all its intelligence activities. Compare this, for example, with the United Kingdom's £550,000, which translated as $2.7 million. All this was consistent with the US government's policy of demobilization in the 1920s and neutrality in the 1930s. While Lincoln pointed at the higher expenditure levels in other countries, he did not mention Germany, but he reckoned that Japan spent $12 million and the Soviet Union $10 million on internal security alone.[17]

Alert to the developing danger, President Roosevelt gradually increased expenditures while seeking to avoid confrontation with Germany and his own country's opponents of militarism. He placed his faith in Hoover. The FBI director drew on his celebrated administrative skills to centralize and coordinate, and his bureau looked abroad for help. The tip-off for the McAlpin plot, of course, came from a British agency. In the summer of 1939, France, Britain, and the United States agreed to share data concerning the activities of German and Italian agents. In the following year, with the war under way in Europe, FBI special agents Hugh Clegg and Lawrence Hince traveled to London to study British intelligence arrangements; they sought to learn lessons and establish future cooperation. It would be a stretch to argue all these counterintelligence developments stemmed from the 1938 spy case, but it was the initial spur.[18]

The impact of growing counterintelligence efforts on civil liberties has commanded the attention of historians and has diverted attention from the spy case's erosion of US neutrality. The issue of civil liberties does, of course, merit scrutiny.

According to a widely credited proposition, the FBI's counterintelligence effort promoted the development of a US surveillance state. Through its overzealousness in protecting freedom, so the indictment goes, the FBI was in danger of becoming just like its foe, the Nazi-ridden Abwehr with its Gestapo ally. The charge gained traction at the time of the 1975–76 US Senate's inquiry into intelligence abuses, following revelations about illegal domestic activities by the CIA and other agencies. Testifying in the Senate inquiry, William C. Sullivan, number 3 in the FBI hierarchy in the 1960s, asserted that the techniques of the "Nazi intelligence services" had been "brought home" in the 1930s and were still evident in the bureau's programs.[19] Thirty years after Roosevelt's death, the idea that he had set in motion the machinery of an incipient police state threatened to dent his image as a liberal icon.

At the time, many expressed significant concern. An editorial in the *New York Times* complained in December 1938 that the American people were being subjected to a confidence trick. Anticipating the neglect of the spy case in future years, the editorial poured scorn on the "petty" proceedings of the recent trial. In an age of transparency, there were no real secrets any more, and the German spies had been engaged in a pointless exercise. Building them up into a serious menace was absurd.

The *Times* accepted there might be a need for modest FBI enhancement, but it warned that a "super-espionage" agency or "secret police" was not "wanted or needed here."[20]

In the ensuing months, further complaints arose that the FBI was becoming a menace to civil liberties. When the FBI raided a group of Spanish Loyalist sympathizers in Detroit, the perception was that the bureau was targeting left-leaning anti-fascists. Liberal circles were in an uproar. The *New Republic* was appalled at the FBI's admission that in the predawn operation, its agents smashed doors, illegally seized papers, and refused arrestees access to telephones and to counsel.[21]

Preparing Roosevelt for a press conference in the wake of the 1938 trial, his speechwriters wrote defensive briefing notes on the civil liberties issue. He found a way of saying that the nation needed to boost its counterintelligence capability and that he would give the matter his "personal attention." He added, however, "I don't believe for one moment that we need an OGPU [Soviet secret political police until 1934, when it was incorporated into the NKVD] or GESTAPO, or any other form of secret police organization." Even as he pressed ahead, the president recognized the real concern about the possibility of an American Gestapo developing. At the same time, he tolerated and benefited from political surveillance. For example, his FBI made an unsuccessful attempt to collect dirt on Senator Nye, the prominent champion of neutrality.[22]

Resentment against the expanding remit of the FBI would become a powerful force in politics, especially when the bureau expanded into South America during World War II. It raised the possibility that in the postwar world, just one, all-powerful US intelligence agency would be responsible for both domestic and foreign security. Upon the establishment of the CIA in 1947, Hoover's organization was required to pull out of foreign engagements because of "super-Gestapo" fears.[23]

The argument that the United States was becoming a police state was, however, overstated. By the end of the war, the FBI had 4,370 special agents—one for every 32,037 citizens—compared with the Gestapo's one for every 2,000 people and, in later years, the East German Stasi's one officer for every 175 citizens.[24] Nor can it be argued that the 1938 spy scandal inspired an exceptional swing against civil liberties. Private surveillance—for example, by private detective agencies—was a long-established practice. Questionable government surveillance had already occurred on several previous occasions, such as when J. Edgar Hoover orchestrated the activities of the FBI's anti-radical division during the Red Scare of 1919–20. It would be fallacious to argue that overreactions to the Nazi spy ring triggered a loss of Americans' freedom. Such ideas have diverted attention from the more important repercussions of the case on foreign relations.

Just as fallacious would be the idea that the spy ring affair inspired an increase in US belligerency, as distinct from an erosion of neutrality. From 1936 to the outbreak of war in Europe, the American Institute of Public Opinion periodically released poll data in response to the question, "Will America be drawn into a European war?" In September 1938—in between the grand jury indictments and the start of the spy trial, and with Hitler threatening Czechoslovakia—the composite poll indicated that 68 percent of those asked believed the United States would be plunged into another conflict. This was a peak and a sharp rise from the previous year, when the figure was 46 percent. However, fear does not always result in anger, and it can trigger caution rather than aggression. Sir Ronald Lindsay, British ambassador to the United States, recognized this when he cabled Foreign Secretary Lord Halifax and claimed that Roosevelt was willing to help Britain withstand the Nazi tide but was being held back by public opinion.[25]

In the spring of 1939, a Gallup poll indicated that the American public's fears of war in Europe had eased. One iconic study of the period concluded that at that point there was "almost unanimous opposition to any involvement in another war." Another study summarizing the scholarship on the issue reports the conventional wisdom was that not until the bombs dropped on Pearl Harbor on December 7, 1941, did Americans favor intervention.[26] The spy events had failed to convert Americans into aggressors.

Nor had the events swayed the German public. The worldwide press covered the spy trial; for example, it was front-page news in the Soviet

Union, where the authorities promoted fears of Nazi spy penetration.[27] But Germany had no coverage at all. Minister of Propaganda Joseph Goebbels had told Ambassador Wilson earlier in the year that he personally ensured that adverse American commentary on Germany did not get into the German press. It was to prevent war fever, he said.[28] Even senior officials had to read the foreign press to find out what was going on in the United States. Udo von Bonin, for example, had read nothing in the German press about Ignatz Griebl's charge that he planned to deploy Kate Moog as a "Mata Hari" mantrap in the US capital. He learned only from the overseas media of the derogatory references to him in the New York trial.[29]

Because Germany was a totalitarian state, German public opinion did not in any case affect Berlin's policies; however, *American* public opinion did influence Berlin. As we have seen, the German diplomatic interpretation of the 1938 spy trial and its media aftermath was that Hitler's regime had lost its hold on Americans' sympathy and failed in the propaganda war. The United States, by increasingly favoring France and Britain, was an obstacle to Hitler's long-harbored designs and thus became a more likely target. So, in contemplating its attack on Pearl Harbor, Japan proceeded in the understandable expectation that Germany would also wage war against the United States.[30] Hitler very quickly satisfied this expectation with his war declaration of December 11, 1941. In the critical realm of expectation, the spy scandal played its part.

Though the spy scandal did not persuade either the American public or the US government to support aggression, as German diplomats rightly noted, it did move American opinion and government policy away from the neutrality that had held the nation in its grip in the mid-1930s. There was no getting away from the Nazi spy story. As soon as the trial ended, Turrou prepared to launch his publishing career. Before a single word appeared, every New York newspaper had published a full-page spread telling the story of the story about to be told. Thereafter, Turrou's propaganda wagon with its anti-Nazi theme rolled on and on.[31]

Poll data indicated that the public's support for the Neutrality Act adopted only three years earlier began to collapse in September 1938.

Arguably, contemporary foreign events, such as the Munich Conference's cession of Sudetenland to Germany, swayed opinion.[32] Such events did worry America's educated elite. In peacetime, however, such foreign events rarely influenced general opinion; people were more concerned with domestic matters, such as westward expansion, race issues, and the economy.[33] In fact, research into attitudes of the 1950s conducted by Samuel Stouffer suggests that people worried most of all about personal matters such as family income, health, and errant daughters, and troubled themselves little about politics.[34]

American politicians of 1938 had no means of knowing that. In supporting preparedness, they heeded the signs of opinion at their disposal. Historians agree that President Roosevelt did study and consider public opinion. Sometimes he was swayed by it; at other times he utilized it to justify policies he already had in mind.[35]

With anti-interventionists in control of Congress, the president's freedom to respond to shifting opinion was apparently limited; however, Congress, too, was reacting to the spy problem. One indication is the frequency with which members of Congress referred to espionage in debates. Taking the period from the mid-1920s to the outbreak of war in 1939, the highest frequency (at forty-five occurrences) was in 1937, when the Senate had protracted exchanges over the La Follette Civil Liberties Committee's exposure of labor espionage, a surefire domestic issue. The next-highest frequency was in 1938 with thirty occurrences. Congress, as well as the White House, gave serious attention to the Nazi spy activities exposed in that year, and by 1939 the proponents of neutrality were losing their grip on Capitol Hill.[36]

Just as Chargé d'Affaires Thomsen feared, the spy case's impact on US public opinion injured Germany's image and its ability to defend its national security interests. Gallup came up with a concrete example of the injury's extent in a February 1939 poll: 65 percent of those polled favored the sale of airplanes to Britain and France in contravention of the neutrality laws. Additionally, 44 percent wanted a ban on such sales to Germany. The message was clear, even if it took the outbreak of war in September to persuade a special session of Congress to revoke the 1936

Neutrality Act in favor of a "cash and carry" provision allowing exports to the European belligerents, which effectively meant Britain and France. By this time, only 2 percent of Americans supported Germany, with 84 percent favoring the Allies.[37]

Chicago's liberal-Protestant *Christian Century* magazine deplored the "campaign" based on the activities of "alleged" spies. It had "far too much the flavor of an effort to arouse a popular anti-Nazi furor. For one thing, it is a little too timely."[38] Its argument was that anti-Nazis had invented the spy menace to assist their propaganda against Hitler's pogroms and aggression. The campaign may indeed have been "timely" in the sense of being opportunistic, but it drew further strength from wider contemporary perceptions of espionage in the 1930s. Perhaps one can set aside the contemporaneous Moscow spy trials on the grounds that American opinion reacts to stimuli closer to home, but spies were very much in the public eye and had a dubious reputation.

The La Follette inquiry in the US Senate had dragged labor spies through the mud. Spy movies magnified the profile of undercover agents, adding glamor but not sanctity. A short spy filmography of that era includes Fritz Lang's *Spies* (1928), Greta Garbo in *Mata Hari* (1931), and Alfred Hitchcock's *The 39 Steps* (1935), *The Secret Agent* (1936), and *The Lady Vanishes* (1938). Though *39 Steps* was hardly pro-German, these films were not anti-Nazi. But they did alert millions of moviegoers, many of whom may not have ordinarily followed foreign affairs, to the phenomenon of espionage. When *Confessions of a Nazi Spy* came along in 1939, with its powerful indictment of fascism, it addressed those millions in a medium that had already made them empathetic and ready to be sympathetic.

Other factors made many Americans change their views on the subject of neutrality. Nazi misbehavior in Europe was one of them, but given that foreign events in peacetime do not shape public opinion as much as domestic considerations do, it is reasonable to suppose that the 1938 spy exposure and its long-running aftereffects rank among those formative domestic considerations. The spy affair with its floods of anti-Nazi newspaper coverage undermined the Americans' sympathy for a neutral stance. The associated ebbing in the public respect for Germany caused Hitler's servants to despair of gaining US support, and this helped open the door for Japan's attack on Pearl Harbor. The scandal was in these ways a discernible eddy in the stream of international history.

DRAMATIS PERSONAE

Canaris, Wilhelm Franz. The head of the Abwehr, Germany's foreign military intelligence service, 1935–44. Admiral Canaris boosted German spying against the United States. Hitler had him executed for his role in an assassination plot.

Dieckhoff, Hans Heinrich. Germany's ambassador in Washington. Driven to despair by the activities of the Abwehr's agents, Dieckhoff left the United States in the wake of the 1938 spy case and was not succeeded by a fully accredited official.

Dix, George C. Jenni Hofmann's defense counsel.

Drechsel, Wilhelm. The maritime official in charge of German shipping line piers in New York, he was also the author of the Drechsel plan, which sought to minimize the reputational damage caused by the 1938 spy scandal.

Duquesne, Frederick Joubert. The flamboyant but ineffective South African spy who gave his name to the 1942 Duquesne spy case.

Eitel, Karl/Carl. An Abwehr agent and aide to Erich Pfeiffer. Toward the end of World War II, Eitel became a British double agent.

Griebl, Ignatz Theodor. A gynecologist, professional anti-Semite, and Nazi agent based in New York, he was one of Leon Turrou's chief informants.

Hardy, Lamar. The district attorney of the Southern District of New York who made a highly unusual trip to Scotland to obtain evidence for the 1938 spy trial.

Hinchley Cooke, William Edward. The MI5 officer who specialized in the interrogation of women and handled the Jessie Jordan case.

Hofmann, Johanna (Jenni). A hairdresser and courier on German shipping lines who was involved in a recruiting mission to Prague, Czechoslovakia. A minor agent, she still received a stiff prison sentence in the New York trial.

Hoover, J. Edgar. The director of the FBI, 1924–72. He became an enemy of Leon Turrou's, but he and the bureau benefited enormously from Turrou's exposure of the Nazi spy ring.

Jordan, Jessie. Born in Glasgow, Scotland, in 1887, Jessie married a German and in 1937 returned to the United Kingdom to spy for Germany. Wanted in connection with the New York spy investigation, she instead spent the years 1938 to 1945 in British prisons and internment institutions.

Lang, Hermann W. A Nazi who was involved in the 1923 Munich Putsch, an early attempt to install Adolf Hitler as the leader of Germany. In 1937 when working as a trusted employee of a US Navy–commissioned company in Manhattan, he betrayed the secret technology of the Norden bombsight.

Moog, Katherina (Kate, a.k.a. Mrs. Kate Busch or Bush). A New York nursing business proprietor. Her lover Ignatz Griebl introduced her to Canaris as the person who would be able to run a honey trap salon in Washington, DC.

Pfeiffer, Erich. A veteran of World War I who had served on the battleship SMS *König* in the Battle of Jutland in 1916. Canaris placed him in charge of espionage against the United States.

Ritter, Nikolaus Adolf Fritz (Niki). The German agent who handled Lang's betrayal of the secret technology of the Norden bombsight.

Robinson, Edward G. A Hollywood actor who played the part of Edward Renard in the 1939 movie *Confessions of a Nazi Spy*. Renard's story was closely based on that of Leon Turrou.

Rumrich, Guenther Gustave Maria (Gus). An early FBI arrestee, he gave his name to what was sometimes called the Rumrich spy ring. Though a minor agent, he was a useful informant in Turrou's developing investigation.

Schlueter, Karl. An Abwehr agent working undercover as a ship's steward. A convinced Nazi, he initiated the plot to kidnap and possibly murder Col. Henry W. T. Eglin of the US Army. Jenni Hofmann's lover.

Sebold, Wilhelm Gottlieb. A double agent who enrolled in the Abwehr but worked for the FBI. His work allowed the FBI to send disinformation to Germany and then arrest large numbers of spies in 1941.

Thomsen, Hans. Dieckhoff's successor in the German Embassy in Washington but with the rank of counselor. In 1940 he complained about the continuing activities of German agents and their counterproductive impact on US public opinion.

Turrou, Leon. The FBI special agent assigned to the Nazi spy case.

NOTES

Abbreviations

BArch   Bundesarchiv.

DbD   Day by Day project, FDR Presidential Library.

FBIT   FBI file on Leon Turrou, obtained via Freedom of Information Act, request number 1366027-000. The notes supply file, section, and serial numbers.

FNAZ   FBI documents on the Nazi spy case sent to the author in response to his Freedom of Information Act request number 1206800-000. All have the classification number 1206800-0-065-HQ-748. The notes supply section and serial numbers.

KV2   Personal files of specific individuals who were investigated, MI5 files from the National Archives, London.

KV3   Subject files on various national security issues, MI5 Files, the National Archives, London.

MHFB   US Army Center of Military History Library, Forrestal Building.

NANY   Court records from criminal case C102-462 (the Nazi spy trial), Record Group 21, National Archives, New York.

SNA   Scottish National Archives.

SSC   Scottish Supreme Court.

VNST   Papers of Lord Vansittart of Denham.

1. Lonkowski's Legacy

1. Louis A. Langille, report, "Guenther Gustave Maria Rumrich," 5 April 1943, p. 72, FNAZ 38/1664 (hereafter "Langille report"); and Hanson W. Baldwin, "A Spy Thriller—in Real Life," *New York Times*, 26 June 1938.

2. A. H. Leviero, "Spy Hunt Here Was Begun by Clue from Abroad to Woman in the Plot," *New York Times*, 21 June 1938; and J. E. Lawler, Memorandum for E. A. Tamm, 6 December 1939, FNAZ 26/1229. So little was known about Lonkowski in the United States that there were doubts as to his real name. His official record dismisses any such doubt,

confirming that he was born on 20 January 1896 in Worleinen, East Prussia. See Personalnachweis, Wilhelm Lonkowski's air force personnel file, PERS 6/154245, BArch.

3. Langille report, 65, 68, 75; and Turrou, *Nazi Spy*, 135, 140.

4. Reile, *Die Geheime Westfront*, 301; and quotation and numbers from Adams, *Historical Dictionary*, 3, 111. Article 160 of the Treaty of Peace with Germany (Treaty of Versailles), which Germany agreed to on 10 January 1920, states that the "maintenance or formation of forces differently grouped . . . is forbidden."

5. Ahlström, *Engineers*, 95; and Anderson, *European Universities*, 158.

6. Lonkowski's signed entry in a technical personnel questionnaire, 28 July 1937, in PERS 6/154245, BArch.

7. Langille report, 61.

8. Bailey, *Kid from Hoboken*, 260.

9. Huchthausen, *Shadow Voyage*, 19; and Whitman, *Hitler's American Model*, 18.

10. Eitel paraphrased in Camp 020, "Interim Report in the Case of Carl Eitel," 9 November 1944, p. 10, KV2/384-2 (hereafter "Camp 020, 'Interim Report'"); and Langille report, 62.

11. Lonkowski's $30,000 claim to Ignatz Griebl recorded in Turrou, *Nazi Spy*, 223; and Guy Liddell, "German Espionage Case in the United States," March–April 1938, p. 12, VNST (hereafter "Liddell, 'German Espionage'"). Liddell was an MI5 officer who gleaned his information from the FBI, from its interrogations that were passed on to him, and from MI5's own sources. According to Liddell, Steuer delivered the bombsight secrets to the Abwehr, but (see chapter 10) the FBI gave Steuer the benefit of the doubt.

12. Turrou, *Nazi Spy*, 137–38; and Langille report, 103.

13. The FBI became aware of the Abwehr's activities in Los Angeles and San Francisco in mid-1937, but the bureau was unable to foil a botched Abwehr effort to extort the Atlas Powder Company's secrets. It resulted in the murder of the wife and daughter of industrialist Weston G. Frome in the Chihuahuan Desert east of El Paso, Texas. See Richmond, *Fetch the Devil*, 185; and chapter 9 of this volume.

14. E. A. Tamm, Memorandum for the Director, 5 April 1938, FNAZ 7/320. Tamm's sources indicated the Driscoll invention was passed to Japan as well.

15. FBI memorandum, "NIKOLAUS FRITZ ADOLPH RITTER," 22 May 1944, KV2/87-1. Here and in the rest of the book, capitalization in both the notes and the text follows the original.

16. FBI memorandum, "NIKOLAUS FRITZ ADOLPH RITTER," 2 September 1945, based on an interrogation of Ritter on 26 July 1944 in Hamburg, KV2/87-1; and Ritter, *Deckname Dr. Rantzau*, 15–20, 27.

17. Josef Starziczny, chief of an Abwehr-related spy ring in Brazil, quoted in FBI memorandum, "RITTER," 22 May 1944; and FBI memorandum, "RITTER," 2 September 1944.

18. Ritter, *Deckname Dr. Rantzau*, 51–52, 72–79.

19. FBI memorandum, "RITTER," 22 May 1944.

20. Career summary in British Army on the Rhine, Preliminary Interrogation Report on Oberstleutnant Nikolaus Fritz Adolf Ritter, 14 December 1945, KV2/88; and Camp 020, "Interim Report," 14. Ritter's brother, Hans, operated on behalf of the Abwehr in California. Thus, one might discern a multitentacled reach of the Lonkowski/Gudenberg ring, even if it maintained its cellular structure.

21. Ritter, *Deckname Dr. Rantzau*, 83–92; and Ronnie, *Counterfeit Hero*, 208.

22. Kahn, *Hitler's Spies*, 328–30; Duffy, *Double Agent*, 319n225; Ritter interview with Ladislas Farago quoted in Farago, *Game of the Foxes*, 41; and Andrew Jeffrey, email to author, 14 December 2017.

23. Statement of Senta de Wanger to FBI special agents George A. Callaghan and J. T. McLaughlin, 31 March 1938, in Leon G. Turrou, report, Guenther Gustave Rumrich et al., 2 April 1938, pp. 75–76, FNAZ 5/213 (hereafter "Turro, report, Rumrich et al."); and Turrou, *Nazi Spy*, 147–48.

24. Turrou, report, Rumrich et al., 82.

25. Statement of Senta de Wanger in Turrou, 76, 79.

26. Data from Historical Branch, G-2, "Materials on the History of Military Intelligence in the United States, 1885–1944" (unpublished document, 1944), Part I, Exhibit B: "Headquarters Personnel and Funds Military Intelligence Activities," MHFB; and Langille report, 72. The quotation is Langille's paraphrase.

27. Translation of a letter in German from Wilhelm Lonkowski to "my dear sister-in-law and brother-in-law," postmarked Montreal, 17 October 1935, and reproduced in Langille report, 74.

28. As of 1 October 1935, Lonkowski was a member of the National-

sozialistische Volkswohlfahrt (NSV, or National Socialist People's Welfare Organization), the party's attempt to nationalize and politicize social welfare. A record of his political loyalties, dated 22 January 1942, is in the Lonkowski personnel file PERS 6/154245, BArch, as are various documents indicating his employment status between 1935 and 1942.

29. Transcript of an order implementing Lonkowski's dismissal of two employees, 31 March 1938; transcript of Lonkowski's agreement to take a pay cut on his transfer to the Luftwaffe's Engineering Corps, 20 April 1938; telegram to the minister for the air force noting Lonkowski's failure to complete further military training, 19 October 1938; Geheime Staatspolizei Stettin (Gestapo, Stettin branch), report on Lonkowski, 8 June 1940; and Lonkowski's defense quoted in a report by the Luftwaff's Engineering Department, 17 September 1940—all in Lonkowski's personnel file PERS 6/154245, BArch.

30. Camp 020, "Interim report," 10.

31. Turrou, *Nazi Spy*, 157; and statement of Senta de Wanger, in Turrou, report, Rumrich et al., 78.

32. The US Secret Service (not the FBI) had taken the lead in combating German agents in World War I, and it had neutralized a Spanish spy network in the Spanish-American War of 1898. However, by the 1920s it concentrated on protecting the president and his entourage, and devoted no resources to counterespionage. See Jeffreys-Jones, *American Espionage*, chap. 3, 5, and 8; Jeffreys-Jones, "United States Secret Service," in Whitnah, *Government Agencies*; and Melanson, *Secret Service*, 36–39.

2. Jessie Jordan

1. "'Unwanted as a Child, Now Unwanted in Two Countries,'" *Daily Express*, 17 May 1938. German spelling and translation as in the original from the staff reporter.

2. Jessie Jordan's serialized memoir, "My Amazing Life," *Sunday Mail*, 5 June 1938 (henceforth "Jordan memoir").

3. Extract of entry in register of births, Edinburgh, 1 December 1937, KV2/193; statement of Sergeant Sutherland of Glasgow Police Alien Registration Department concerning Jordan's visit to the department on 1 July 1937, 11 March 1938, KV2/3534; and Jordan memoir, *Sunday Mail*, 12 June 1938. For the construction of Jessie Jordan's family tree, thanks go

to Ross Nisbet, a great grandson of Lizzie Wallace (later Haddow), and to Pat Storey, who very kindly put at the author's disposal her genealogical skills.

4. Karl Wilhelm Friedrich Jordan death certificate, Hamburg, 9 August 1918, kindly supplied by Jessie Jordan's kinsman Donald Haddow; and Marga quoted in "'Unwanted as a Child,'" *Daily Express*. The *Express*'s anonymous correspondent interviewed Marga.

5. Jordan memoir, 29 May 1938.

6. Jordan memoir, 5 June 1938; and "'Unwanted as a Child,'" *Daily Express*.

7. Ferguson, *Paper and Iron*, 31–39, 199.

8. Jordan memoir, 12 June 1938.

9. Jordan quoted in "'Unwanted as a Child,'" *Daily Express*. For elaboration on Jessie Jordan's spying motives, see Jeffreys-Jones, "Jessie Jordan," 769–72.

10. MI5 Counter Intelligence War Room, London, Liquidation Report No. 206 KDM Hamburg, 28 March 1946, p. 3, KV3/204; Situation Report KDM Hamburg, 1 August 1946, KV3/204; British Army on the Rhine, Preliminary Interrogation Report on Oberstleutnant Nikolaus Fritz Adolf Ritter, 5 December 1945, p. 4, KV2/88; and Kluiters and Verhoeyen, "International Spymaster," 2.

11. Leonard O. Mosley, "Our Counter-Spy Machine Moves Swiftly," *Empire News* (Manchester), 22 May 1938; Andrew, *Defence of the Realm*, 210; Lt. Col. William Edward Hinchley Cooke statement addition, Precognition of Witnesses against Jessie Wallace or Jordan (for proposed High Court trial in Edinburgh), Dundee, 22 March 1938, p. 1, KV2/3534; and Kluiters and Verhoeyen, "International Spymaster," 8.

12. "New Breconshire Enterprise," *Brecon County Times*, 30 July 1925. Pat Storey's research indicates that in 1911, Mary Wallace was working as a qualified sick nurse in the home of a widow in Bath. She is in the 1926–56 telephone directories with Felin Newydd as her address. Huw Evans-Bevan, the manager of Felin Newydd, in an email to the author, 23 February 2013, wrote that his great grandfather owned the house in the 1940s, and records confirm that Mary Jean Mackay Wallace was the owner in 1930.

13. Report by Lieutenant Colonel Hinchley Cooke on Jordan's espionage activities, 29 March 1938, KV2/3534.

14. Letter postmarked Brecon, purporting to be from Mary Wallace to her niece Jessie Jordan in Perth and offering money, 12 September 1937, KV2/3534; and an accompanying undated report by an MI5 handwriting analyst concluding that the foregoing letter was written in the same hand as another letter written by Jessie Jordan, making the Mary Wallace epistle a forgery. See also Jeffrey, *Dangerous Menace*, 16.

15. Letter translated from German and narrative in report by Lieutenant Colonel Hinchley Cooke on Jordan's espionage activities, 29 March 1938, pp. 5–7, KV2/3534.

16. Guy Liddell (of MI5), "German Espionage Case in the United States," 28 April 1938, p. 16b, KV2/3533 (hereafter Liddell, "German Espionage Case"); "'Unwanted as a Child,'" *Daily Express*; and Oppenheim, *Evil Shepherd*, 11, 21, 21, 28, 29.

17. Boghardt, *Spies of the Kaiser*, 62. Sir John Lavery's painting titled *The American Battle Squadron in the Firth of Forth: "New York" (flagship), "Texas," "Florida," "Wyoming," "Delaware"* is in the Imperial War Museum, London. The canvas depicts nine ships, not only the five stated in the artwork's title.

18. Draft deposition by Alexander Jack, September 1938, KV2/194.

19. Detective Lieutenant J. Carstairs, report to Chief Constable, Dundee City Police, 29 November 1937, KV2/193; John Curran statement, 10 March, 1938, Precognition of Witnesses, 101, 105, KV2/3534; and the Currans' narrative of events as related by J. W. Fraser, staff reporter, in *Daily Record*, 23 and 24 May 1938.

20. Chief Constable Joseph Neilans to Col. Sir Vernon Kell, 8 December 1937, KV2/193.

21. "They Unmasked Spy Mrs. Jordan," banner headline of front-page story in *Daily Record* (Glasgow), 24 May 1938, the first in a series; and Dingle Foot, M.P., to Sir Victor Warrender, M.P., 23 November 1938, KV2/194. Acting on behalf of the Currans, Foot—the Liberal member of parliament for Dundee and a barrister—argued that the *Daily Record* payment should not be regarded as an obstacle to further government recompense for his clients, who had acted from patriotic motives. Warrender was the financial secretary for the War Office, with the authority to make compensation payments in relation to MI5 matters.

22. Signed copy of Sir Vernon Kell's statement, 5 December 1938, KV2/194.

23. The historian Andrew Jeffrey states that MI5 obtained an additional HOW on 1 Kinloch Street as the result of Mrs. Curran's discoveries, per Jeffrey's written commentary in November 2017 on the author's article "Jessie Jordan." As will be seen in the next chapter, a crucial letter intercepted on 29 January 1938 was addressed to 1 Kinloch Street.

3. Murder in the McAlpin

1. Jones, *German Spy in America*, 292.
2. Jeffreys-Jones, "Montreal Spy Ring," 119–34.
3. Text of message copied in Langille report, 107.
4. Guy Liddell, "Liaison with the United States Intelligence Organizations Arising from the German Espionage Case," March–April 1938, p. 5, KV2/3533 and VNST II 2/21.
5. "Rt." to "Mr. S.," 1 December 1937, enclosed in an envelope addressed to Jessie Jordan at 1 Kinloch Street, KV2/3534.
6. Crown letters in envelopes addressed to Jessie Jordan, 19 and 31 January 1938 and 15 February 1938, KV2/3421.
7. Gustav to Guenther Rumrich, 24 January 1938, KV2/3421. Copies of some of the Crown letters are found in FBI files as well. They are redacted to disguise MI5's involvement in the tip-off, but the McAlpin plot letter of 17 January 1938 is available in its entirety, for example, in Langille report, 94–95.
8. Crown to Sanders, 17 January 1938, in KV2/3421.
9. "Re Mrs. J. JORDAN formerly WALLACE," undated typed memorandum bearing the handwritten note "shown to PUS [Permanent Undersecretary of State] and HO [Home Office]," KV2/193.
10. President Roosevelt quotations in Swift, *Kennedys*, 3, 6; and Whalen, *Founding Father*, 213–14.
11. House of Lords debate reported in *The Times* (London), 17 February 1938.
12. Robert Allen, "Behind the Scenes at Whitehall," *Evening Standard*, 21 October 1938, clipping in Cadogan Papers.
13. Sir Alexander Cadogan diary, 18 and 26 January 1938, and 1 March 1938, Cadogan Papers; and copy of 17 January 1938 Crown/McAlpin letter in VNST II 2/21.
14. [MI5], "Memorandum for U.S. Military Attaché [Lt. Col. Raymond E. Lee]," 29 January 1938, KV2/193.

15. Liddell, "German Espionage," 2–3; and Batvinis, *Origins of FBI Counterintelligence*, 10.
16. J. E. Lawler, Memorandum for Edward A. Tamm, 5 January 1939, p. 2, FNAZ 28/1281; and Batvinis, *Origins of FBI Counterintelligence*, 10. The *New York Times* first mentioned Colonel Eglin by name on 27 February 1938: "Leader Confesses."
17. [MI5], "Memorandum for U.S. Military Attaché."

4. Enter Leon Turrou

1. Tamm, Memorandum for the Director, 5 April 1938, p. 1, FNAZ 7/320.
2. Turrou claimed fluency in French, German, Russian, Polish, Ukrainian, Malay, and English, and when Hoover had him tested on these languages, he proved his linguistic ability. Turrou's application to the Department of Justice, 24 June 1928, FBIT 1/1/1; Hoover, "Memorandum for Mr. Baley," 19 March 1921, FBIT 1/1/1; Tolson, "L. G. Turrou . . . remarks," 6 November 1935, FBIT 1/2/1; and D. Milton Ladd, Inspector Report on Turrou, 1 April 1929, FBIT 1/2/1.
3. Tolson, "L. G. Turrou . . . remarks"; J. M. Keith, Inspector, Memorandum for the Director on Turrou, 22 April 1929, FBIT 1/1/1; Anon. (indecipherable signature), Memorandum for the Director re: Leon G. Turrou, applicant for appointment as special agent, 17 December 1928, FBIT 1/1/1; Turrou, *Nazi Spy*, 268; and Turrou, *Where My Shadow Falls*, 70.
4. Walter F. Stillger to Department of Justice, 8 March 1929, FBIT 1/1/1. In later years, Turrou wrote a novel with autobiographical elements in which a Russian character called Boris, an internationally renowned ballet dancer, sustained a leg injury in a horse-riding accident. See Turrou, *Bonheur en Sursis*, 177.
5. Louis Loebl, Memorandum for the Director re: Leon G. Turrou, formerly Leon George Turovsky, 22 July 1938, FBIT 1/3/1.
6. Transcript of Turrou's address to the Breakfast Club of Los Angeles broadcast over local radio, 7 March 1939, FBIT 1/3/1.
7. Leon Turrou's grandson Bob Turrou gave this reaction in an email to the author, 6 May 2017: "Kind of funny, but my father never mentioned that his father was an orphan. He [Leon Turrou] had two brothers, Rudolph and Joseph (I think it was). I think they were actual brothers, but not sure. Joseph never came to the U.S. Rudolph was the father of Sandy and

David. He died in [approximately] 1938." The researcher Richard Bareford determined that Rebecca Turovsky journeyed to Seattle from Singapore, arriving 27 July 1916 on a ship whose manifest of alien passengers
listed her as of "Russian Nationality" and "Hebrew Race." Rebecca settled
in Brooklyn with her son Rudolph, who registered for the draft on 12
September 1918. Bareford's email comments sent to the author, 5 March
2019.

8. Communication from Bob Turrou's sister, Teresa Turrou-Bressert, to
Bertrand Vilain, kindly forwarded to the author in email of 28 October
2019. Vilain is a French journalist and author who has researched Leon
Turrou's background in connection with his investigation of the alleged
murder of Pierre Quéméneur in May 1923. See Baker and Vilain, *L'affaire Seznec*; and Vilain's volume, *Affaire Seznec: Les archives du FBI ont
parlé*.

9. Transcript of Turrou's address to Breakfast Club.

10. "I did the DNA 23 and Me thing and I'm not 25% Jewish like I should
be if Granddad was 100% Jewish, I'm only about 3/16, which would have
made my dad 3/8 and his dad ¾, which would have meant that one of
his parents was 100% Jewish and the other ½ Jewish, unless both of them
were 3/4 Jewish." Bob Turrou email to author, 6 May 2016.

11. Turrou, *Nazi Spy*, 268 (emphasis in the original).

12. Except for the maxim, the quotations are from transcript of Turrou's address to Breakfast Club.

13. Information from Thomas Shoemaker, assistant commissioner of immigration and naturalization, given to Louis Loebl and cited in Loebl, Memorandum for the Director; and transcript of Turrou's address to Breakfast
Club.

14. Louis Loebl to Director, FBI, re: Leon George Turrou, 24 August 1938,
FBIT 1/3/1.

15. Loebl.

16. Loebl, Memorandum for the Director. Vilain has ascertained that Turrou
was not in the Legion Bajończyków, the Polish fighting force formed in
France in World War I. Vilain, email to author, 6 November 2019.

17. Kusielewicz, "Paderewski and Wilson's Speech," 66ff.

18. Robert M. Turrou, supplement to "Leon G. Turrou: Biography," IMDb,
http://www.imdb.com/name/nm0878103/bio (accessed 26 June 2017).

19. Transcript of Turrou's address to Breakfast Club.

20. Turrou, "An Unwritten Chapter," a typescript that Turrou offered to "the next edition of the ARA 'Review,'" enclosed with Turrou to Brooks, 12 September 1926, in Collection no. YY545, Hoover Institution Library and Archives, and supplied by kind courtesy of Richard Bareford; and Patenaude, *Big Show in Bololand*, 685.

21. Turrou, "Unwritten Chapter." In an email to the author, 25 October 2019, Bertrand Vilain speculated that Turrou later had business dealings with Dzerzhinsky.

22. Patenaude, *Big Show in Bololand*, 685; and Turrou, supplement to "Leon G. Turrou."

23. Loebl to Director FBI, re: Leon George Turrou. Davidowsky may have confused Turrou's Catholic mother-in-law with his Jewish mother.

24. Hoover letter to Turrou, 29 March 1921, FBIT 1/1/1.

25. Thomas C. Desmond (New York Young Republican Club) letter to Donovan, 10 December 1928; Alan Fox letter to Donovan, 31 January 1929; Donovan letter to Turrou, 16 March 1929; Hoover letter to Turrou, 16 March 1929; and Turrou's oath of allegiance, 1 April 1929—all in FBIT 1/1/1.

26. Turrou, *Where My Shadow Falls*, 20–21. Although Turrou's account has persuasive detail, there is no listing in the historic files of Leavenworth Penitentiary of an inmate named Skropinski. He does not say so, but Turrou may have anonymized the name for legal reasons.

27. Rosendahl, "Loss of the *Akron*," 928; Leon G. Turrou and James R. Crowell, "Akron Saboteur Boasted of Causing Air Crashes," *New York Post*, 23 July 1941 (one of a nine-part series titled "Sabotage"); and Leon G. Turrou and James R. Crowell, "How Saboteur Froze Rivets on Akron," *Pittsburgh Press*, 24 July 1941 (another part of the same syndicated series).

28. Ladd to Hoover, 17 November 1933, FBIT 1/1/1. Further details in Special Agent F. S. Smith Memorandum for SAC Oklahoma City R. H. Colvin, 14 November 1933, FBIT 1/1/1.

29. Horace Cate, "Attempt Take Life U.S. Officer Fails," *Jonesboro (AR) Daily Tribune*, 15 November 1933; and "U.S. Agent Blames Gang for Highway Death Plot," *Memphis Press-Scimitar*, 15 November 1933.

30. R. H. Colvin to Hoover, 21 November 1933, FBIT 1/1/1.

31. Turrou, *Where My Shadow Falls*, 107, 122.

32. Hoover to Francis X. Fay, scientific evidence expert, 5 January 1935, FBIT 1/2/1.

5. Crown Identified

1. Turrou, *Nazi Spy*, 31.
2. Tamm, Memorandum for the Director, 4; and text of message in Langille report, 107.
3. Tamm, Memorandum for the Director, 14.
4. Turrou, *Nazi Spy*, 52; Rumrich's protest paraphrased in Tamm, Memorandum for the Director, 23; and Leon Turrou, Report on Rumrich/Espionage, 27 February 1938, p. 3, FNAZ EBF 74 (hereafter "Turrou, Report on Rumrich/Espionage").
5. "Inquiry Is On Here in Spy Ring Scare," *New York Times*, 27 February 1938; "Spionenjagd in Amerika [Spy chase in America]," *Hamburger Nachrichten*, 28 February 1938; "US Guards Air Base as 3 Wait Jury in Spy Scare," *Washington Post*, 28 February 1938; and Welles paraphrased in R. C. Lindsay to UK Foreign Secretary Lord Halifax, 1 March 1938, KV2/3533.
6. Turrou, *Nazi Spy*, 63–64.
7. Batvinis, *Origins of FBI Counterintelligence*, 21.
8. Turrou, *Nazi Spy*, 56.
9. Jones, *German Spy in America*, 24, 74, 97, 205, 231.
10. Turrou, *Nazi Spy*, 64.
11. Later on, Rumrich would say that "furs" referred to passports. See L. A. Langille, report on Hofmann/Internal Security, 19 February 1942, p. 5, FNAZ 26/1651 (hereafter "Langille, Rumrich report").
12. Turrou, *Nazi Spy*, 53–57.
13. Rumrich confession, 21 February 1938, p. 3, in Turrou, Report on Rumrich/Espionage.
14. "US Guards Air Base," *Washington Post*.
15. Rumrich confession, in Turrou, Report on Rumrich/Espionage; Langille, Rumrich report; and J. T. McLaughlin, Parole Report, Rumrich/Espionage, 14 December 1938, p. 8, FNAZ 27/1258.
16. Photocopy of the advertisement placement in Turrou, Report on Rumrich/Espionage, 2 April 1938, p. 153, FNAZ 5/213.
17. Rumrich's paraphrase in his confession, 9, in Turrou, Report on Rumrich/Espionage, 27 February 1938.

18. Statement by Mrs. Juanita Carol Raney, in Julius S. Rice report, Rumrich/Espionage, 21 October 1943, p. 10, FNAZ 42/1988.

19. Information on splitting from "Spies, Guerrillas & Violent Fanatics" (London, ca. 1971–72), an analysis by psychologists at the Tavistock Institute of Human Relations that Lily Pincus supplied to the author.

20. Rumrich confession, in Turrou, Report on Rumrich/Espionage, 27 February 1938, 12.

21. Rumrich confession, 11.

22. Tamm, Memorandum for the Director, 11. Earlier speculation about the Soviet penetration plan, based on "cable dispatches from Moscow," appeared in "US Guards Air Base," *Washington Post.*

23. "H. Spielman" to "Dear Friend," 1 January 1938, reproduced in Langille, Rumrich report, 4–5.

24. See chapter 19 in this volume regarding Schlueter's alleged agency in the plot. Schlueter frequented New York bars using the name Schmidt. See also Farago, *Game of the Foxes*, 55.

25. Turrou, *Nazi Spy*, 89; and Erich Glaser confession, 21 February 1938, 3, in Turrou, Report on Rumrich/Espionage, 27 February 1938.

26. Turrou, *Nazi Spy*, 20; and Rumrich confession, in Turrou, Report on Rumrich/Espionage, 14.

27. Turrou, *Nazi Spy*, 57–58.

6. Tales of Hofmann

1. All quotations from Turrou, *Nazi Spy*, 64–68.

2. Hofmann's version of the event reflected coaching by her defense counsel, and there are minor discrepancies as to dates and words spoken when compared with Turrou's account. US District Court, Southern District of New York, United States v. Johanna Hofmann et al., Johanna Hofmann petition, 16 September 1938, p. 2, NANY.

3. Ferguson, *Paper and Iron*, 31.

4. Lorenz, *Spy Who Loved Castro*, 5, 7, 8, 11, 31, 36.

5. Turrou, *Nazi Spy*, 73; Hofmann petition, 1, 3; and Turrou, Report on Rumrich/Espionage, 27 February 1938, 3. Hofmann's confession of 25 February 1938 is included in Turrou's report, 43–46.

6. Confession of Wilhelm Drechsel, 28 March 1938, in Turrou, Report on Rumrich/Espionage, 2 April 1938, p. 18; and Turrou, *Nazi Spy*, 91–93.

7. Drechsel, follow-up interview, 29 March 1938, in Turrou, Report on Rumrich/Espionage, 27.

8. Drechsel, follow-up interview, 28–29.

9. Hoover paraphrased in a Reuters report in an unidentified clipping from a British newspaper, in KV2/193; "US Defence Chiefs Act after Girl Spy Arrest," *Daily Mirror* (London), 28 February 1938; and "Army & Navy: Espionage," *Time*, 7 March 1938.

10. Farago, *Game of the Foxes*, 56.

11. C. K. Lee, Parole Report on Johanna Hofmann, 14 December 1938, FNAZ 27/1255; and Stephenson, *Nazi Organisation of Women*, 11–12.

12. Summary of Hofmann trial testimony and Schlueter biographic details in Langille report, 85, 87.

13. Hofmann confession, in Turrou, Report on Rumrich/Espionage, 27 February 1938, 45; and Langille report, 84–85.

14. Turrou, *Nazi Spy*, 87.

15. All quotations from memorandum, "GERMANY: Cover Addresses in Dublin and Dundee for German Espionage," 3 May 1938, KV2/3421; and Hofmann's account in Langille report, 17.

7. Avoiding a High Court Trial

1. "Mrs Jordan's Shop Gave Spy Ring Clue," *Daily Express* (London), 22 June 1938.

2. Andrew, *Defence of the Realm*, 56, 78, 143.

3. Joseph Neilans statement, 10 March 1938, in High Court case file on Jessie Jordan, pp. 73–82, KV2/3534; and "Woman Arrested on Secrets Charge," *Daily Express,* 3 March 1938.

4. Author's conversation with Dr. Andrew Jeffrey, 24 October 2017; and Neilans statement (KV2/3534) listing items corresponding to evidential productions 19, 21–31(a), 32–34, and 46 (b) in Indictment against Jessie Jordan or Wallace Con. Official Secrets Act, 1911 and 1920, Sec. 1 (1), Edinburgh, High Court, May 1938, JC 26/1938/46, SSC. The indictment cited here and in further notes is the original text that predated alterations following legal maneuvers.

5. "Police Raid Flat of German Woman," *Daily Express*, 4 March 1938; Neilans statement; Christiansen, *Headlines All My Life*, 171; and Allen, *Voice of Britain*, 64–66.

6. "Secrets Act Probe Extends to Fife," *Courier*, 4 March 1938.

7. "Mrs. Jordan Unseen by Crowd," *Courier*, 11 March 1938.

8. Report by Lieutenant Colonel Hinchley Cooke on Jordan's espionage activities, 29 March 1938, p. 63, KV2/3534.

9. "Lt.-Col. Hinchley Cooke," *Evening Standard*, 3 March 1938.

10. "Four Years Sentence on Woman Spy," *Courier*, 6 May 1938.

11. Nigel West remark to the author in conversation, Gregynog, 24 May 2013.

12. "Unwanted," *Empire News*, undated clipping, KV2/194.

13. Quoted in Jeffreys-Jones, *FBI*, 100.

14. Statement by William George Quinlan, chief inspector in charge, Royal Marine Police, Scottish Area, in Hinchley Cooke report, 114.

15. Hinchley Cooke report, 63.

16. Hinchley Cooke report, 2.

17. "Secrets Case Woman in Mystery Drive," *Daily Herald*, 4 March 1938.

18. *Washington Post*, 4 March 1938; and "Mrs Jordan's Shop Gave Spy Ring Clue," *Daily Express*, 22 June 1938.

19. Jordan to "Dear Sir," 19 March 1938, Scottish Office File, Criminal Case File: Jessie Jordan, 1938–1952, HH 16/212/1597/1, SNA.

20. J. Mayo, governor of Perth Prison, to Secretary of State for Scotland, 22 March 1938, HH 16/212/1597/1, SNA; W. Steele Nicoll, solicitor of 3 Great King Street, Edinburgh, to Undersecretary of State for Scotland, 27 April 1938, HH 16/212/1597/1, SNA; and the *Sunday Mail* series, or "Jordan memoir" (see notes 2, 3, 5, and 8 of chapter 2).

21. According to Andrew Jeffrey, conversation with author, 24 October 2017.

22. Instructions approved by the Lord Justice Clerk re: Trial on 16 May 1938, JC26/1938/46, SSC.

23. Note of Objections to Relevancy of Indictment in H. M. Advocate v. Mrs. Jessie Wallace or Jordan, stamped 10 May 1938, JC26/1938/46, SSC; and undated note indicating defense counsel's acceptance of "relevancy" objection, accused's intention now to plead guilty, and agreement over procedure whereby there would be a speech in mitigation followed by sentencing, JC26/1938/46, SSC.

24. Handwritten deletions in indictment against Jessie Jordan, 1, JC26/1938/46, SSC.

25. New indictment reproduced in Leonard O. Mosley, "How Jessie Jordan Was Shadowed from the Very Start," *Empire News*, 22 May 1938; and

"Woman Convicted as Spy in Scotland," *New York Times*, 17 May 1938 ("wireless" report).

26. "Espionage in the East of Scotland," *Scotsman*, 10 May 1948.
27. Duffes quoted in Mosley, "How Jessie Jordan."

8. What Griebl Knew

1. Langille report, 27–28.
2. Turrou, *Nazi Spy*, 104.
3. Hamilton, *Salute the Jew!*; Langille report, 39; and E. A. Tamm, Memorandum for the Director, "re Contemplated Prosecution in connection with the GUENTHER GUSTAVE RUMRICH ESPIONAGE CASE on October 14, 1938," 10 October 1838, p. 5, FNAZ 23/1043.
4. Quotation from Turrou, *Nazi Spy*, 108.
5. Turrou, 106–7; and quotation from Turrou, *Where My Shadow Falls*, 150.
6. Langille report, 26; and Maria Griebl quoted in Turrou, *Nazi Spy*, 212.
7. Benjamin Lichtman, attorney at law, Brooklyn, action of 7 November 1933, quoted in J. T. McLaughlin report, "Guenther Gustave Rumrich with aliases," 20 July 1938, p. 20, FNAZ 15/696.
8. Turrou, *Nazi Spy*, 99–100, 218; and "Woman Accuses Greibl," *New York Times*, 29 March 1935.
9. McLaughlin, report on Rumrich, 18; and Langille report, 44.
10. Diamond, *Nazi Movement*, 132.
11. Turrou, *Where My Shadow Falls*, 151.
12. Report of Special Agent Leon G. Turrou on von Bonin and others, 13 March 1938, p. 2, FNAZ 4/141 (hereafter "Turrou report on von Bonin and others.")
13. Tamm, Memorandum for the Director, 4.
14. "Camp 020 Report on the Case of Erich Pheiffer [Pfeiffer]," September 1945, p. 58, KV2/267 (hereafter "Camp 020 Pheiffer Report"). According to the historian Andrew Jeffrey, Herbert Wichmann of the Hamburg office of the Abwehr recruited Griebl and allocated him to Pfeiffer, who would be his case officer. Jeffrey adds that Griebl worked up contacts in the United States and passed them on to Lonkowski. See Jeffrey, *Dangerous Menace*, 14.
15. Pfeiffer's account in "Camp 020 Pheiffer Report," 62; and Liddell, "German Espionage Case," 12.

16. Langille report, 75.
17. Perlman, *Theory*, 123.
18. "Camp 020 Pheiffer Report," 13.
19. "Camp 020 Pheiffer Report," 27.
20. Carl Eitel seems to have believed Pfeiffer's Kronprinzenstrasse address was his family home, possibly mistaking his mistress for his wife. See "Interim Report in the Case of Carl Eitel," 28 October 1944, p. 8, KV2/384-1. A municipal change of address entry from 1951 (Staatsarchiv Bremen) retrospectively records Pfeiffer's quitting of the Misslerstrasse address on 13 July 1941 and gives his family's period of residence there as starting on 1 October 1935. Comments on the Misslerstrasse neighborhood kindly supplied by Marion Alpert of Staatsarchiv Bremen.
21. Ronge, *Kreigs- und Industrie Spionage*, 5, 10, 364–65.
22. Weinberg, "Hitler's Image," 1009; Heinemann, "Abwehr," in Dear and Foot, *Oxford Companion*, 1; Simms, *Hitler*, 119 ff., 331; and Hitler quoted in Compton, *Swastika and the Eagle*, 17.
23. Canaris talk in Bremerhaven, 2 February 1935, quoted in Breuer, *Spy Who Spent*, 5.
24. Pfeiffer quoted in "Camp 020 Pheiffer Report," 21.

9. Miss Moog Says No

1. Langille report, 56.
2. Maria Griebl quoted in Turrou, *Nazi Spy*, 216; and J. T. McLaughlin, "Guenther Gustave Maria Rumrich/Espionage," 20 July 1938, p. 8, FNAZ 15/676.
3. Turrou, *Nazi Spy*, 218; Tamm, Memorandum for the Director, 32; and Flint-Larsen personnel summary, 4 September 1945, KV2/1973.
4. A search of six collection indexes and lists in the Franklin D. Roosevelt Library, for which thanks are due to archivist Virginia Lewick, revealed no reference to Kate Moog/Busch/Bush by either her family or married name. For example, there is no mention of the future spy in the "Cumulative List of Employees, Roosevelt Estate, 1867–1970" complied for the Roosevelt Estate Historic Resource Study (National Park Service, 2004). The Roosevelt family may have employed her in a casual, short-term capacity, but Moog and her lover Griebl exaggerated, if they did not invent, her role in

this phase in her past. One book that describes in some detail the nursing arrangements made for FDR does not mention Moog. See Cook, *Eleanor Roosevelt*, 308–14.

5. Moog paraphrased in Tamm, Memorandum for the Director, 2.

6. McLaughlin, "Guenther Gustave Rumrich with aliases," 3. Kate Moog's married name appears as Bush in this report but was elsewhere given as Busch.

7. Langille report, 56; and Pfeiffer quoted in Turrou, *Nazi Spy*, 222.

8. Pfeiffer's account of the meeting in "Camp 020 Pheiffer Report," 21.

9. Pfeiffer quoting Griebl in "Camp 020 Pheiffer Report," 21.

10. Pfeiffer paraphrased and quoted in "Camp 020 Pheiffer Report," 21.

11. Pfeiffer paraphrased in Langille report, 54.

12. Griebl gave two versions of how he achieved contact with the Abwehr hierarchy. In one version, he said that Schlueter introduced him and Moog to Canaris's deputies Menzel and von Bonin on the *Europa* on the way to his meeting with Pfeiffer. See Batvinis, *Origins of FBI Counterintelligence*, 20. In another version, he said that his brother, who held (in the FBI's paraphrase) "a responsible position with the German Labor Ministry," introduced him to "Colonel Busch" (Canaris) once Griebl and Moog had traveled on to Berlin. Canaris had then "summoned his chief assistants" Menzel and von Bonin to meet him. See Langille report, 29.

13. Pfeiffer quoted in "Camp 020 Pheiffer Report," 22.

14. Kahn, *Hitler's Spies*, 92.

15. Promotions data related to a military pension claim, 16 November 1978, in Udo von Bonin PERS 6/12477, BArch; biographical summary, "Udo Wilhelm Bogislav von Bonin," Civilian Interrogation Centre, Civilian Military Mission Denmark, 31 August 1945, KV2/1973; and Farago, *Game of the Foxes*, 143.

16. Ashdown, *Nein!*, 79.8, 139.8; and quotation in Langille report, 29. According to one of Griebl's accounts, von Bonin first proposed the idea that Moog should perform services in Washington when he met her and Griebl on the *Europa* as they traveled to the Pfeiffer rendezvous in Bremen. See Batvinis, *Origins of FBI Counterintelligence*, 20.

17. Langille report, 29; Liddell, "German Espionage," 5; and Turrou, *Nazi Spy*, 8–12.

18. Von Bonin biographical summary, 7.

19. Statement of Katherina Moog Busch, 24 March 1938, pp. 2–3, FNAZ 5/213.

20. Moog statement, 4.

21. Camp 020 Memo, R. G. Fletcher to D. M. Ladd, with observations by Dr. Erich Pheiffer, "head of Nest Bremen from 1934 to 1941," on the London edition of Turrou's *Nazi Spy Conspiracy in America* (1939, commenting on p. 120), 16 January 1946, p. 7, FNAZ 45/1875.

22. Langille report, 43. Turrou put the values at $100,000 and $20,000. See Turrou, *Nazi Spy*, 217–18.

23. For a strong data match, see "Isidor Berliner," https://www.geni.com/pe ople/Isidor-Berliner/6000000001850878371 (last updated 17 November 2014).

24. Gempp in *Köilnische Zeitung*, 31 January 1929, quoted in Craig, *Tangled Web*, 256. Craig suggests that at a time when France was pressing for the payment of war reparations, Gempp was trying to defame the French by inferring that they had executed an innocent woman. A French declassification of the files in 2017 became available at https://bit.ly/3blDOKx.

25. Reile, *Frauen im Geheimdienst*, 43, 44, 92. Reile may have been influenced by the more feminist temper of the 1970s, the decade in which he wrote his book.

26. "Two Women Held as Spy Witnesses," *New York Times*, 15 June 1938.

27. Langille report, 38.

28. FBI Report on Hans Ritter, 21 May 1942, KV2/2130.

29. Richmond, *Fetch the Devil*, 277.

10. A Season of Inquiry

1. Leland Stowe, "International Spy Systems Increase," *Washington Post*, 26 June 1938.

2. Tamm, Memorandum for the Director, 3 April 1938, 43–44.

3. Turrou, Report on Rumrich/Espionage report, 2 April 1938, 4–5.

4. Associated Press, "US Guards Air Base as 3 Wait Jury in Spy Scare," *Washington Post*, 28 February 1938. Vetterli worked on the tragic Charles Mattson case of 1936–37.

5. Statement of Wilhelm Drechsel, 28 March 1938, in Turrou, Report of Rumrich/Espionage, 16–20, 34.

6. Paraphrase of Drechsel statement in Turrou, 26, 42. Because of declining passenger numbers, the two firms were placed in administration, and their management fell under the control of the National Socialist Party.

7. Statements of Drechsel and of Wilhelm Boehnke, political officer on the SS *Bremen*, 3 June 1938, in McLaughlin, "Guenther Gustave Rumrich with aliases," 6–11.

8. Turrou, Report on Rumrich/Espionage, 28.

9. Tamm, Memorandum, 7. On the seizure of phone records, see Turrou report on von Bonin and others, 69–72. On the polygraphic testing of Drechsel, Moog, Griebl, and others, see R. E. Vetterli to Director, FBI, 30 April 1938, p. 2, FNAZ 9/335.

10. C. K. Lee, Parole Report on Voss, 14 December 1938, p. 2, FNAZ 27/1254.

11. Turrou report on von Bonin and others, 35; Tamm, memorandum, 56–57; and Turrou, *Nazi Spy*, 140–43.

12. Turrou, Report on Rumrich/Espionage, 106.

13. Turrou, 83–90.

14. Turrou, 79–81.

15. Tamm, Memorandum, 49.

16. Herrmann statement, 28 March, 1938, in Turrou, Report on Rumrich/Espionage, 48–55.

17. Rossberg statement, 29 March 1938, in Turrou, 59–62.

18. "Another US Espionage Arrest," *Daily Telegraph* (London), 6 June 1938.

11. The Flight of the Spies

1. Turrou, *Nazi Spy*, 165.

2. Kruse statement, 25 March 1938, in Turrou, Report on Rumrich/Espionage, 2 April 1938, p. 9; and Turrou, *Nazi Spy*, 167. Often accidentally but sometimes reflecting Abwehr deception, spellings varied considerably in FBI, MI5, and German documents. Theodore Schuetz may have been identical with an agent called Schultz, who, according to Pfeiffer, was Schlueter's replacement on the *Europa*. See F. G. Beith, "Interim Report in the Case of Erich Pheiffer," September 1945, p. 13, KV2/267 (hereafter "Beith report").

3. Paraphrase of Drechsel's statement to the FBI, 31 March 1938, in Turrou, Report on Rumrich/Espionage, 32; and Janichen is identified in Beith report, 13.

4. Turrou, *Nazi Spy*, 130.

5. Turrou, 235; and Langille report, 27–28.

6. Statement of Harry Grundling, Room and Table Steward, SS *Bremen*, 19 July 1938, FNAZ 15/696; and Griebl to Vetterli cable, 16 May 1938, reproduced in Langille report, 39.

7. Grundling statement, 22; and Pfeiffer paraphrased and Griebl quoted in translation, in Beith report, 31. MI5 personnel habitually used the spelling "Pheiffer," as they saw it as the phonetic rendering of Pfeiffer's name. Wurzburg is in Bavaria, where Griebl must by this time have taken possession of the house the Abwehr had promised him for his services.

8. Turrou, *Nazi Spy*, 259; Pfeiffer evidence recounted in Beith report, 15; British Army on the Rhine, Preliminary Interrogation Report on Ritter, 14 December 1945, 3; and Langille report, 103–5.

9. Turrou, Report on Rumrich/Espionage, 20 June 1938, enclosed with J. Edgar Hoover to Rear Admiral R. S. Holmes, Director of Naval Intelligence, 8 July 1938, and quoting German communications, 1-4, FNAZ 12/546; and Turrou, *Nazi Spy*, 263.

10. Hinsley and Simkins, *British Intelligence*, 4:11–12; and Andrew, *Defence of the Realm*, 209.

11. Weiner, *Enemies*, 79.

12. Batvinis, *Origins of FBI Counterintelligence*, 25. Friske would reappear to testify at the spy trial in the fall.

13. "Hitler Aides Indicted in American Spy Plot," *Los Angeles Times*, 21 June 1938.

14. Abortive inquiry into Dr. Karl Otto reported in "Blamierte Spionjäger," *Hamburger Nachrichten*, 19 June 1938, 1. On behalf of the author, Leonie Werle perused the files of the *Völkischer Beobachter* for selected dates, finding no references to the American spy affair: Werle to author, email, 15 October 2018. *Frankfurter Zeitung* reported sympathetically on US politics and covered the contemporary Moscow spy trials, but it steered clear of the Abwehr spy scandal in the United States.

15. Crawford in *Congressional Record*, 75 Cong., 2 sess., Senate Proceedings 83/6, 3 May 1938, 6186; Ashurst in *Congressional Record*, 75 Cong., 3 sess., House Proceedings 83/8, 10 June 1938, 8672–73; Dickstein in *Congressional Record*, 75 Cong., 3 sess., Appendix 83/10, 31 May 1938, 2303–4; and Duffy, *Double Agent*, 308–9n54.

16. Both quotations from Turrou, *Nazi Spy*, 264.

17. Jeffreys-Jones, *FBI*, 91.

18. Tamm, Memorandum for the Director, 5 April 1938, p. 1; and Hardy and others paraphrased in "Inquiry Is On Here in Spy Ring Scare," *New York Times*, 20 February 1938.

19. "Leader Confesses," *New York Times*, 27 February 1938.

20. Lamar Hardy obituary, *New York Times*, 19 August 1950.

21. Both quotations from "Hoover and Hardy Clash in Spy Case," *New York Times*, 2 June 1938.

12. Blame Games

1. Theoharis, *Chasing Spies*, 35; Lokhova, *Spy Who Changed History*, chap. 1nn2, 7; Haynes and Klehr, *Venona*, 50, 174; and Christopher Andrew quoting Hoover from MI5 files in Andrew, *Defence of the Realm*, 388.

2. Erickson, "Soviet War Losses," 256–68.

3. Pfeiffer's quotations in Beith report, 29–30.

4. Pfeiffer quoting Canaris, from Beith report, 29–30.

5. Turrou article in *New York Post*, 3 January 1939. According to Turrou, the promotion was from kapitänleutnant to full kapitän, with the US equivalents being lieutenant commander to full commander.

6. Hoare, *Camp 020*, 361.

7. MI5 Counter Intelligence War Room, Liquidation Report No. 206, KV3/204.

8. Pfeiffer's naval design assertion could well have related more to his espionage activities against the United Kingdom. Extensive from 1937 on, these activities gave MI5 great concern. See Andrew, *Defence of the Realm*, 211.

9. "Report from FBI re Dr. Eric Pfeiffer, with aliases," undated, p. 2, KV2/267.

10. Griebl quoting Pfeiffer in Turrou, *Nazi Spy*, 15.

11. Turrou, 15.

12. Turrou, *Where My Shadow Falls*, 143.

13. Memorandum (probably by E. A. Tamm), 5 April 1938, pp. 45–47, FNAZ 7/320.

14. Turrou, Report on Rumrich/Espionage, 2 April 1938, pp. 99–118. The Burgess aluminum design was tried but abandoned when cracks appeared in the destroyers' hulls.

15. Turrou report on von Bonin and others, 58.

16. Turrou, Report on Rumrich/Espionage, 140–42.

17. Turrou report on von Bonin and others, 65; and Turrou, Report on Rumrich/Espionage, 140.

18. Editorial, "Spies," *New York Times*, 1 December 1938.

19. Liddell, "German Espionage Case," 15.

20. McLaughlin, "Guenther Gustave Rumrich," 2; Turrou, Report on Rumrich/Espionage, 20 June 1938, p. 11; and Dix quoted in "Turrou Spy Story Barred in Press," *New York Times*, 23 June 1938.

21. "Turrou Spy Story," *New York Times*.

22. Press release, "Statement of Lamar Hardy, United States Attorney. Re: Spy Investigation," 20 June 1938, pp. 2, 5–6, FNAZ 14/661.

13. Dismissed with Prejudice

1. Turrou to Hoover, 20 June 1938, FBIT 1/2/1.

2. "4 High-Ranking Nazis Names as Spy 'Brains'," *Washington Post*, 23 June 1938.

3. "Ace G-man Bares German Conspiracy to Paralyze United States!" *New York Post*, 22 June 1938.

4. "4 High-Ranking Nazis," *Washington Post*; "G-Men and Publicity," *Newsweek*, 11 July 1938; and "Turrou Reported Signed by Warners," *New York World*, 9 July 1938. These reports indicated that the contract was signed fifteen minutes after Turrou's resignation. There was no doubt agreement in principle, but the operative contract was signed on 19 July. See chapter 16 for the actual amounts paid.

5. Turrou to Tamm, 11 August 1938, FBIT 1/2/1.

6. Hoover, memo for Tolson, 14 May 1938; Vetterli to Hoover, 1 June 1938; Hoover to Vetterli, 6 June 1938; and Tamm, memo for files, 10 June 1938—all in FBIT 1/2/1.

7. Stern quoted in "4 High-Ranking Nazis," *Washington Post*.

8. P. E. Foxworth, Memorandum for Mr. Tamm re: Rumrich Case, 23 June 1938, FBIT 1/2/1.

9. "Free Press Argued at Turrou Hearing," *New York Times*, 24 June 1938.

10. Rifkind quoted in Foxworth memo.

11. "President Urges Fund to Fight Spies," *New York Times*, 25 June 1938.

12. Hoover to Rear Adm. R. S. Holmes, 8 July 1938, enclosing two reports by Leon G. Turrou dated 14 and 20 June 1938, FNAZ 12/546.

13. Purvis, *Vendetta*, 11, 182.

14. Hoover, Memorandum for Mr. Tamm, reciting a briefing Hoover had given to a journalist from the *Buffalo Evening News*, FBIT 1/3/1; and "Hoover Jealous, Turrou Declares," *New York Times*, 2 July 1938.

15. Critique by John D. Pennekamp, managing editor of the *Miami Herald*, of Hoover's 13 August 1938 *Collier's* article, as reported in *Newsweek*, 22 August 1938.

16. Hoover, two separate memorandums to Assistant Attorney General Joseph B. Keenan, both dated 24 June 1938, FBIT 1/2/1.

17. Denniston, "Yardley's Diplomatic Secrets," 81, 122–23.

18. Percy E. Foxworth headed the FBI's Special Intelligence Service in South America, created in 1941, until he was killed in a plane crash in Dutch Guiana (later Suriname) in January 1943.

19. Text of *New York Times* editorial reproduced in P. E. Foxworth, Memorandum for Mr. Tamm, 22 June 1938, FBIT 1/2/1; Foxworth, Memorandum for the Director, 24 June 1938, FBIT 1/2/1; and facsimile of the text of the 1933 "Yardley Act" in Kahn, *Reader of Gentlemen's Mail*, 170.

20. The full text of Totten v. United States, 92 US 105 (1875) is at https://supreme.justia.com/cases/federal/us/92/105/case.html.

21. Turrou, sworn statement, FBIT 1/2/1 (emphasis added).

22. Cummings to Turrou, "20" June 1938; Hoover, dismissal recommendation, 25 June 1938; and Hoover to all Special Agents in Charge, 27 June 1938—all in FBIT 1/2/1; "Turrou Dismissed 'with Prejudice' by FBI," *New York Times*, 1 July 1938; and "Hoover Jealous," *New York Times*.

23. Hoover, memo for Mr. Tolson, 30 June 1938, FBIT 1/2/1.

24. Turrou quoted in the *Washington Post*, 24 June 1938.

25. Turrou quoted in "G-men and Publicity," *Newsweek*, 11 July 1938.

26. Turrou quoted in "Turrou, Ex-GMan, to Fight Back," *New York Sun*, 1 July 1938.

27. "Hoover Writes, Why Can't I?," *Washington Post*, 24 June 1938.

28. "Spy Catcher Quits G-Men," *Daily Mirror* (New York), 22 June 1938.

29. George C. Dix, Supplementary Affidavits in Support of Motion for Commission, US District Court, Southern District of New York, 2 July 1938, NANY.

14. Seeking the Evidence

1. Turrou to Hoover, 30 September 1937, FBIT 1/2/1; E. A. Tamm, Memorandum for the File re: Turrou, 1 December 1938, FBIT 1/3/1; and Hoover memorandum for Tolson, 25 August 1938, FBIT 1/3/1.

2. Motion for Bill of Particulars and Affidavit, 18 July 1938, US District Court, Southern District of New York, NANY.

3. Barnes, *Life of Hans Wasemann*, 170n8; and Christgau, *Enemies*, 172.

4. Dix quoted in "Accuser Weakens on Turrou Charge," *New York Times*, 30 June 1938.

5. George C. Dix affidavit, 2 July 1938, NANY.

6. Davidson quoted in "Visiting Judge Holds Lawyer in Contempt," *New York Times*, 9 August 1938. John N. Garner, from Texas, was prominent at the time because he was vice president of the United States (1933–41).

7. George C. Dix supplemental affidavit, 22 August 1938, NANY.

8. Dix, Order to Show Cause and Affidavits, 27 June 1938, NANY; Dix, Supplementary Affidavits in Support of Motion for Commission, 2 July 1938, NANY; and "Woman in Spy Case Denies She's Guilty," *New York Times*, 3 July 1938.

9. Order, USA v Karl Schluter et al., 29 July 1938, NANY.

10. "Sail to Question Griebl," *New York Times*, 8 September 1938.

11. Langille report, 41.

12. E. A. Tamm memorandum for the files re: Rumrich case, 6 October 1938, FBIT 1/3/1.

13. Griebl quoted in Strassman, *Strassmans*, 137.

14. Attorneys' report paraphrased by FBI special agent Brantley, in Tamm memo of 6 October 1938.

15. All quotations from Tamm memo. Dwight Brantley was by now special agent in charge, New York.

16. Liddell, "Liaison with the United States Government Intelligence," 1–2; Liddell paraphrased in Turrou, Report on Rumrich/Espionage, 2 April 1938, p. 41; P. E. Foxworth, Memorandum for Mr. Tamm, 26 May 1938, FNAZ 10/450; and Curry, *Security Service*, 137.

17. "Woman Convicted as Spy in Scotland," *New York Times*, 17 May 1938.

18. D. H. Moir, "Jordan Witnesses May Go to USA," *Daily Herald*, 22 June 1938.

19. "Hardy to Follow Spy Trail Abroad," *New York Times*, 29 June 1938; and R. A. Pugh, "Spy Hunter Tells of English Visit," *Daily Mail*, 4 July 1938.

20. "Jailed Woman Spy Expecting Freedom Soon," *Daily Express*, 26 July 1938.

21. P. J. Rose (assistant secretary of state, Scottish Office) to Vernon Kell (head of MI5), 26 July 1938, HH16/212, file 4139, SNA.

22. Lorenz biography in Pfeiffer's list of personnel associated with his Abwehr work, "Camp 020 Pheiffer Report," appendix XX, p. 26.

23. "Camp 020 Pheiffer Report," 32.

15. The Nazi Spy Trial

1. Turrou, *Nazi Spy*, 267.

2. Percy Hoskins, "Our Own Spies Are Not So Bad, Come to That," *Daily Express*, 20 October 1938; "Trial Stirs the Soviet," *New York Times*, 22 October 1938; "Nazis Profess No Concern in NY Spy Trial," *Washington Post*, 9 October 1938; and *Völkischer Beobachter* as well as a sample of other German newspapers scanned by the author's research assistant, Leonie Werle.

3. Liddell, "German Espionage," 14; and Kimball, "Dieckhoff and America," 218.

4. Rowan, *Story of Secret Service*, 1.

5. "Confessed Spy Tells of Part in Plot," *Los Angeles Times*, 18 October 1938; "Spy Witness Bares 'Mata Hari' Offer," *New York Times*, 28 October 1938; and "Reich's Relief Fund Financed Plots, Spy Says," *Washington Post*, 25 October 1938.

6. "Spy Plot to Gas US Army Chief," *Daily Mirror*, 19 October 1938.

7. Certificate of Dr. T. J. Schück, Hoboken, NJ, 23 August 1938, NANY; Lamar Hardy, Opinion, U.S. v. Udo Von Bonin, In the Matter of the Application of Maria Griebl, #963, 16 September 1938, p. 3, NANY; Records of the Property Control Branch of the US Allied Commission for Austria, 1945–50, "Petition for Control and Appointment of Administrator by the American Property Control Office, 14 September 1945," US Allied Commission for Austria, Vienna Area Command, National Archives and Records Administration DN1929, Record Group 260, accessed online via Fold3, PC/V/1/13 Marie Griebl, p. 26; Collins quoted in Batvinis, *Origins of FBI Counterintelligence*, 26; "Grand Jury Hears Mrs Griebl," *New York Times*, 29 July 1938; and "Spy Ring Witness Released from Bail," *New York Times*, 23 September, 1938.

8. Tamm, Memorandum for the File re: Rumrich Case, 10 October 1938, FBIT 1/3/1.

9. Dix quoted in "Griebl Deposition Read at Spy Trial," *New York Times*, 10 November 1938; Tamm, Memorandum for the Files re: Rumrich Case, 6 October 1938, FBIT 1/3/1; and Turrou, *Nazi Spy*, 268.

10. "Reich's Relief Fund Financed Plots, Spy Says," *Washington Post*, 25 October 1938; "Spy Explains Aid to Germany," *Los Angeles Times*, 17 and "Confessed Spy Tells of Part in Plot," *Los Angeles Times*, 22 October 1938.

11. Defense attorneys' quotation in "Confessed Spy Tells of Part in Plot," *Los Angeles Times*, 22 October 1938; and "Reich's Relief Fund," *Washington Post*.

12. Lee, Parole report on Johanna Hofmann.

13. Hofmann quoted in "Woman Spy Suspect Cries during Trial," *Los Angeles Times*, 21 October 1938.

14. Hofmann-Dix petition, 16 September 1938, NANY.

15. Digest of Dix's statement in P. E. Foxworth, Memorandum for Mr. E. A. Tamm, 17 October 1938, FBIT 1/3/1.

16. Steuer statement, 14 March 1938, in Turrou, Report, 13 March 1938, p. 33, FNAZ 4/141.

17. "Turrou under Fire Again at Spy Trial," *New York Times*, 22 November 1938.

18. Dix quoted in "US Attorney, G-Man Flayed at Trial," *Washington Post*, 29 November 1938.

19. Dialogue and *Sun* quotation from Patenaude, *Big Show in Bololand*, 689; and dialogue from "Turrou under Fire Again," *New York Times*.

20. Tamm, Memorandum, 10 October 1938.

21. Hoover, handwritten note on Foxworth, Memorandum for the Director re: Rumrich Case, 19 November 1938, FBIT 1/3/1.

22. Hoover, Memorandum for Mr. Tamm, 26 October 1938, FBIT 1/3/1.

23. Kessler, *Bureau*, 40. The bureau's website exhibits a document suggesting that the invention of the term "FBI" and of the accompanying motto are attributable to Special Agent W. H. Drane Lester, who in September 1935 was the editor of the employee magazine, *The Investigator*.

24. P. E. Foxworth, memorandum for Mr. E. A. Tamm, 17 October 1938, FBIT 1/3/1.

25. Tamm, Memorandum of the files in re: Rumrich Case, 2 November 1938, FBIT 1/3/1.

26. Tamm, Memorandum for the files re: Former Agent Turrou, 30 November 1938, FBIT 1/3/1.

27. Foxworth, Memorandum for the Director re: Leon G. Turrou, 5 December 1938, FBIT 1/3/1.

28. Foxworth, Memorandum for the Director re: Rumrich Case, 7 December 1938, FBIT 1/3/1; and Hardy's fifteen-minute appointment recorded in Stenographer's Diary and Tully's Appointments Diary, 8 December 1937, DbD.
29. "Suspect Found Guilty as Spy," *Los Angeles Times*, 1 December 1938.
30. Photograph of a weeping Hofmann in "Judge Shows Her Mercy," *Los Angeles Times*, 3 December 1938; and Knox quotations, from the same source, and also in Turrou, *Nazi Spy*, 273.

16. Of Propaganda and Revenge

1. E. A. Tamm, Memorandum for the File, 1 December 1938, FBIT 1/3/1.
2. Quotations from Lore, "Spies, Plain and Fancy"; Rowan, *Secret Agents against America*; and Turrou, *Nazi Spy*, 114. At various times a socialist, communist, and Trotskyist, Lore had in the early 1930s spied for the Soviet Union but was respected for his independence of mind.
3. "Camp 020 Pheiffer Report," 32; and Leonie Werle's computer-aided survey of the online mentions of the 1930s German press, drawing on resources in the State Library of Berlin, the Cooperative Library Network Berlin-Brandenburg, and the libraries of the Free University of Berlin and Humboldt University.
4. Earl Richert, "Turrou Says US Infested by Saboteurs," *Indianapolis Times*, 3 February 1940.
5. Dick Scholz, "US Is Pitted with Spies, Says Former G-Man Turrou," *Washington News*, 28 April 1939.
6. "US Filled with Spies, Turrou Says," *Pittsburgh Post*, 2 May 1939.
7. Hoover's annotation to a clipping from the *Boston Herald*, 17 November 1939, FBIT 1/3/1. On Hoover and the origins of the FBI's Crime Records Division, see Cecil, *Branding Hoover's America*, 14–15.
8. Transcript of Turrou lecture enclosed with SAC B. R. Sacket to Director FBI, 5 February 1940, FBIT 1/5/1.
9. Turrou quoted in Lowell Lawrence, "Former G-Man Speaks Out in Defense of Maligned Kansas City," *Kansas City Journal*, 6 April 1939.
10. Earl Richert writing in the *Indianapolis Times*, 3 February 1940; and text of "Sylvan Seal" WCAU radio broadcast, 2 May 1939, FBIT, 1/4/1.

11. Diggins, *Mussolini and Fascism*, 113; White House Usher's Diary, 8 July 1937, DbD; and Donovan and Mowrer, *Fifth Column Lessons*. Hemingway's play *The Fifth Column* was not produced until 1944.

12. Doherty, *Hollywood and Hitler*, 335–36.

13. Quotation from Gabler, *Empire of Their Own*, 2, 6.

14. Rosenzweig, *Hollywood's Spies*, 93.

15. Doherty, *Hollywood and Hitler*, 12.

16. Jack Warner quoted in Herzstein, *Roosevelt and Hitler*, 280.

17. Vaughan, "Spies," 366; Warner Bros. Studios press release, 30 January 1939, in FBIT 1/3/1; Lya Lys's obituary, *Los Angeles Times*, 8 June 1986; Doherty, *Hollywood and Hitler*, 338; and Kullen, "Little Caesar," 97.

18. Quotations from Kullen, "Little Caesar," 37. See also Moldovan, "Romanian Jew in Hollywood," 43–44; and "They're Confessin'," *Washington Sunday Star*, 15 January 1939.

19. The Warners arrived at 3:30 p.m., and the president had nothing further scheduled until 6:15 p.m., per Stenographer's Diary and Tully's Appointments Diary, 17 March 1939, DbD.

20. *New York Daily News*, 5 May 1939.

21. Donald McNicol, "Ex-'G'-Man Relates Facts behind Spy Film," *Daily Worker*, 23 June 1939; and Greene's reviews in *The Spectator*, 23 June and 7 July 1939.

22. Sandeen, "Anti-Nazi Sentiment," 73; Hoellering, review of *Confessions*, 595–96; Louella O. Parsons, "'Confessions of a Nazi Spy' Epochal Film," *Los Angeles Examiner*, 28 April 1939; and Lorentz quoted in Halliwell, *Halliwell's Film Guide*, 149.

23. Pfeiffer paraphrased in "Camp 020 Pheiffer Report," 32.

24. William J. Donovan and Edgar Mowrer, "French Debacle Held Masterpiece of Fifth Columnists under Hitler," *New York Times*, 22 August 1940. On the FBI's suspicions, see the bureau documents cited in Lownie, "Tyler Kent," in Jeffreys-Jones and Lownie, *North American Spies*, 67–68, 77nn92–106.

25. Vetterli to Director, FBI, 28 June 1938, FBIT 1/2/1.

26. Loebl to Director, FBI, re: Leon George Turrou, 24 August 1938, FBIT 1/3/1.

27. Leon G. Turrou, "Hitler Could Be Kidnapped if Ace US Snatchers Were Put on the Job," *Pittsburgh Press*, 26 July 1941. Dr. Samuel Harden

Church, president of the Carnegie Institute, had offered a million-dollar reward for the capture of Hitler and his delivery to a court of justice.

28. Turrou to La Guardia, 23 July 1940; Hoover to La Guardia, 27 July 1940; Hoover comment on Ed Tamm to Director, 5 June 1942; and Hoover comment on dinner conversation report by informant (name redacted), 3 July 1942—all in FBIT 1/5/1; and Batvinis, *Hoover's Secret War*, 296–97n23.

29. Purvis, *Vendetta*, 312.

30. Turrou, *Where My Shadow Falls*, 199–212; and Corson, *Armies of Ignorance*, 87.

31. "Fabrik der Gerechtigkeit," 18–19.

32. Tamm to Hoover, 5 June 1942, FBIT 1/5/1.

33. Turrou quoted in Getty, *As I See It*, 254; and Corson, *Armies of Ignorance*, 88.

34. Turrou to Hoover, 13 April 1965; C. R. Davidson Memorandum, 20 April 1965; Hoover airmail to Turrou, 1 June 1965; Turrou to Hoover, 20 July 1965; and FBI Notification, signed 21 June 1965—all in FBIT 1/6/1.

17. Spy Sequels

1. Brantley memorandum, 15 December 1938, FNAZ 27/1251.

2. Hermann Wobrock interview with Theo Long, 1955, denying he had divorced Marga, cited in Jeffrey, *Dangerous Menace*, 24; and prison invigilator's notes on conversation between Jessie Jordan and her daughter, Marga, 25 October 1938, HH16/212, file 4139, SNA. It is unclear whether, at the time of the Gretna Green ceremony, Tom Reid was yet divorced from Jessie Horan, the woman he had married in 1930 in Ayr when he was seventeen years old, per Andrew Jeffrey's comments sent to the author in November 2017.

3. Photograph of four-year-old Jessie peeping from behind a cabin door on the SS *Gothland*, in the Glasgow *Bulletin*, 14 November 1938.

4. Hinchley Cooke to Colonel Leith-Ross of the Prisons Department for Scotland, 26 August 1938, HH16/212, file 4139, SNA; and John Sturrock (Royal Infirmary, Edinburgh) to Mr. Sloan, 23 September 1938, HH16/212, file 4139, SNA.

5. Hamburg death certificate, dated 26 January 1939 and referring to the patient's perforated uterus, kindly supplied to the author by Donald Haddow; prison warder's transcript of conversation between Jessie Jordan and

Tom Reid, who had just returned from a futile visit to Germany aimed at bringing the child Jessie to Scotland, 7 March 1939, HH16/212, file 4139/2, SNA; and Andrew Jeffrey's notes sent to the author, November 2017, indicating Reid's marriage to Grace Nisbet in Hillhead, Glasgow, in 1940.

6. Transcript of conversation between Tom Reid and Jessie Jordan signed by the governor, Edinburgh Prison (Saughton), 30 January 1939, and sent to the Secretary of State, Scottish Office, London, HH16/212, file 4139/2, SNA.

7. Report on Jordan by governor of Aberdeen Prison, 23 December 1939, enclosing Jordan's handwritten note to governor, same date, HH16/212, file 4139/2, SNA; and Crown (Rumrich) to anonymous Abwehr controller, 17 January 1938, KV2/3421.

8. For a comparison of Mata Hari with Jessie Jordan, see Jeffreys-Jones, "Verraden," 45–49.

9. Report to the secretary of state, governor of Aberdeen Prison, 23 December 1939, HH16/212, file 4139/3, SNA; and Rose letter to the governor, 9 January 1940, HH16/212, file 4139/3, SNA.

10. Particulars of Convict recommended for License, Jessie Wallace or Jordan, 30 November 1940, HH16/212, file 4139/4, SNA; Donald Haddow, "Jessie Wallace—'The Platinum Blonde Spy,'" an essay by the half grandnephew of Jessie Jordan, based on family interviews and other research. Completed in 2016, it was written for inclusion in a private family history book, and Haddow kindly supplied it to the author.

11. Haddow, "Jessie Wallace."

12. "Griebl Arrested in Austria," *New York Times*, 20 August 1945.

13. Flindt-Larsen summary, interrogation of Bonin at the British Military Mission Denmark, 31 August 1945, and accompanying correspondence, KV2/1973.

14. Batvinis, *Hoover's Secret War*, 232–47; and handwritten comment "shown to FBI 4.12.45," Flint-Larsen summary.

15. FBI report on Ritter, 2 September 1945, and accompanying British documents, KV2/87.

16. Report re: CELERY (double agent Walter Dicketts) and SNOW, 1 April 1941, KV2/86; and Andrew, *Secret Service*, 440–41.

17. British Army on the Rhine, Preliminary Interrogation Report on Oberstleutnant Nikolaus Fritz Adolf Ritter, alias Rantzau etc., 20 No-

vember 1945, KV2/88; and Ritter, *Deckname Dr. Rantzau*, 9–10, 28–32, 51–52.

18. Langille report, 5 April 1943, FNAZ 38/1664.

19. Edward C. Kemper, Jr. report, 25 September 1943, FNAZ 39/1713.

20. Julius H. Rice report, 21 October 1943, FNAZ 42/1788.

21. J. T. McLaughlin, round up report on the spy case fugitives, 25 February 1939, FNAZ 39/1333.

22. C. K. Lee, report on Rumrich case, 28 December 1938, FNAZ 28/1279; and quotation from Judge John C. Knox's memorandum in the case USA v. Erich Glaser et al., 16 December 1938, NANY.

23. C. K. Lee, report of 21 June 1939 enclosed with Hoover to SAC NY, 12 July 1939, FNAZ 30/1369; and Langille report.

24. Lee, Parole report on Johanna Hofmann; and Langille report, FNAZ 38/1664.

25. C. K. Lee, parole report on Otto Hermann Voss, 14 December 1938, FNAZ 27/1254; criminal case docket C102-462, NANY; and Louis A. Langille, case report on Rumrich (and associates), 5 April 1943, FNAZ 44/1847.

18. The Case Named for Duquesne

1. Ronnie, *Counterfeit Hero*, 6, 140.

2. Ritter, *Deckname Dr. Rantzau*, 45–58, 87–88; Ronnie, *Counterfeit Hero*, 213–14; and Breuer, *Spy Who Spent*, 17–18.

3. MI5 Counter Intelligence War Room, Liquidation Report No. 206, with enclosures, KV3/204.

4. Memorandum for the file re: Frederick Joubert Duquesne/Espionage, 13 September 1941, enclosed with J. Edgar Hoover to SAC Cincinnati, 5 November 1941, FNAZ 36/1527.

5. J. M. Gwyer letter to anonymous colleague in MI6, 26 March 1942, KV2/87.

6. Duffy, *Double Agent*, 64–65.

7. Duffy, 114, 124.

8. Ronnie, *Counterfeit Hero*, 220–21.

9. Stafford, *Roosevelt and Churchill*, 9, 29; and Field, *All This*, 30.

10. Busch's criticism of his colleagues may have been colored by the fact that he was an anti-Nazi. See J. C. Hales's interrogation report dated 13 August 1945 and Leroy Vogel's US interrogation report dated 11 January 1946—both for the US Army and located in KV2/529.

11. Miller, "Spies in America," 44; list of the unindicted in Batvinis, *Origins of FBI Counterintelligence*, 265–66; Hoover quoted in "US Spy Round-Up," *Scotsman* (Edinburgh), 1 July 1941; and "US Bomb Sight Sold to Germany, Jury Is Told," *New York Times*, 9 September 1941.

12. Hoover quoted in Ronnie, *Counterfeit Hero*, 258.

13. Quotations from the DVD of Litvak's *Confessions of a Nazi Spy*; Klemperer, *German Resistance against Hitler*, 154; and Kollander, "Boomerang Resistance," in Zeiler and Dubois, *Companion to World War II*, 639.

14. Dulles cited in Adams, *Historical Dictionary*, 4.

15. Handlin, *Uprooted*, 272, 285.

16. "Spies, Guerrillas and Violent Fantasies" (Tavistock Institute). The finding was based on interviews with contemporary Palestinians, but Tavistock had a link to World War II studies of spy personality through the work of former SOE psychiatrist P. M. Turquet. See Bailey, "Psychiatrists and Secret Agents," 2864.

17. List of those indicted on 1 July 1941 in Batvinis, *Origins of FBI Counterintelligence*, 263–64; and Kater, *Nazi Party*, 236, 238.

18. On von Bonin's role, see J. A. Cimperman, from 1 Grosvenor Square (the American Embassy) to Winston M. Scott, War Department, 14 November 1945, KV2/1873. On the Meiler affair, see Batvinis, *Hoover's Secret War*, 232–47.

19. Counter Intelligence War Room London, Liquidation Report No. 206, 16.

20. According to a later, more detailed report, by the time news of Sebold's defection came through, the German authorities were already done with Ritter and had moved him to new responsibilities. He was in any case recovering from injuries sustained in an African air crash. British Army on the Rhine, Preliminary Interrogation Report on Ritter, 14 December 1945, 3–4.

19. Pfeiffer's Story

1. "Camp 020 Pheiffer Report," appendix I, 89.

2. "Erich Pfeiffer, Details of Property," 9 October 1945, KV2/267. Pfeiffer had much more luggage than his fellow voyagers did.

3. "Agnostio" report on Eitel, 24 July 1944, KV2/383; Camp 202, "Interim Report in the Case of Karl Eitel," 28 October 1944, p. 1, KV2/384; and "Camp 020 Pheiffer Report," 89.

4. Speech by Sir Ralph Glyn (Conservative, Abingdon), House of Commons, 22 May 1940, *Hansard*, vol. 361, column 197.

5. Hoare, *Camp 020*, 20, 368; Fry, *London Cage*, 18, 46; and McKinstry, *Operation Sealion*, 40.

6. Captain Beith's account and Pfeiffer's own account in "Camp 020 Pheiffer Report," 90.

7. The quotation is an 020 heading for Turkish Abwehr desertion cases, from Minute sheet, 6 September 1944, KV2/267.

8. Maj. C. O'Brien to A. J. Kellar, 1 September 1945, KV2/267.

9. Robin Stephens, "A Digest of Ham," an account of Camp 020 printed in Hoare, *Camp 020*, 59.

10. A. J. Kellar to Aubrey Jones, 6 September 1945, KV2/267; Jones to Kellar, 8 September 1945, KV2/267; and Murphy, *Diplomat among Warriors*, 240.

11. Fry, *London Cage*, 46.

12. "Camp 020 Pheiffer Report," appendix III, 1, 8, 13; and a replica of appendix III incorporated in R. G. Fletcher to D. M. Ladd, Memorandum re: Rumrich/Espionage, 16 January 1946, FNAZ 45/1875. D. Milton Ladd was the director of the FBI's Domestic Intelligence Division from 1942 until he was promoted to assistant to the director in 1949. He oversaw the bureau's wartime counterintelligence effort.

13. Author's extended conversations with Mulhouse's Striby family, of later political note, in the early 1960s.

14. Burgland report on "Charles" Eitel, 25 September 1944, p. 39, KV2/382.

15. H. P. Milmo to C. P. Hill of the Aliens Department, Home Office, 5 October 1944, KV2/382; and Eitel translated and paraphrased in Burgland report, 7.

16. Eitel translated and paraphrased in Camp 202, "Interim Report on Eitel," 10, 11.

17. "Camp 020 Pheiffer Report," 1, 90.

18. Stephens, "Digest of Ham," in Hoare, *Camp 020*, 326.

19. "Camp 020 Pheiffer Report," 14.

20. "Camp 020 Pheiffer Report," appendix III, 9, 11, 13.

21. "Camp 020 Pheiffer Report," 1, 90, and appendix XX: Near East Personalities; Abwehr Personnel: Agents Other Contacts.

22. "Camp 020 Pheiffer Report," 59.

23. Quotations from "Camp 020 Pheiffer Report," 17, 18; and O'Halpin, *Spying on Ireland*, 38.
24. *Breiza Isel Arvor* translates as "lower Brittany shore."
25. "Camp 020 Pheiffer Report," 59; Robinson, *Invasion, 1940*, 204; and McKinstry, *Operation Sealion*, 182.
26. Ronge, *Kriegs -und Industrie Spionage*, 367–69; and "Camp 020 Pheiffer Report," 67.
27. "Camp 020 Pheiffer Report," 60.
28. Summary of Pfeiffer communications, 5 May 1940 to 11 March 1945, KV2/267; and "Camp 020 Pheiffer Report," 57, 59.
29. Memorandum, Lt. Col. A. H. Stimson to Major M. N. Forrest, 9 October 1945, KV2/267.
30. The postwar fate of Erich Pfeiffer is a mystery. A personnel file on him in the Deutsche Dienststelle (WASt) military records in Berlin is available only to family members, and it mistakenly holds that he died in the war, per Mietle for Deutsche Dienststelle email to Leonie Werle, 17 August 2018. In 1953 a CIA source noted that a certain Erich Pfeiffer, whom it identified as "a former SS war correspondent," had been the editor of the Austrian newspaper *Linzer Tagblatt* and that he was interested in and informed about the formation of a new German intelligence service. See Exhibit 1, Dr. Anton Boehm to Dr. Anton Fellner, 15 May 1953, https://www.cia.gov/library/readingroom/docs/HOETTL,%20WILHELM%20%20%20VOL.%206_0062.pdf (accessed 11 February 2019). The BND has not responded to the author's inquiries. Erich Pfeiffer is quite a common name.
31. Stephens, "Digest of Ham," in Hoare, *Camp 020*, 361; and "Camp 020 Pheiffer Report," 91.

20. Diplomatic Fallout

1. Adler, "War-Guilt Question," 16–18, 25, 27.
2. Smith, "Foreign Organization," in Trefousse, *Germany and America*, 179.
3. Welles, "Memorandum of Conversation," in Axton et al., *British Commonwealth*, 2:447–51, d359.
4. Welles, 2:447–51, d359.
5. Dieckhoff, "Memorandum on the Political Consequences of a Possible Rupture of Diplomatic Relations with the United States, 20 November

1939," in Lambert, Sweet, and Baumont, *Documents on German Foreign Policy*, series D, 4:Document 504.

6. Thomsen, telegrams "for the Personnel Department," 30 November and 1 December 1938, in Lambert, Sweet, and Baumont, *Documents on German Foreign Policy*, series D, 4:Document 505; and Compton, *Swastika and the Eagle*, 52–53.

7. Thomsen memorandum for Reich Minister of Foreign Affairs Joachim von Ribbentrop, 22 May 1940, in Lambert, Sweet, and Baumont, *Documents on German Foreign Policy*, series D, 9:Document 299.

8. Weizsäcker telegram to Thomsen, 10 June 1940, in Lambert, Sweet, and Baumont, *Documents on German Foreign Policy*, series D, 9:Document 411; and Thomsen memorandum, on which Ribbentrop wrote, "[For] F[ührer]."

9. Ribbentrop-Canaris meeting reported by the new head of the American desk at the Abwehr's Berlin headquarters, Friederich Busch, in FBI, *History of the Special Intelligence Service Division*, 2:435.

10. McPherson, *SHAFR Guide Online,* reveals a twenty-first-century drop-off in interest in the causes of America's entry into World War II. Dr. Andrew Johnstone, an authority on the United States' entry in World War II, noted the paucity of literature on the spy scandal's political repercussions in an email to the author, 15 January 2018: "I would have to say that the case has not really been integrated into the wider literature on 'the road to war' at all." Johnstone mentioned the scholarship of Michaela Hoenicke Moore. The latter historian notes President Roosevelt's anti-Nazi stance in the 1940 presidential election and offers the view that the Bund's Nazi propaganda was counterproductive, a judgment that is consistent with the argument that German spies adversely affected US public opinion. See Hönicke Moore, *Know Your Enemy*, 93, 94. In an unpublished master's thesis, Joan Irene Miller did address the political impact of the spies. She argues that it was considerable, and out of proportion to the actual threat proposed, for the media concocted a national spy phobia. See Miller, "Spies in America."

11. To the examples given at the start of the chapter may be added another, one that involved Germany and preceded the events of 1938 by little more than two decades. For varying views on how and to what extent the affair of the Zimmermann telegram contributed to the United States' entry in

World War I, see Tuchman, *Zimmermann Telegram*, 199; Boghardt, *Zimmermann Telegram*, 9–22; and Larsen, *Plotting for Peace*.

12. See, for example, Batvinis, *Origins of FBI Counterintelligence*, 257; and Luff, "Covert and Overt Operations," 752.

13. Liddell, "German Espionage," 6.

14. Hoskins, "Our Own Spies Are Not So Bad."

15. "President Urges Fund to Fight Spies," *New York Times*, 25 June 1938; "US to Get Help of Britain, France in Spy War," *Los Angeles Times*, 18 July 1939; and Draper, "Nazi Spies in France," 72.

16. "Roosevelt Seeks $108,000 for FBI in Emergencies," *Washington Post*, 11 May 1938; and "Table 1.1. Number of FBI Personnel and FBI Appropriations Annually, 1908–97," in Theoharis, *FBI*, 4–5.

17. Roosevelt press conference reported in "President Urges Funds to Fight Spies," *New York Times*, 25 June 1938; Historical Branch, G-2, "Materials on the History of Military," part 1, exhibit B: "Headquarters Personnel," MHFB; and F. H. Lincoln (assistant chief of staff, G-2), "The Military Intelligence Division, War Department General Staff" (typescript of lecture delivered at Fort Humphreys, Washington, DC, 5 January 1937), p. 3, Records of the War Department General Staff.

18. "US to Get Help of Britain," *Los Angeles Times*; and Jeffreys-Jones, *In Spies We Trust*, 72–73.

19. Schwartz testimony, 18 November 1975, in U.S. Senate Select Committee, *Hearings before the Select Committee*, 24.

20. Editorial, "Spies," *New York Times*, 1 December 1938.

21. "G-Man Hoover's Spy Hunt," *New Republic*, 10 June 1940, 778–79.

22. Undated draft in Box 55, folder "Justice: 1938-39," President's Secretary's File, FDR Library; Jeffreys-Jones, *FBI*, 128; and Charles, *J. Edgar Hoover*, 42.

23. Walter Trohan, "New Deal Plans to Spy on World and Home Folks; Super Gestapo Agency Is under Consideration," *Chicago Tribune*, 9 February 1945. President Truman agreed that "we have to guard against a Gestapo" in an off-the-record press conference, 18 April 1946, noted in general file, folder "Intelligence Service," Eben A. Ayers Papers.

24. Jeffreys-Jones, *We Know*, 91.

25. Leigh, *Mobilizing Consent*, 42; and summary of Lindsay telegram of 12 September 1938 in Reynolds, *Creation*, 34.

26. Langer and Gleason, *Challenge to Isolation*, 1:50–51; and Berinsky, *In Time of War*, 46.

27. According to "Trial Stirs the Soviet," *New York Times*, 22 October 1938.

28. Ambassador Hugh R. Wilson, Memorandum of the Conversation with Reich Minister of Propaganda Dr. Goebbels, 22 March 1938, in Schewe, *Franklin D. Roosevelt*, 9:458–59, document 1037a.

29. Lieutenant Flint-Larsen, transcript of von Bonin interrogation at the Civilian Interrogation Centre, British Military Mission Denmark, 31 August 1945, p. 7, KV2/1973. The author's research assistant, Leonie Werle, used a variety of German media search engines but found no references to the New York spy trial.

30. See Friedländer, *Prelude to Downfall*, 128–29.

31. Ed Tamm, Memorandum for the Director, 5 December 1938, FNAZ section 3, serial 1.

32. See, for example, Doenecke, *Storm on the Horizon*, 1.

33. Divine, *Foreign Policy*, vii.

34. Stouffer, *Communism, Conformity*, 59–66, 220.

35. For a summary of historians' assessments of Roosevelt's sensitivity to public opinion on foreign policy, see Kimball, *Juggler*, 204n13.

36. Author's frequency survey of the digitized *Congressional Record*.

37. Langer and Gleason, *Challenge to Isolation*, 1:50; and October 1939 Gallup poll cited in Kennedy, *Freedom from Fear*, 427.

38. "Is America Infested," *Christian Century*, 1316.

BIBLIOGRAPHY

Archival Sources

Ayers, Eben A. Papers. Harry S. Truman Library, Independence, MO.

Bundesarchiv, Berlin, Freiberg and Koblenz, Germany.

Cadogan, Sir Alexander George Montagu. Papers. Churchill Archives Centre. Cambridge University.

Court records, criminal case C102-462 (the Nazi spy trial). Record Group 21. National Archives, New York.

Deutsches Schiffahrtsmuseum (German Maritime Museum), Bremerhaven, Germany.

Fries Museum (Friesian Museum), Leeuwarden, the Netherlands.

Hoover Institution Library and Archives, Stanford, CA.

Library of Congress, Washington, DC.

National Archives, Washington, DC.
> Records of the Property Control Branch of the US Allied Commission for Austria, 1945–50.
> Records of the War Department General Staff. Military Intelligence Division, 1917–41.

National Library of Scotland, Edinburgh.

Roosevelt, Franklin D., (FDR) Presidential Library. Hyde Park, NY.
> Day by Day. Project of the Pare Lorentz Center. http://www.fdrlibrary.maris t.edu/daybyday/.
>> Stenographer's Diary.
>> Tully's Appointments Diary.
>> White House Usher's Diary.
> President's Secretary's File.
> Roosevelt, Franklin D. Papers.

Scottish National Archives, Edinburgh.

Scottish Supreme Court. Old Parliament Building, Edinburgh.

Staatsarchiv Bremen, Bremen, Germany.

The UK National Archives. Kew Gardens, London.
> MI5 files KV2 and KV3.

US Army Center of Military History Library. Forrestal Building, Washington, DC.

Vansittart, Lord, of Denham. Papers. Churchill Archives Center. Cambridge University.

Published Sources

Adams, Jefferson. *Historical Dictionary of German Intelligence*. Lanham, MD: Scarecrow, 2009.

Adler, Selig. "The War-Guilt Question and American Disillusionment, 1918–1928." *Journal of Modern History* 23 (March 1952): 1–28.

Ahlström, Göran. *Engineers and Industrial Growth*. London: Croom Helm, 1982.

Allen, Robert, ed. *Voice of Britain: The Inside Story of the Daily Express*. Cambridge: Stephens, 1983.

Anderson, Robert D. *European Universities from the Enlightenment to 1914*. Oxford: Oxford University Press, 2004.

Andrew, Christopher. *The Defence of the Realm: The Authorized History of MI5*. London: Allen Lane, 2009.

———. *Secret Service: The Making of the British Intelligence Community*. London: Heinemann, 1985.

Asada, Sadao, ed. *Japan and the World, 1853–1952: A Bibliographical Guide to Japanese Scholarship in Foreign Relations*. New York: Columbia University Press, 1989.

Ashdown, Paddy. *Nein! Standing Up to Hitler, 1935–1944*. London: William Collins, 2018. Ebook.

Bailey, Bill. *The Kid from Hoboken: An Autobiography*. San Francisco: Circus Lithographic Prepress, 1993.

Bailey, Roderick. "Psychiatrists and Secret Agents." *Lancet* 388 (December 2018): 2864–65.

Bajohr, Frank. *"Aryanisation" in Hamburg: The Economic Exclusion of Jews and the Confiscation of Their Property in Nazi Germany*. Translated by George Wilkes. New York: Berghahn Books, 2002.

Baker, Alain, and Bertrand Vilain. *L'affaire Seznec: Nouvelles révélations*. Cesson-Sévigné, France: Coëtquen, 2011.

Barnes, James J. *The Life of Hans Wasemann, 1895–1971*. Westport, CT: Praeger, 2001.

Batvinis, Raymond J. *Hoover's Secret War against Nazi Spies: FBI in World War II*. Lawrence: University Press of Kansas, 2014.

———. *The Origins of FBI Counterintelligence*. Lawrence: University Press of Kansas, 2007.

Bell, Leland V. "The Failure of Nazism in America: The German-American Bund, 1936–1941." *Political Science Quarterly* 85 (December 1970): 585–99.

Bellaby, Ross W. *The Ethics of Intelligence: A New Framework*. Abingdon, UK: Routledge, 2014.

Berinsky, Adam J. *In Time of War: Understanding American Public Opinion from World War II to Iraq*. Chicago: University of Chicago Press, 2009.

Boghardt, Thomas. *Spies of the Kaiser: German Covert Operations in Great Britain during the First World War Era*. Basingstoke, UK: Palgrave Macmillan, 2004.

———. *The Zimmermann Telegram: Intelligence, Diplomacy, and America's Entry into World War I*. Annapolis, MD: Naval Institute Press, 2012.

Booth, Alan R. "The Development of the Espionage Film." In *Spy Fiction, Spy Films, and Real Intelligence*, edited by Wesley K. Wark, 136–60. London: Frank Cass, 1991.

Bowd, Gavin. *Fascist Scotland: Caledonia and the Far Right*. Edinburgh: Birlinn, 2013.

Breitman, Richard. *U.S. Intelligence and the Nazis*. Cambridge: Cambridge University Press, 2005.

Breuer, William. *Nazi Spies in America*. New York: St. Martin's Press, 1990.

———. *The Spy Who Spent the War in Bed: And Other Bizarre Tales from World War II*. Hoboken, NJ: John Wiley, 2003.

Cadogan, Alexander. *The Diaries of Sir Alexander Cadogan, 1938–1945*. Edited by David Dilks. London: Cassell, 1971.

Cantril, Hadley, ed. *Public Opinion, 1935–1946*. Princeton, NJ: Office of Public Opinion Research, 1951.

Cecil, Matthew. *Branding Hoover's America: How the Boss's PR Men Sold the Bureau to America*. Lawrence: University Press of Kansas, 2016.

Charles, Douglas M. *J. Edgar Hoover and the Anti-Interventionists: FBI Political Surveillance and the Rise of the Domestic Security State, 1939–1945*. Columbus: Ohio State University Press, 2007.

Christgau, John. *Enemies: World War II Alien Internment*. Lincoln: University of Nebraska Press, 2009 (1985).

Christian Century. "Is America Infested with Spies?" 55 (2 November 1938): 1316.

Christiansen, Arthur. *Headlines All My Life.* London: Heinemann, 1961.

Cobain, Ian. *Cruel Britannia: A Secret History of Torture.* London: Portobello, 2012.

Cole, Wayne S. *Roosevelt and the Isolationists, 1932–45.* Lincoln: University of Nebraska Press, 1983.

———. *Senator Gerald P. Nye and American Foreign Relations.* Minneapolis: University of Minnesota Press, 1962.

Compton, James V. *The Swastika and the Eagle: Hitler, the United States and the Origins of the Second World War.* London: The Bodley Head, 1968.

Cook, Blanche W. *Eleanor Roosevelt.* London: Bloomsbury, 1993.

Corson, William R. *The Armies of Ignorance: The Rise of the American Intelligence Empire.* New York: Dial, 1977.

Craig, Mary W. *A Tangled Web: Mata Hari—Dancer, Courtesan, Spy.* Stroud: The History Press, 2018.

Cummings, Homer S., and Carl McFarland. *Federal Justice: Chapters in the History of Justice and the Federal Executive.* New York: Macmillan, 1937.

Curry, John Court. *The Security Service, 1908–1945: The Official History.* London: Public Record Office, 1999.

Dallek, Robert. *Franklin D. Roosevelt and American Foreign Policy, 1932–1945.* New York: Oxford University Press, 1979.

Davies, Sarah, and James R. Harris. *Stalin's World: Dictating the Soviet Order.* New Haven, CT: Yale University Press, 2014.

Denniston, Robin. "Yardley's Diplomatic Secrets." *Cryptologia* 18 (April 1994): 48–70.

Der Spiegel. "Fabrik der Gerechtigkeit: Mit Gott für J. Edgar Hoover." 22 December 1949.

Diamond, Sander A. *The Nazi Movement in the United States, 1924–1941.* Ithaca, NY: Cornell University Press, 1974.

Diggins, John P. *Mussolini and Fascism: The View from America.* Princeton, NJ: Princeton University Press, 1972.

Divine, Robert A. *Foreign Policy and U.S. Presidential Elections, 1940–1948.* New York: New Viewpoints, 1974.

Doenecke, Justus D. *Debating Franklin D. Roosevelt's Foreign Policies, 1933–1945.* Lanham, MD: Rowman & Littlefield, 2005.

————. *Storm on the Horizon: The Challenge to American Intervention, 1939–1941*. Lanham, MD: Rowman & Littlefield, 2000.

Doerries, Reinhard R., ed. *Hitler's Last Chief of Foreign Intelligence: Allied Interrogations of Walter Schellenberg*. London: Frank Cass, 2003.

Doherty, Thomas P. *Hollywood and Hitler, 1933–1939*. New York: Columbia University Press, 2013.

Donovan, William, and Edgar Mowrer. *Fifth Column Lessons for America*. Washington, DC: American Council on Public Affairs, [1940?].

Draper, Theodore. "Nazi Spies in France." *New Republic*, 23 August 1939, 72.

Duffy, Peter. *Double Agent: The First Hero of World War II and How the FBI Outwitted and Destroyed a Nazi Spy Ring*. New York: Scribner, 2014.

Erickson, John. "Soviet War Losses: Calculations and Controversies." In *Barbarossa: The Axis and the Allies*, edited by John Erickson and David Dilks, 255–77. Edinburgh: Edinburgh University Press, 1994.

Farago, Ladislas. *The Game of the Foxes: British and German Intelligence Operations and Personalities Which Changed the Course of the Second World War*. London: Hodder & Stoughton, 1971.

Federal Bureau of Investigation (FBI). *History of the Special Intelligence Service Division*. Vol. 2, *Accomplishment: Argentina–Japan*. Washington, DC: 1947. https://vault.fbi.gov/special-intelligence-service/SIS%20History%20Part%2003%20of%2008/view.

Ferguson, Niall. *Paper and Iron: Hamburg Business and German Politics in the Era of Inflation, 1897–1927*. Cambridge: Cambridge University Press, 1995.

Field, Rachel. *All This, and Heaven Too*. London: Collins, 1939.

Friedländer, Saul. *Prelude to Downfall: Hitler and the United States, 1939–1941*. Translated by Aline B. Werth and Alexander Werth. London: Chatto & Windus, 1967.

Fry, Helen P. *The London Cage: The Secret History of Britain's World War II Interrogation Centre*. London: Yale University Press, 2017.

Frye, Alton. *Nazi Germany and the American Hemisphere, 1933–1941*. New Haven, CT: Yale University Press, 1967.

Gabler, Neal. *An Empire of Their Own: How the Jews Invented Hollywood*. London: W. H. Allen, 1989.

Gentry, Curt. *J. Edgar Hoover: The Man and the Secrets*. New York: Norton, 1991.

Getty, J. Paul. *As I See It: The Autobiography of J. Paul Getty.* Englewood Cliffs, NJ: Prentice-Hall, 1976.

Geyer, Michael. "National Socialist Germany: The Politics of Information." In *Knowing One's Enemies: Intelligence Assessment between the Two World Wars*, edited by Ernest R. May, 310–46. Princeton, NJ: Princeton University Press, 1986.

Goldstein, Robert Justin. *American Blacklist: The Attorney General's List of Subversive Organizations.* Lawrence: University Press of Kansas, 2008.

Goodman, Walter. *The Committee: The Extraordinary Career of the House Committee on Un-American Activities.* New York: Farrar, Straus and Giroux, 1968.

Griffiths, Dennis. *The Encyclopedia of the British Press, 1422–1992.* London: Macmillan, 1992.

Halliwell, Leslie. *Halliwell's Film Guide.* London: Granada, 1979.

Hamilton, William [pseudonym for Ignatz Theodor Griebl]. *Salute the Jew!* Metairie, LA: Sons of Liberty, 1978. Reprint, privately printed, 1935.

Handlin, Oscar. *The Uprooted: The Epic Story of the Great Migrations That Made the American People.* New York: Grosset & Dunlap, 1951.

Hart, Bradley W. *Hitler's American Friends: The Third Reich's Supporters in the United States.* New York: St. Martin's Press, 2018.

Haynes, John E., and Harvey Klehr. *Venona: Decoding Soviet Espionage in America.* New Haven, CT: Yale University Press, 1999.

Hearden, Patrick J. *Roosevelt Confronts Hitler: America's Entry into World War II.* DeKalb: Northern Illinois Press, 1987.

Heinemann, Winfried. "Abwehr." In *Oxford Companion to the Second World War*, edited by I. C. B. Dear and M. R. D. Foot, 1–3. Oxford: Oxford University Press, 1995.

Hemingway, Ernest. *The Fifth Column and the First Forty-Nine Stories.* New York: Scribner, 1938.

Hemming, Henry. *M: Maxwell Knight, MI5's Greatest Spymaster.* London: Arrow, 2018.

Herzstein, Robert E. *Roosevelt and Hitler: Prelude to War.* New York: Paragon House, 1989.

Hinsley, Francis H., and C. A. G. Simkins. *British Intelligence in the Second World War.* Vol. 4, *Security and Counter-Intelligence.* London: Her Majesty's Stationery Office, 1990.

Hoare, Oliver, ed. *Camp 020: MI5 and the Nazi Spies: The Official History of MI5's Wartime Interrogation Centre*. Richmond, UK: Public Record Office, 2000.

Hoellering, Franz. Review of *Confessions of a Nazi Spy*, directed by Anatole Litvak. *Nation*, 20 May 1939, 595–96.

Hogan, Michael J. *Paths to Power: The Historiography of American Foreign Relations to 1941*. Cambridge: Cambridge University Press, 2000.

Hönicke Moore, Michaela. *Know Your Enemy: The American Debate on Nazism, 1933–1945*. Cambridge: Cambridge University Press, 2010.

Huchthausen, Peter A. *Shadow Voyage: The Extraordinary Wartime Escape of the Legendary SS* Bremen. Hoboken, NJ: Wiley, 2005.

Iriye, Akira. *Japan and the Wider World: From the Mid-Nineteenth Century to the Present*. London: Longman, 1997.

Jeffrey, Andrew. *This Dangerous Menace: Dundee and the River Tay at War, 1939 to 1945*. Edinburgh: Mainstream, 1991.

Jeffrey, Keith. *MI6: The History of the Secret Intelligence Service, 1909–1949*. London: Bloomsbury, 2010.

Jeffreys-Jones, Rhodri. *American Espionage: From Secret Service to CIA*. New York: Free Press, 1977.

———. *The FBI: A History*. New Haven, CT: Yale University Press, 2007.

———. *In Spies We Trust: The Story of Western Intelligence*. Oxford: Oxford University Press, 2013.

———. "Jessie Jordan: A Rejected Scot Who Spied for Germany and Hastened America's Flight from Neutrality." *The Historian* 76 (Winter 2014): 766–83.

———. "The Montreal Spy Ring of 1898 and the Origins of 'Domestic' Surveillance in the United States." *Canadian Review of American Studies* 5 (Fall 1974): 119–34.

———. "United States Secret Service." In *Government Agencies*, edited by Donald R. Whitnah, 592–97. Westport, CT: Greenwood, 1983.

———. "Verraden." *Geschiedenis Magazine* 52, no. 1 (January/February 2017): 45–49.

———. *We Know All about You: The Story of Surveillance in Britain and America*. Oxford: Oxford University Press, 2017.

Johnston, Flora (FJ), and Siân Reynolds (SR). "Jordan, Jessie." In *The New Biographical Dictionary of Scottish Women*, edited by Elizabeth Ewan, Rose

Pipes, Jane Rendall, and Siân Reynolds, 223. Edinburgh: Edinburgh University Press, 2018.

Johnstone, Andrew. *Against Immediate Evil: American Internationalists and the Four Freedoms on the Eve of World War II*. Ithaca, NY: Cornell University Press, 2014.

———. "'A Godsend to the Country'? Roosevelt, Willkie, and the Election of 1940." In *US Presidential Elections and Foreign Policy, Candidates, Campaigns, and Global Politics from FDR to Bill Clinton*, edited by Andrew Johnstone and Andrew Priest, 19–39. Lexington: University Press of Kentucky, 2017.

———. "To Mobilize a Nation: Citizens' Organizations and Intervention on the Eve of World War II." In *The US Public and American Foreign Policy*, edited by Andrew Johnstone and Helen Laville, 26–40. London: Routledge, 2010.

Jones, John P. *The German Spy in America: The Secret Plotting of German Spies in the United States and the Inside Story of the Sinking of the* Lusitania. London: Hutchinson, 1917.

Kahn, David. *Hitler's Spies: German Military Intelligence in World War II*. New York: Macmillan, 1978.

———. "Intelligence Studies on the Continent." *Intelligence and National Security* 23 (April 2008): 249–75.

———. *The Reader of Gentlemen's Mail: Herbert O. Yardley and the Birth of American Codebreaking*. New Haven, CT: Yale University Press, 2004.

Kater, Michael H. *The Nazi Party: A Social Profile of Members and Leaders, 1919–1945*. Oxford: Blackwell, 1983.

Kennedy, David M. *Freedom from Fear: The American People in Depression and War, 1929–1945*. New York: Oxford University Press, 2001.

Kessler, Ronald. *The Bureau: The Secret History of the FBI*. New York: St. Martin's Press, 2002.

Kimball, Warren F. "Dieckhoff and America: A German's View of German-American Relations, 1937–1941." *The Historian* 27 (February 1965): 218–43.

———. *The Juggler: Franklin Roosevelt as a Wartime Statesman*. Princeton, NJ: Princeton University Press, 1991.

Klemperer, Klemens von. *German Resistance against Hitler: The Search for Allies Abroad, 1938–1945*. Oxford: Clarendon Press, 1992.

———. *Mandate for Resistance: The Case for German Opposition to Hitler*. Northampton, MA: Smith College, 1969.

Kluiters, Frans A. C., and Etienne Verhoeyen. "An International Spymaster and Mystery Man: Abwehr Officer Hilmar G. J. Dierks (1889–1940) and His Agents." Online summary of the authors' *Spionnen aan de achterdeur: de Duitse Abwehr in België, 1936–1945*. Antwerp: Maklu Uitgevers, 2015.

Kollander, Patricia. "Boomerang Resistance: German Emigrés in the U.S. Army during World War II." In *A Companion to World War II*, edited by Thomas W. Zeiler and Daniel M. Dubois, 638–51. Oxford: Blackwell, 2013.

Kullen, George S. "Little Caesar Joins the G-Men." *Screen Book*, June 1939.

Kusielewicz, Eugene. "Paderewski and Wilson's Speech to the Senate, January 22, 1917." *Polish American Studies* 13, no. 3/4 (July–December 1956): 65-71.

LaFeber, Walter. *The American Age: United States Foreign Policy at Home and Abroad since 1750*. New York: Norton, 1989.

Lambert, Margaret, Paul R. Sweet, and Maurice Baumont, eds. *Documents on German Foreign Policy, 1918–1945*. Series D, vol. 9, *The War Years: March 18–June 22, 1940*. London: Her Majesty's Stationery Office, 1956.

Langer, William L., and S. Everett Gleason. *The Challenge to Isolation*. Vol. 1, *The World Crisis of 1937–1940 and American Foreign Policy*. New York: Harper, 1952.

Larsen, Dan. *Plotting for Peace*. Cambridge: Cambridge University Press, forthcoming.

Leigh, Michael. *Mobilizing Consent: Public Opinion and American Foreign Policy, 1937–1947*. Westport, CT: Greenwood Press, 1976.

Litvak, Anatole, dir. *Confessions of a Nazi Spy*. Written by Milton Krims and John Wexley. 1939; Burbank, CA: Warner Home Video, 2009. DVD.

Lokhova, Svetlana. *The Spy Who Changed History: The Untold Story of How the Soviet Union Won the Race for America's Top Secrets*. London: William Collins, 2018. Ebook.

Lore, Ludwig. "Spies, Plain and Fancy." *The Nation*, 8 July 1939.

Lorenz, Marita. *The Spy Who Loved Castro*. London: Ebury, 2017.

Lownie, Andrew. "Tyler Kent: Isolationist or Spy?" In *North American Spies: New Revisionist Essays*, edited by Rhodri Jeffreys-Jones and Andrew Lownie, 49–78. London: Thistle Publishing, 2013 (1992).

Luff, Jennifer. "Covert and Overt Operations: Interwar Political Policing in the United States and United Kingdom." *American Historical Review* 122 (June 2017): 727–57.

MacDonnell, Francis. *Insidious Foes: The Axis Fifth Column and the American Home Front*. New York: Oxford University Press, 1995.

Mahoney, M. H., ed. *Women in Espionage: A Biographical Directory*. Santa Barbara: ABC-CLIO, 1993.

Marshall-Cornwall, James, Bernadotte E. Schmitt, and Maurice Baumont. *Documents on German Foreign Policy, 1918–1945*. Series D, vol. 4, *The Aftermath of Munich, October 1938–March 1939*. London: Her Majesty's Stationery Office, 1951.

McKercher, Brian. "Reaching for the Brass Ring: The Recent Historiography of Interwar American Foreign Relations." In *Paths to Power: The Historiography of American Foreign Relations to 1941*, edited by Michael J. Hogan, 176–223. Cambridge: Cambridge University Press, 2000.

McKinstry, Leo. *Operation Sealion: How Britain Crushed the German War Machine's Dreams of Invasion in 1940*. London: John Murray, 2014.

McPherson, Alan, ed. *SHAFR Guide Online: An Annotated Bibliography of U.S. Foreign Relations since 1600*. Leiden: Brill, 2017.

Melanson, Philip H. *The Secret Service: The Hidden History of an Enigmatic Agency*. New York: Carroll & Graf, 2002.

Middendorf, Stefanie. "'Verstoßenes Wissen': Emigranten als Deutschlandexperten im 'Office of Strategic Services' und im Amerikanischen Außenministerium 1943–1955." *Neue Politische Literatur* 46, no. 1 (2001): 23–52.

Miller, Joan Irene. "Spies in America: German Espionage in the United States, 1935–1945." Master's thesis, Portland State University, 1984.

Moldovan, Raluca. "A Romanian Jew in Hollywood: Edward G. Robinson." *American, British and Canadian Studies* 22 (2014): 43–62.

Mueller, Michael. *Canaris: The Life and Death of Hitler's Spymaster*. Translated by Geoffrey Brooks. London: Chatham, 2007.

Murphy, Robert. *Diplomat among Warriors*. New York: Doubleday, 1964.

Naftali, Timothy. "Reinhard Gehlen and the United States." In *U.S. Intelligence and the Nazis*, edited by Richard Breitman, Norman J. W. Goda, Timothy Naftali, and Robert Wolfe, 375–418. Cambridge: Cambridge University Press, 2005.

Office of Naval Intelligence. "German Espionage and Sabotage against the United States in World War II." *Office of Naval Intelligence Review* 1, no. 3 (January 1946): 33–38.

O'Halpin, Eunan. *Spying on Ireland: British Intelligence and Irish Neutrality during the Second World War*. Oxford: Oxford University Press, 2008.

Olmstead, Kathryn S. *Real Enemies: Conspiracy Theories and American Democracy, World War I to 9/11*. New York: Oxford University Press, 2009.

Omand, David, and Mark Phythian. *Principled Spying: The Ethics of Secret Intelligence*. Washington, DC: Georgetown University Press, 2018.

Oppenheim, E. Phillips. *The Evil Shepherd*. London: Hodder & Stoughton, 1922.

Paehler, Katrin. *The Third Reich's Intelligence Services: The Career of Walter Schellenberg*. Cambridge: Cambridge University Press, 2017.

Patenaude, Bertrand M. *The Big Show in Bololand: The American Relief Expedition to Soviet Russia in the Famine of 1921*. Stanford, CA: Stanford University Press, 2002.

Perlman, Selig. *A Theory of the Labor Movement*. New York: Augustus M. Kelley, 1949 (1928).

Persico, Joseph E. *Roosevelt's Secret War: FDR and World War II Espionage*. New York: Random House, 2001.

Phillips, Timothy. *The Secret Twenties: British Intelligence, the Russians and the Jazz Age*. London: Granta, 2017.

Powers, Richard Gid. *Broken: The Troubled Past and Uncertain Future of the FBI*. New York: Free Press, 2004.

———. "J. Edgar Hoover and the Detective Hero." *Journal of Popular Culture* 9 (1975).

———. *Secrecy and Power: The Life of J. Edgar Hoover*. London: Hutchinson, 1987.

Purvis, Alston W. *The Vendetta: FBI Hero Melvin Purvis's War against Crime, and J. Edgar Hoover's War against Him*. New York: Public Affairs, 2005.

Quinlan, Kevin. *The Secret War between the Wars: MI5 in the 1920s and 1930s*. Woodbridge, UK: Boydell Press, 2014.

Reile, Oscar. *Die Geheime Westfront: Die Abwehr, 1935–1945*. Munich: Welsermühl, 1962.

———. *Frauen im Geheimdienst*. Illertissen, Germany: Federmann, 1979.

Remak, Joachim. "Friends of the New Germany: The Bund and German-American Relations." *Journal of Modern History* 29 (March 1957): 33–41.

Reynolds, David. *The Creation of the Anglo-American Alliance, 1937–41: A Study on Competitive Co-operation*. London: Europa, 1981.

Richmond, Clint. *Fetch the Devil: The Sierra Diablo Murders and Nazi Espionage in America*. Lebanon, NH: ForeEdge, 2014.

Ritter, Nikolaus. *Deckname Dr. Rantzau: Die Aufzeichnungen des Nikolaus*

Ritter, Offizier im Geheimen Nachrichtendienst. Hamburg: Hoffmann & Campe, 1972.

Robinson, Derek. *Invasion, 1940: The Truth about the Battle of Britain and What Stopped Hitler.* London: Constable, 2005.

Ronge, Maximilian. *Kriegs- und Industrie Spionage.* Leipzig: A. H. Payne, 1930.

Ronnie, Art. *Counterfeit Hero: Fritz Duquesne, Adventurer and Spy.* Annapolis, MD: Naval Institute Press, 1995.

Rose, Norman. *Vansittart: Study of a Diplomat.* London: Heinemann, 1978.

Rosendahl, Charles E. "The Loss of the *Akron*." *U.S. Naval Institute Proceedings*, July 1934, 921–33.

Rosenzweig, Laura B. *Hollywood's Spies: The Undercover Surveillance of Nazis in Los Angeles.* New York: New York University Press, 2017.

Rout, Leslie B., Jr., and John B. Bratzel. *The Shadow War: German Espionage and United States Counterespionage in Latin America during World War II.* Frederick, MD: University Publications of America, 1986.

Rowan, Richard W. *Secret Agents against America.* New York: Doubleday, Doran, 1939.

———. *Story of Secret Service.* Garden City, NY: Doubleday, Doran, 1937.

Sandeen, Eric J. "Anti-Nazi Sentiment in Film: *Confessions of a Nazi Spy* and the German-American Bund." *American Studies*, 20 (Fall 1979): 69-81.

Schewe, Donald B., ed. *Franklin D. Roosevelt and Foreign Affairs.* 11 vols. New York: Clearwater Publishers, 1979–83.

Simms, Brendan. *Hitler: Only the World Was Enough.* London: Allen Lane, 2019.

Smith, Arthur L., Jr. "The Foreign Organization of the Nazi Party and the United States, 1931–39." In *Germany and America: Essays on Problems of International Relations and Immigration*, edited by Hans L. Trefousse, 173–82. New York: Brooklyn College Press, 1981.

Smith, Geoffrey S. *To Save a Nation: American Countersubversives, the New Deal, and the Coming of World War II.* New York: Basic Books, 1973.

Sparrow, James T. *Warfare State: World War II Americans and the Age of Big Government.* Oxford: Oxford University Press, 2013 (2011).

Spivak, John L. *Secret Armies: The New Technique of Nazi Warfare.* New York: Modern Age, 1939.

Stafford, David. *Roosevelt and Churchill: Men of Secrets.* London: Little, Brown, 1999.

Stephenson, Jill. *The Nazi Organisation of Women*. London: Croom Helm, 1981.

Stouffer, Samuel Andrew. *Communism, Conformity, and Civil Liberties: A Cross-Section of the Nation Speaks Its Mind*. Gloucester, MA: Peter Smith, 1963 (1955).

Strassman, W. Paul. *The Strassmans: Science, Politics, and Migration in Turbulent Times, 1793–1993*. New York: Berghahn Books, 2008.

Summers, Anthony. *Official and Confidential: The Secret Life of J. Edgar Hoover*. New York: G. P. Putnam's Sons, 1993.

Swift, Will. *The Kennedys amidst the Gathering Storm: A Thousand Days in London, 1938–1940*. New York: Collins, 2008.

Taylor, Les. *Luftwaffe over Scotland*. Dunbeath: Whittles, 2010.

Theoharis, Athan G. *Chasing Spies: How the FBI Failed in Counterintelligence but Promoted the Politics of McCarthyism in the Cold War Years*. Chicago: Ivan R. Dee, 2002.

———, ed. *The FBI: A Comprehensive Reference Guide*. New York: Facts on File, 2000.

———. *Spying on Americans: Political Surveillance from Hoover to the Huston Plan*. Philadelphia: Temple University Press, 1978.

Theoharis, Athan G., and John Stuart Cox. *The Boss: J. Edgar Hoover and the Great American Inquisition*. London: Harrap, 1989.

Trefousse, Hans L. "Failure of German Intelligence in the United States, 1935–1945." *Mississippi Valley Historical Review* 42 (June 1955): 84–100.

Tuchman, Barbara W. *The Zimmermann Telegram*. New York: Macmillan, 1966 (1958).

Turrou, Leon G. *Le Bonheur en Sursis*. Paris: Del Duca, 1960.

———. *How to Be a G-Man*. With Tom Tracy and George Daws. New York: R. M. McBride, 1939.

———. *The Nazi Spy Conspiracy in America*. With David G. Wittles. London: George G. Harrap, 1939. Published in the United States as *Nazi Spies in America*.

———. *Where My Shadow Falls: Two Decades of Crime Detection*. Garden City, NY: Doubleday, 1949.

Underhill, Stephen M. *The Manufacture of Consent: J. Edgar Hoover and the Rhetorical Rise of the FBI*. East Lansing: Michigan State University Press, 2020.

US Senate Select Committee to Study Governmental Operations with Respect to Intelligence Activities (Church Committee). *Hearings before the Select Committee to Study Governmental Operations with Respect to Intelligence Activities of the United States Senate*, Ninety-Fourth Congress, First Session. Vol. 6, *Federal Bureau of Investigation*. Washington, DC: Government Printing Office, 1976.

Vasey, Christopher. *Nazi Intelligence Operations in Non-occupied Territories: Espionage Efforts in the United States, Britain, South America and Southern Africa*. Jefferson, NC: McFarland, 2016.

Vaughan, Stephen. "Spies, National Security, and the 'Inertia Projector': The Secret Service Files of Ronald Reagan." *American Quarterly* 39 (Fall 1987): 355–80.

Vilain, Bertrand. *Affaire Seznec: Les archives du FBI ont parlé*. Saint Eloy, France: Monsieurbrocanteur, 2020.

Waller, John H. "The Double Life of Admiral Canaris." *International Journal of Intelligence and Counterintelligence* 9 (Fall 1996): 271-89.

Wark, Wesley K., ed. *Spy Fiction, Spy Films and Real Intelligence*. London: Frank Cass, 1991.

———. *The Ultimate Enemy: British Intelligence and Nazi Germany, 1933–1939*. Oxford: Oxford University Press, 1985.

Watt, Donald Cameron. "The Relationship between the Far Eastern and European Wars, 1922–1941." In *Pearl Harbor Revisited*, edited by Robert W. Love, 1–12. Basingstoke, UK: Macmillan, 1995.

Weinberg, Gerhard. "Hitler's Image of the United States." *American Historical Review* 69 (July 1964): 1006–21.

Weiner, Tim. *Enemies: A History of the FBI*. London: Penguin, 2012.

Welles, Sumner. "Memorandum of Conversation, by the Under Secretary of States (Welles), 1 November 1938." In *Foreign Relations of the United States, 1938*. Vol. 2, *The British Commonwealth, Europe, Near East, and Africa*, edited by Matilda F. Axton, Rogers P. Churchill, N. O. Sappington, John G. Reid, Francis C. Prescott, Louis E. Gates, and Shirley L. Phillips, 2:447–51, d359. Washington, DC: Department of State, 1954. https://history.state.gov /historicaldocuments/frus1938v02/d359.

West, Nigel. *MI5: British Security Service Operations, 1909–1945*. London: Triad, 1983.

Whalen, Richard J. *The Founding Father: The Story of Joseph P. Kennedy*. New York: New American Library, 1966.

White, Rosie. *Violent Femmes: Women as Spies in Popular Culture*. London: Routledge, 2007.

Whitman, James Q. *Hitler's American Model: The United States and the Making of Nazi Race Law*. Princeton, NJ: Princeton University Press, 2018.

Wighton, Charles. *The World's Greatest Spies*. London: Odhams Press, 1962.

Williams, David. "'Without Understanding': The FBI and Political Surveillance, 1908–1941." PhD diss., University of New Hampshire, 1981.

Yardley, Herbert O. *The American Black Chamber*. New York: Bobbs-Merrill, 1931.

INDEX

Page numbers in italics signify photos.

ABOUT THE AUTHOR

Educated at Cambridge and Harvard Universities, Rhodri Jeffreys-Jones is a professor emeritus of US history at the University of Edinburgh, Scotland. Previously he held positions at Harvard, the Free University of Berlin, and Toronto University. A prize-winning author, he has written histories of both the CIA and the FBI. He founded and is honorary president of the Scottish Association for the Study of America.